AF675348

ENHANCED EDITION

HNWI Survival Manual

When your wealth becomes a target

Mia Galgau

High Net Worth Individuals Survival Manual

SOS - a Strategic Operating System for HNWIs

This enhanced edition goes far beyond the original book. It isn't just a survival guide anymore, it's a complete operating system for people whose lives have reached a point where mistakes are expensive and improvisation is dangerous.

This is not a manual about making money. It is a guide to staying in control when money turns you into a target. It helps you understand where real risk comes from and how to build a life that cannot be shaken by a headline, a leak, a lawsuit, or a sudden change in your environment.

In these pages, you will learn practical skills that most people in your position never receive: how to protect your privacy without disappearing, how to act with strength without being visible, and how to build structures, legal, personal, digital, and emotional, that keep working for you even when you step away.

The enhanced edition adds what many readers of the original wished they had: clearer strategies, deeper explanations, and a step-by-step understanding of how power, exposure, and stability truly work for someone in your situation. It connects the emotional side of pressure with the structural solutions you can implement immediately.

Everything here is designed to give you more clarity, more peace of mind, and a sense of direction when the world around you becomes unpredictable.

Above all, this book gives you something rare: a way to live with freedom and confidence, even when your name, your assets, or your position attract more attention than you want.

This document is intended for private use only. It contains high-level strategies for individuals in positions of risk, visibility, or power. Use with discernment.

© 2025 Mia Galgau · Taxhells Strategic Series · All rights reserved

Published by taxhells.com

INDEX

About this book

Being wealthy is a dream for much of the world. From the outside, it looks like freedom, comfort, and possibility. But anyone who has lived long enough with significant assets knows another truth: wealth is not only a privilege. It is also a system you must learn to navigate, or it will start navigating you.

This expanded edition was written for individuals whose lives have reached a level of complexity where instinct is no longer enough. With nearly four hundred pages of analysis, real-world patterns, and strategic explanations, this book goes far deeper than the original version. It examines every layer of a high-net-worth life, legal, financial, digital, emotional, relational, and geopolitical, and shows how each one can become either an asset or a point of exposure depending on how you handle it.

Wealth amplifies everything: opportunities, risks, misunderstandings, and vulnerabilities. When it's not managed with clarity, it can turn into pressure, conflict, or even a quiet kind of chaos. Many people dream of reaching this level; very few understand how demanding it becomes once you're inside it. This book exists to help you see the reality that public narratives rarely describe, and to give you a framework that allows you to adapt to the circumstances that your fortune inevitably creates around you.

Throughout these chapters, you will find practical explanations, examples drawn from decades of legal and strategic experience, and scenarios that may resemble situations you have faced or will face. They are presented to help you recognize patterns, anticipate consequences, and build systems that protect you, always legally, ethically, and without unnecessary noise.

Still, this book has limits, and they are important to acknowledge. No written guide, no matter how comprehensive, can cover every possible situation. Every individual has a unique combination of history, relationships, jurisdictions, obligations, and risks. For deeper or highly specific issues, nothing replaces the judgment of seasoned professionals who can examine your case directly and guide you with precision. If something in these pages resonates with your current challenges, consider it a signal: consult advisors who understand the territories you are navigating.

This book is not here to create fear, nor to encourage paranoia. Its purpose is clarity. It aims to describe different realities that some readers will recognize immediately, while others may never encounter them, and some situations may fall outside anything described in these pages. That is the nature of real life: no manual can capture every possibility.

What this book does offer is a framework, a guide, to help you recognize patterns, risks, and pressures that could one day affect you, your assets, or your peace of mind. Some chapters may resonate deeply with your own experience; others may feel distant or purely theoretical. Both are valuable, because understanding what *could* happen is often as important as understanding what *has* already happened.

The intention is simple: to help you identify the elements in your environment that might cause conflict, instability, or harm if left unattended, and to give you the tools to operate wisely despite those pressures. I don't aim to teach you invincibility, instead I write about architecture, so your life, your freedom, and your stability are not left to chance.

If wealth has placed you in a position where mistakes carry consequences, where visibility creates pressure, or where silence sometimes feels safer than speaking, then these pages were written for you.

And if you are ready to understand your world with more depth, more honesty, and more control than ever before, then you are exactly where you need to be.

Enhanced Edition Note

When I published the first edition of this book, I believed its structure and message were complete. What I did not expect was the volume of private requests and consultations that followed. Readers from different countries and backgrounds reached out to me personally, asking for deeper explanations, practical examples, and guidance tailored to their own situations. Many shared concerns that were remarkably similar, even though their lives were entirely different.

Those conversations made something clear: the need for more detail was not individual, it was universal. Instead of offering expanded explanations only through private consultations, I decided to make that same clarity available to everyone.

This ***Enhanced Edition*** does not replace the original; it extends it. It adds nuance where readers asked for more depth, reinforces concepts that prompted the most questions, and expands the practical guidance they told me they needed.

It is the same book – just more complete, more detailed, and designed so that every reader can benefit from the insights that so many requested directly.

About the author

Mia Galgau is a lawyer and strategic consultant with nearly two decades of experience advising individuals, families, executives, investors, diplomats and public figures across multiple jurisdictions. Her work combines legal precision with a deep understanding of human behavior, power dynamics and cross-border exposure. Throughout her career, she has guided clients through complex transitions, international mobility, wealth restructuring, political visibility, private disputes, and high-pressure environments where every decision carries consequences.

Her books reflect the same philosophy that guides her professional practice: everything she teaches is fully compliant, jurisdiction-agnostic, and grounded in the belief that legality is the strongest form of protection an individual can build. Through clear explanations and practical structures, she helps readers understand realities that most people never see, empowering them to safeguard their freedom, their stability and their long-term peace of mind.

She publishes her work under the Taxhells Strategic Series, an editorial imprint dedicated to bringing clarity to complex global lives. Through this series, Taxhells develops books and strategic guides that help readers understand how power, mobility, wealth, and legality interact across jurisdictions. The focus is simple: to teach individuals how to protect themselves through structure, informed decisions, and a deep respect for the law. Each publication offers practical insight, real-world patterns, and tools that readers can apply immediately—whether they need to strengthen their privacy, redesign their mobility, or build a life that remains stable no matter where the world pulls them next.

Also by Mia Galgau

Silent Power, the *discreet formula for global influence and control,* or how to disappear when you need to, stay visible only when it serves you, and build a life that no one can weaponize.

This book teaches something that almost no one will ever tell you directly: visibility is optional, but power is not. Silent power shows you how to make invisibility a strategic asset, how to reduce your digital footprint, control what others can see, and move through the world without leaving openings that others can exploit. It explains how to manage perception, how to create a life that cannot be easily read, and how to operate with freedom even when the world around you becomes noisy or intrusive. For readers who feel observed, pressured, or too exposed, this book offers a blueprint for reclaiming privacy without giving up influence.

The Gatekeeper, *a strategic guide for diplomats and political elites on how to survive exposure and remain untouchable*

This book reveals the real mechanisms of political influence, diplomatic negotiation, and high-level decision-making, and humbly suggests how to survive them without being swallowed by the system.

Unlike most books that talk about power from the outside, the gatekeeper explains how things actually work once you step into the rooms where decisions are made. It reveals the structures, the personalities, the hidden incentives and the invisible pressures that define political and diplomatic environments. You'll learn how to build authority, how to avoid being manipulated, how to position yourself without appearing confrontational, and how to navigate environments where information is currency and silence is often a negotiation tool. This book is essential for anyone who deals with governments, embassies, international organizations, or high-stakes networks where the wrong move can cost influence, or reputation.

Nomad Structures - *Design your life*, or how to build a global life without losing legal and mental stability.

This book is a practical guide to designing a lifestyle across multiple jurisdictions, fully legal, tax-efficient, mobile, and emotionally sustainable. It is intended for people who want freedom without chaos. It explains how to build a global lifestyle where you can live between countries without falling into legal traps, tax complications, residency conflicts, or administrative problems that can follow you for years.

With clear examples and simple structures, it shows you:

- Where to live depending on your goals and personal circumstances,
- How to choose tax residences legally and coherently,
- How to protect your assets while you move,
- How to manage banking, compliance, and documentation across borders,
- How to avoid the typical mistakes that ruin the digital nomad dream.

If you want to live globally with peace of mind, and without risking fines, audits, or instability, this book will show you how to do it.

Who is this book for

This book is for people who have crossed a quiet threshold without noticing it. For individuals whose lives no longer move through the world the way they once did. For those who wake up one day and realize that ordinary rules no longer apply to them, even if nobody ever told them why.

It is for people who have become visible, sometimes by choice, sometimes by accident, sometimes simply because life pulled them into circles where attention is currency and silence is interpreted as intention. It is for anyone who carries wealth, influence, reputation, or symbolic power in places where these things provoke curiosity, resentment or scrutiny. Some earned their position; others inherited it. Some stepped into it slowly; others were thrown into it without preparation. But all of them share one thing: they cannot afford the illusions that protect everyone else.

This book is for you if your life has begun to attract patterns, the kind you can feel before you can explain. A phone call that suddenly sounds different. A journalist who mentions knowledge they should not have. A former partner who speaks with too much confidence about things they shouldn't know. A member of your team who starts behaving as if they have been listening to conversations you don't remember having out loud. Exposure rarely announces itself. It whispers before it speaks.

It is for you if people around you treat your decisions as signals, even when you intend nothing of the sort. If a property you buy becomes a discussion. If a donation you make becomes a headline. If a trip you take becomes a theory. If a friendship you maintain becomes a problem for someone else. You may not see yourself as important, but importance is not decided by how you feel. It is decided by how the world interprets your existence, and how others can use it.

This book is also for those who are not wealthy by conventional standards, but who live in environments where visibility is dangerous in other ways: diplomats, activists, journalists, minority shareholders, whistleblowers, founders, heirs, partners to powerful figures, or anyone caught between political, legal, or family systems that reward silence and punish misalignment. In such worlds, risk does not always come from your actions. Sometimes it comes from the position you occupy in the minds of others.

It is for the entrepreneur who built something valuable, only to discover that success attracts both admiration and surveillance, often in equal measure. For the heir who inherits not only assets, but expectations, resentments, and narratives written by people who have never met them. For the investor who finds themselves entangled in structures that looked clean on paper but become murky under pressure. For the discreet partner whose very discretion becomes suspicious the moment something goes wrong. For the political affiliate who did nothing but stand next to the wrong person at the wrong moment in history.

It is for those who have begun to feel watched, not always by institutions, not always by enemies, but sometimes by people who simply want access, relevance or proximity. And it is especially for those who have been made to feel responsible for carrying the weight of that attention alone, because those around them rely on their stability while contributing to its erosion.

If you are reading this, there is a reason. People in your position do not read books like this for entertainment. They read them because something, somewhere, has shifted. A change in tone. A breach of trust. A strange request. A subtle warning. A silence that felt heavier than it should have. A moment when you looked at your life and realized that you had built an extraordinary existence, but not an invulnerable one.

This book is not meant to flatter you, frighten you or promise safety. It is meant to help you see your world with clarity, so you can operate with structure instead of improvisation. It is for those who understand that power is fragile, that wealth is loud even when unspoken, and that reputation travels faster and farther than intention. It is for the person who senses that the margin for error has narrowed, and that the cost of a single mistake is no longer measured in inconvenience, but in consequences that echo across jurisdictions, institutions, families and time.

It is for the individual who lives surrounded by advisors, staff, partners or relatives, yet carries the deep, private awareness that in the moments that matter, the moments where decisions shape destiny, you stand essentially alone. Wealth creates teams, but crisis reveals solitude. This book is written for that solitude: the part of your life that no one else can protect for you, because no one else carries the risks that come with your name.

It is also for those who feel the quiet fatigue of being a target without understanding why. People who want peace without surrendering their autonomy. People who want control without needing applause. People who have realized that disappearing is not always possible, and that being unreadable is more powerful than being invisible.

Finally, this book is for the person you are becoming, not the person you were before the pressure began. That earlier version of you had the luxury of believing that the world was neutral and that intentions were enough. The version of you reading these pages now knows better. You understand that systems have memory, that information travels without your consent, and that silence must be constructed, not hoped for.

If you are here, it is because your life has entered a different chapter. *This book is written for that chapter, and for the one after it.*

Introduction

This book is not about success; it is about what happens you're your success becomes a liability.

At a certain point, wealth stops being a number, it becomes a signature, a pattern, or even a target.

Whether your visibility came through inheritance, business, politics, (un)wanted fame or exposure in a globalized world, at some point, you will no longer be able to move without being watched, recorded, or interpreted. And when that moment comes, the risks change shape.

You are not simply rich. You are readable.

The threats are no longer hypothetical. They are legal, reputational, emotional, digital, and strategic. They may come from litigation, tax authorities, regulatory bodies, media, internal leaks, public controversies, or private betrayals. They may originate from your circle, your country, your structure, or yourself.

This is not paranoia. This is pattern recognition.

The world has changed. Power is no longer protected by distance or privilege. The infrastructure that once offered insulation now generate exposure. Every registry, every post, every advisor, every flight, every structure carries metadata. And at scale, metadata becomes narrative.

This manual exists because most responses to threat are improvised, emotional, reactive... and become costly. And sometimes irreversible.

What you will find in the following pages is not theory, it is structure.

You will learn how to identify exposure events, how to reduce risk without creating suspicion, how to operate under pressure, how to dismantle noise, and how to rebuild your life even under fire.

You will not be told what to feel. You will be told what to build.

You won't read hundreds of pages of motivational text, instead you will approach a survival protocol, a framework that helps you *understand* how certain things work whether you like it or not and learn how to survive no matter what life brings you.

Remember, the moment you realize you've become a target, this book begins.

Chapter I. The moment of exposure

Profiles at risk

Exposure does not happen to everyone with money. It happens to people whose position, history, or environment carries a particular weight. Wealth is only part of the equation; the real trigger is the intersection between assets, influence, visibility, and narrative vulnerability. The following profiles are not stereotypes but recurring patterns, observed across families, jurisdictions, generations, and crises.

Some individuals become targets because they hold wealth that affects others. Others become targets because they stand too close to power, or because their presence shifts the balance inside fragile systems. Some are attacked for what they own, others for what they represent, and many simply for being convenient to someone else's agenda.

The first-generation builder is exposed because their story is documented in real time: companies founded, growth accelerated, exits announced, hires and partnerships recorded. Their past decisions exist in the public domain, their success has left a visible trail, and their name has been circulated widely enough that any disruption becomes newsworthy. Their strength is momentum; their weakness is traceability.

The heir or successor carries a different kind of exposure. They inherit not only assets but a pre-existing narrative, one shaped by parents, siblings, trustees, rivals, and the public imagination. Even if they live discreetly, the system around them is not private. The legacy they receive functions like a beacon, attracting attention even when they do nothing at all.

The political adjacency profile, someone connected to a political figure, a diplomatic circle, a lobbying network, a controversial regime, or a shifting geopolitical landscape, faces exposure that is symbolic rather than financial. They become relevant not because of their own actions but because of the story others can tell using their proximity.

The quiet capital partner is vulnerable precisely because they believed discretion was protection. They invested early, deeply, or strategically, but the structures they relied on are now under pressure. When a principal becomes the subject of investigation or interest, silent partners are pulled into the light whether they like it or not.

The cross-jurisdiction individual lives across borders, domicile in one place, assets in another, income in a third, and relationships or political ties in a fourth. This complexity creates exposure simply because too many systems can claim jurisdiction over pieces of their life.

The symbolic target is not necessarily wealthy. They are artists, founders, dissidents, journalists, or public critics whose influence outweighs their assets. Their vulnerability comes from their visibility and the ease with which someone can turn them into an example.

If you see part of yourself in any of these profiles, even faintly, then the dynamics in this chapter apply to you. Exposure is rarely total; it begins at the edges, and only those who understand their profile can anticipate where the first crack appears.

The wealth threshold where visibility starts

Visibility almost never begins with a dramatic moment. More often, it starts quietly: a line that appears in a corporate registry, a picture taken at an event, a property transfer published automatically, or a financial movement that someone, somewhere, is paid to examine. The shift from anonymity to attention is rarely emotional; it is often accidental, and suddenly the environment starts to change the way things used to work before.

There is no single number that turns a private individual into a public subject. For some, the shift begins around a few million in assets; for others, it takes a hundred million or more. But the number itself is not what matters. What matters is how visible you are across systems, how many jurisdictions your life touches, how easily your ownership structures can be traced, and how frequently your name appears in digital pathways that never forget.

Thus said, your wealth is not the problem. Being trackable is.

The four archetypes of vulnerability

This book is not written for everyone with capital. It is written for individuals who stand at the intersection of exposure and consequence, people whose circumstances make them visible even when they intended to remain private.

The heir inherits exposure along with the assets. They often underestimate how much information about their family wealth circulates in the background, and how many people have an interest in watching them for signs of change or conflict.

The entrepreneur builds something valuable quickly, which inevitably produces documents, filings, negotiations, and partnerships that can resurface at the worst possible moment. Their success generates a reputation tail long after the deal is done.

The political affiliate becomes relevant because they exist near power, even if they never sought it. Their vulnerability shifts with elections, ideologies, alliances, and geopolitical consequences.

The silent partner remains invisible until the structure they invested in comes under pressure, and suddenly silence becomes exposure.

These archetypes are broad, but they reveal a truth: if your story can be used by someone else, legally, politically, emotionally, or financially, you are already inside the zone of risk.

Triggers that shift you into the spotlight

Exposure is not always a result of misconduct. More often, it is activated by transitions, moments of structural or emotional change that others interpret as opportunity. A divorce filing becomes public before anyone is ready. An inheritance dispute reopens old conflicts. A transaction leaks because someone with access sees value in sharing it. A failed investment mutates into litigation that drags your name into places you never intended.

Sometimes the trigger is political: a change in government, a shift in alliances, or a narrative that requires a target of convenience. And sometimes the trigger is simply timing: you lived in complete privacy yesterday, and tomorrow someone decides that revealing your name serves their interests.

The danger is not in the cause but in the speed. The transition from private individual to public subject can unfold in less than forty-eight hours. Once it begins, the strength of your legal, financial, and relational architecture determines whether the impact remains contained or becomes a fracture that reshapes your life.

Misconceptions among HNWIs

Many high-net-worth individuals believe they are too insignificant to become targets. They assume their structures are sound, their advisors are competent, and their lives are irrelevant to the wider world. These assumptions are comforting, and often catastrophic.

Some heirs assume inherited wealth attracts less scrutiny than created wealth. Some entrepreneurs believe privacy settings are the same as protection. And many equate silence with invisibility, forgetting that visibility today is generated not by noise but by data.

The most dangerous misconception is the belief that there will be time to prepare once something begins. In reality, the window for preparation closes long before exposure becomes visible. By the time something feels urgent, the systems around you have already moved.

Definitions, geography, and strategic exposure

Banks, law firms, and asset managers use "high-net-worth individual" to categorize clients with at least one million dollars in liquid assets. "ultra-high-net-worth" typically starts around thirty million. These figures are operational, not strategic. In some countries, one million dollars grants influence; in others, it barely grants access. Exposure is always, always relative to context.

Not all targets are wealthy. Some are symbolic, artists, whistleblowers, minority shareholders, journalists, dissidents, diplomats, etc. They can be targeted for representing an idea, a position, or a threat to someone else's narrative. In unstable or authoritarian environments, targeting a single individual serves as a warning to many.

This book does not assume wealth is the defining factor. It assumes that visibility, symbolism, and perceived influence are just as dangerous, especially when institutions shift and power rearranges itself.

The exposure event: anatomy of the shift

The moment you lose control of your narrative.

Exposure rarely feels like an explosion. It feels like a drift, quiet at first, then sudden, then irreversible. You may still believe you are in control long after the shift has begun. But by the time you realize something has changed, your name may already be attached to narratives that did not originate from you.

This is your first tactical disadvantage: you feel it and you are no longer the author of your story.

Public perception moves faster than due process, and institutions often respond to perception before they respond to fact. If a journalist, an algorithm, or an adversary frames you as a threat, a suspect, or a symbol, regulators, banks, and governments may begin reacting accordingly, even if nothing illegal has occurred.

Passive vs. Active exposure

Some exposure is structural. When a country publishes a corporate ownership registry, names that used to be shielded become searchable. When a media outlet automates data-mining, patterns emerge that no human ever intentionally revealed. This is passive exposure: it happens because the system evolves.

Other exposure is targeted. A former partner leaks documents. A political rival triggers a regulatory complaint. An employee initiates a claim that forces a legal audit. These are deliberate actions designed to damage or destabilize.

Both forms are dangerous. Passive exposure gives you no warning, and active exposure comes with intent and often with inside knowledge.

Understanding which one you are facing determines your first defensive move.

Systems that amplify the damage

Exposure never unfolds in isolation. It travels through systems, media algorithms, legal databases, compliance networks, social platforms, cross-border regulatory frameworks. These systems are interconnected, fast, and indifferent to your intentions.

A single blog post triggers a google alert - the alert triggers a compliance flag - the flag triggers an internal review - the review triggers institutional caution - caution leaks – and the leak becomes a story.

Even when nothing substantive has occurred, the chain reaction can feel like freefall. Without a containment plan, a localized incident can escalate across jurisdictions in hours. Systems amplify attention faster than individuals can correct it.

The role of time: how fast exposure escalates

The most underestimated variable in any exposure scenario is time. HNWIs often believe they will have the chance to gather information, call advisors, and build a narrative. That belief belongs to another era.

Today, seventy-two hours is often enough for an incident to reach a point of no return. A publication. A regulatory notice. A social thread. An automated database update. Once the event crosses that threshold, systems begin reinforcing each other, creating momentum you can no longer slow. Speed is the real threat, not complexity.

The three phases of strategic shock

Phase one: denial

The first reaction is often not emotional denial but strategic hesitation. Wealth, advisory teams, and established structures create the illusion that things will resolve on their own. This delay is lethal because it consumes the only asset you cannot regain: time.

Phase two: vulnerability

The exposure becomes public or begins accelerating. Legal inquiries appear. Journalists circle. Partners request explanations. Institutions hesitate. Trust fractures. Your internal stability erodes just as your external demands multiply. Many break here, not because they lack intelligence, but because they lack a protocol.

Phase three: shielding

Eventually, instinct or strategy forces a shift from explanation to protection. Emergency teams assemble. Assets are frozen or relocated. Communication channels tighten. A perimeter forms. But if the underlying structures were not built to absorb shocks, shielding becomes improvisation, and improvisation attracts more attention.

The goal in this phase is not victory but rather stopping the bleeding.

Moving from panic to structure

Crisis does not reward improvisation, it rewards architecture.

The only way to regain control after exposure is to convert panic into protocol. Defined roles, communication limits, decision trees, and accurate maps of your risks turn pressure into something navigable. Energy is not a strategy. Clarity is.

Those who survive exposure without long-term damage do so because they prepared long before the moment arrived. They know what to freeze, what to reveal, what to remove, and what to let die.

Structure is the real shield while everything else is dust.

Damage assessment: real vs. Perceived risk

Separating noise from threat.

One of the most important skills in exposure scenarios is distinguishing what is loud from what is lethal. Headlines are loud; regulators are lethal. Social commentary is loud; cross-border legal action is lethal. Public noise rises quickly and fades just as fast. Legal pressure moves slowly but changes everything or even destroy everything.

Clarity begins by asking three questions: Who controls the narrative? Who has jurisdiction? Who benefits from your reaction?

If you cannot answer these, you are reacting blindly. And in crisis, blindness is a luxury you cannot afford.

The map of exposure

You cannot defend what you cannot see. Every individual who carries wealth, influence, or symbolic weight needs to maintain a living map of exposure, one that evolves as life moves, as relationships shift, and as systems around them change their rules without warning. This map is not an abstract exercise but rather a tool of survival.

Exposure exists across four dimensions: personal, legal, financial, and digital. Personal exposure comes from the closest sphere, family members, partners, ex-partners, long-term staff, friends who know too much, and former allies whose frustration or resentment may one day find an outlet. Legal exposure grows from unresolved disputes, dormant liabilities, opaque structures inherited from previous advisors, and obligations left unattended for too long. Financial exposure appears in centralized banking, illiquid assets, concentrated ownership, or reliance on jurisdictions that may not protect you when you need them most. Digital exposure, though less visible, is often the most corrosive: years of email trails, informal messages, archived pictures, forgotten accounts, metadata, and cross-network linkages that form an unintentional biography of your movements.

Each of these elements may feel insignificant when examined in isolation. But together, they form the blueprint for another person's leverage. The map must remain alive, reviewed regularly, updated without hesitation and, most importantly, understood directly by you. Advisors can help interpret exposure, but they cannot own the map on your behalf. Delegating visibility is, in practice, delegating your survival.

The cost of overreaction

Exposure triggers instinct, and instinct in high-pressure environments is almost always the wrong guide. Panic leads to actions that feel decisive but signal instability: abrupt liquidation of assets, sudden restructuring, changing advisors without strategy, or dismantling long-standing entities in the hope that movement equals safety. In reality, these actions create more visibility, not less.

Some jurisdictions treat abrupt changes as automatic red flags, triggering audits or reviews. Banking systems notice sudden fund movements and generate alerts that travel faster than you imagine. Even well-intentioned public statements can be misread as defensiveness; legal threats can be interpreted as intimidation; visible withdrawal from public roles can create the illusion of guilt where none exists.

Overreaction is rarely interpreted as strength. It is interpreted as confession. And stillness, when chosen deliberately and not out of fear, is often the strongest signal you can send. Strategy is not always action, sometimes the correct move is the one the outside world never sees.

Knowing when to stay still

Acting under pressure can destroy more than inaction ever would. Silence is not passivity. Stillness is not surrender. There are moments in which speaking, moving, or reacting would escalate the situation far beyond its actual significance. Media speculation without legal foundation is one such moment. The desire to correct the record is natural, but every public correction invites another wave of attention, another interpretation, another reshaping of your narrative by people who do not have your interests in mind.

Strategic stillness is not built on hope. It is grounded in assessment, legal facts, jurisdictional dynamics, reputational maps, and an understanding of how systems behave when they sense movement. The discipline is in recognizing when the storm is noise rather than threat, and when doing nothing protects more value than any immediate intervention. Mastering this discipline is one of the defining traits of individuals who endure exposure without losing structural integrity.

Early-warning signals before exposure becomes public

Exposure rarely arrives unannounced. It casts a shadow before it becomes a headline. The warning signs are subtle: unusual questions from someone who normally asks none, a shift in tone from a partner or advisor, delays from institutions that were once responsive, or the quiet appearance of people you do not know asking about details they should not have. Sometimes the clue is as small as an unexpected request for documentation; other times, it is a silence that feels coordinated, not accidental.

Recognizing these signals does not require paranoia. It requires listening to the tone beneath the facts, those small changes that indicate someone, somewhere, is gathering information or preparing a narrative. Early detection gives you time to shift position before the exposure crystallizes.

How exposure begins inside families, companies, and political circles

Exposure does not always come from institutions. It often originates inside the environments you believe to be safe. In families, exposure begins with conflict, inheritance tensions, or emotional ruptures that spread beyond private walls. In companies, it begins with employees seeking leverage, partners seeking renegotiation, or advisors who feel undervalued and begin trading information. In political circles, it begins with shifting allegiances, electoral cycles, or the need to distance oneself from certain names.

These are not attacks in the traditional sense. They are tectonic shifts inside human structures, and once they begin, they often spill outward.

Damage assessment: real vs. Perceived risk

You cannot navigate exposure without distinguishing noise from threat. Some events generate a storm of attention but hold no real legal or institutional danger. Others unfold quietly, without public comment, but reshape entire futures. Many high-net-worth individuals react incorrectly because they misinterpret which category they are facing.

Clarity comes from asking three questions: who controls the narrative? Who has jurisdiction? Who benefits from your reaction? The answers determine whether the event is a reputational ripple, a legal precursor, or a systemic threat. Noise distracts. Threat reshapes landscapes. And yeah, knowing the difference often decides the outcome.

From movement to pattern: the architecture behind the attack

Exposure is not random, it always follows a pattern, even when the pattern feels chaotic. First, someone gathers information. Then they test reactions. Then they build a narrative. Then systems amplify and chaos often arise. Understanding this sequence gives you control over timing and response. Once you know the architecture, you can predict where pressure will appear next and where you should never place your attention.

When exposure becomes leverage

In many cases, exposure is not an end, it is a tactic. A leaked document, a rumor, a threat of publication or investigation becomes a bargaining tool. People use exposure the way others use money: to negotiate, coerce, destabilize, or force agreements. Those who understand this dynamic learn to differentiate between genuine risk and manufactured leverage, avoiding traps that were designed to provoke a reaction.

Final note

Exposure is not a question of if, it is a matter of when, and under what circumstances. It often enters quietly: a headline, a request, a lawsuit, a silence that feels heavier than it should. By the time you sense it, the first phase has already passed. This chapter was not designed to alarm you. It was designed to illuminate the landscape, to show you where the real dangers live and where the illusions of danger disguise themselves as threats.

Exposure does not mark the end. It marks the beginning of a shift, from perception to protocol, from instinct to architecture, from reaction to structure. What happens next depends entirely on what you have prepared before this moment arrived.

Chapter II. Legal shields and strategic defense

Understanding jurisdictional fragility

Your legal identity: the four anchors that shape your life

Your legal identity is built on four elements that determine how different countries interpret your presence, your obligations, and your connection to their systems. These elements are residency, domicile, citizenship, and the geographical patterns of your daily life. Although they appear simple, they influence almost every aspect of your legal and personal landscape and play a significant role in how institutions, authorities, and private actors respond to you.

Most people think of identity as something personal: your name, your profession, or your family background. In the legal world, identity is defined instead by the jurisdictions that can claim you, tax you, regulate you, or expect compliance with their rules. Understanding these four anchors is essential for anyone whose life crosses borders or whose activities take place in more than one country. The more international your life becomes, the more important it is to know how each jurisdiction interprets your connection to it. This knowledge is what prevents contradictions, misunderstandings, and unnecessary exposure.

Residency tells a state where you live. Domicile links you to the legal culture that governs your personal and family affairs. Citizenship ties you to a political entity that may require disclosures, obligations, or allegiance. Your geographic identity reflects your real behavior and movements, often captured automatically through data. When these anchors point in the same direction, your legal environment is relatively predictable. When they conflict, they create doubt, and doubt is what triggers scrutiny.

The aim is not to simplify your life into a single jurisdiction, because most international individuals do not operate in one. The goal is to understand how your connections are perceived and to ensure they do not contradict each other. That clarity is what allows you to design a stable and coherent legal position.

Residency: your operational anchor

Residency is the most immediate and practical aspect of your legal identity. It concerns where you actually live and how your daily patterns align with the laws of the country you call home. Many people believe that residency is determined by permits, declarations, or intentions. In reality, residency follows your real life, not your stated preferences.

Authorities use a range of factual indicators to determine residency, including where you spend most of your time, where your family lives, where you keep a home, and how your financial and social routines are structured. International organizations such as the OECD also apply a sequence of criteria to resolve conflicts, beginning with the place where you maintain a permanent home and continuing through your center of personal and economic interests, your habitual presence, and, in certain cases, your nationality.

Residency affects everything from personal taxation to administrative duties. It determines which country expects your declarations, how your income is interpreted, and what benefits or obligations apply to you. If the story you tell about where you live does not match the reality reflected in your travel patterns, spending habits, contracts, and digital traces, authorities will usually rely on the latter. For this reason, residency must always be aligned with verifiable facts rather than preference or convenience.

Domicile: your lifetime legal anchor

Domicile is a deeper and more enduring concept than residency. While residency may change frequently, domicile often stays with you for many years and, in some countries, for life. It is the jurisdiction that governs your personal law, particularly in areas such as inheritance, marital regimes, succession rights, and family matters.

Your domicile can determine how your estate is distributed after death, how disputes within the family are resolved, and which laws apply to major life events. Even if you live abroad for extended periods, your domicile may continue to influence your legal and financial affairs unless you take deliberate and formal steps to change it. Some jurisdictions make this especially difficult.

Domicile is one of the most overlooked elements in the planning of wealthy families, yet its implications are significant. Conflicts between domicile and residency can lead to disputes over which country has authority over your estate, which courts can hear family-related matters, and whether certain structures–such as trusts, foundations, or marital agreements–will be recognized or challenged.

Citizenship: your geopolitical anchor

Citizenship defines your political and legal connection to a state. It affects how you are treated by immigration systems, financial institutions, and international authorities. For individuals with high visibility or substantial assets, citizenship can either reduce friction or create additional layers of scrutiny.

Different nationalities are interpreted differently by institutions. Some passports are associated with stability, low geopolitical risk, and predictable legal frameworks. Others are treated with caution due to sanctions, political tensions, or regulatory constraints tied to the issuing state. This affects everything from banking procedures to travel requirements.

Your citizenship determines where you enjoy certain rights, where you may be required to comply with tax or reporting rules, and how authorities react when you move across borders. It can also influence extradition risk, visa access, and the level of due diligence required to open accounts, invest, or establish a presence in another country. When an individual holds multiple citizenships, these considerations increase rather than decrease, and each state may apply its own expectations and obligations independently of the others.

Geographic identity: your real pattern of life

Geographic identity is the practical expression of your movements and routines. It is formed by the places you frequent, the routes you travel, the cards you use, the properties you rent or own, and the digital traces you leave behind. While residency, domicile, and citizenship reflect legal categories, geographic identity reflects observable behavior.

Authorities, banks, and automated systems often rely on geographic identity to verify the credibility of your declared circumstances. Airline data, transaction records, hotel registrations, mobile geolocation, and other everyday signals reveal where you truly spend your time. If these patterns align with your declared residence, they strengthen your position. If they contradict it, they may prompt questions, audits, or administrative decisions that are difficult to reverse.

Geographic identity is not inherently positive or negative. It simply provides a factual description of your life. The challenge arises when it contradicts the legal narrative you present. Ensuring consistency between your behavior and your declarations is a fundamental aspect of maintaining a stable legal profile.

When your anchors conflict

Conflicts between residency, domicile, citizenship, and geographic identity are common among individuals with international lives. A person may claim residence in one country, remain domiciled in another, hold citizenship from a third, and spend most of their actual time in a fourth. Although common, this mix can produce uncertainty for the institutions interpreting the situation.

When these anchors point in different directions, authorities may question the legitimacy of declarations, claim jurisdiction unexpectedly, or deny benefits and protections normally available to residents or citizens. Conflicts can result in tax audits, challenges to inheritance or family arrangements, migration issues, or the denial of treaty advantages that depend on a clear and verifiable link to one jurisdiction.

Inconsistent anchors do not necessarily indicate wrongdoing, but they can create ambiguity. And in the legal world, ambiguity invites scrutiny. The objective is not to eliminate complexity but to ensure that each anchor has a clear purpose and that the overall picture is coherent.

When these elements are aligned, your legal position becomes more stable and predictable across borders.

Understanding jurisdictional fragility

Every jurisdiction has its own logic, its own priorities, and its own way of interpreting the behavior of individuals who live, invest, or operate within its borders. Legal exposure is not fixed; it shifts depending on geography, political climate, institutional culture, and even public sentiment. A perfectly lawful action in one country may be questioned elsewhere, and an activity tolerated for decades may suddenly fall under new scrutiny after a political change or regulatory reform.

The stability of a jurisdiction is often assumed, but in practice it is never guaranteed. Democracies adjust their definitions of compliance, authoritarian states reinterpret ordinary behavior as misconduct when it serves political goals, and countries under economic pressure may adopt a more aggressive fiscal or regulatory posture. These shifts rarely happen in isolation. Countries communicate, exchange information, and react to each other's decisions. A development in one place may influence how your activities are viewed somewhere else.

When your life crosses borders, you must recognize that you operate within overlapping systems. Each system has its own expectations, but also its own vulnerabilities. Some states rely heavily on data-driven enforcement; others are influenced by politics or public mood; some are efficient and process-driven; others are inconsistent, slow, or arbitrary. Your exposure is shaped by the weakest or most unpredictable jurisdiction in your personal landscape, not necessarily the one you interact with the most.

A high-net-worth individual can be fully compliant in one country while being unexpectedly exposed in another country. This is not because of wrongdoing, but because governments interpret the same facts through different lenses. One state may see opportunity in your presence, another may view it as leverage, and another may treat it as a responsibility. The fragility of jurisdictions lies in these competing interpretations.

Understanding this diversity does not eliminate exposure, but it gives you the perspective needed to manage it. Knowing how each jurisdiction perceives you–your wealth, your mobility, your business activity, and your political or social proximity–allows you to anticipate behavior instead of reacting to it. The more you understand the systems that surround you, the easier it becomes to shape a legal and structural position that remains stable even when the external environment changes.

Civil risk and narrative-based exposure

Civil exposure does not begin in a courtroom. It often starts much earlier, in the informal spaces where impressions form, conversations circulate, and personal moments acquire a life of their own. In today's world, private actions are rarely contained, and public noise can escalate into legal pressure more quickly than most people expect. For individuals with visibility or resources, the boundary between everyday life and civil liability is especially thin.

Civil risk includes defamation, privacy claims, retaliation through litigation, business disputes, and conflicts arising from partnerships or investments. Some of these situations develop gradually; others appear suddenly when someone interprets a gesture, a comment, or a decision in a way that places you on the defensive. Wealth or public presence often amplifies these dynamics, not because the claims are stronger, but because people assume you will settle, negotiate, or compromise in order to protect your reputation.

This dynamic is heavily influenced by narration. A story that takes shape online, within a community, or through private conversations can become the foundation of a civil claim even if the original details were incomplete or misunderstood. The legal process often arrives last; the erosion of trust, credibility, or perceived legitimacy tends to happen first.

The civil battlefield

Civil disputes today unfold across different arenas at the same time. Social media, professional networks, private messaging groups, and industry circles all contribute to how a situation is interpreted. A minor disagreement can become a reputational event. A miscommunication can lead to escalating demands. A private dispute can be reframed as misconduct. Each of these steps increases your exposure long before a lawyer becomes involved.

People respond to stories, not evidence. By the time a civil claim is formally made, many minds may already be shaped by the narrative that preceded it. This is why civil exposure often feels disproportionate. The legal claim may be small, yet the reputational implications are far larger.

Social media as evidence

HNWIs use the same platforms as everyone else, but they are not interpreted in the same way. A photograph, a comment, or a location tag can be taken out of context and used to support claims about your habits, your wealth, or your intentions. Algorithms surface old content without warning. Posts made in a lighthearted moment may be viewed through a legal or political lens years later.

Even silent digital behavior produces an impact. A "like" on a sensitive topic can be read as a public stance. Sharing an article can be treated as endorsement. A message exchanged casually can be copied, forwarded, or misrepresented. For individuals who operate across borders, these interpretations may influence immigration decisions, banking relationships, contract negotiations, or ongoing legal matters.

The illusion of private spaces

Many platforms present themselves as private environments, but very few actually are. Closed groups leak. Private messages are forwarded. Screenshots circulate. Context is lost. Automated systems flag content without understanding nuance. What feels intimate in practice is often porous, and the fragments that escape can be interpreted as complete stories.

This matters because civil claims today rarely rely solely on formal correspondence or official documents. They are built from pieces—photos, messages, comments, impressions. None of these elements need to be dramatic to influence a judge, a journalist, or a counterpart in a negotiation. Once out of your hands, your information becomes material for interpretation.

Narrative escalation and legal consequences

A narrative does not need to be malicious to become dangerous. It only needs momentum. A comment taken the wrong way may shape someone's perception of your intentions. A frustrated business partner may describe events in a way that frames you as responsible for an outcome you did not cause. A personal conflict may later appear in the form of a demand letter.

When the story grows louder than the facts, civil exposure increases. Contracts are terminated, partnerships dissolve, opportunities vanish, and institutions become more cautious. Visa applications may be delayed, banks may request additional documentation, and regulators may begin asking questions. All of this can happen without any wrongdoing on your part.

For these reasons, managing civil risk is not only about responding to claims. It is about understanding how your actions, your online presence, and your interactions can be interpreted, and about maintaining a posture that limits the opportunity for narratives to grow unchecked.

Criminal exposure: the quiet door everyone forgets

Criminal exposure does not always arise from intentional wrongdoing. For many individuals with complex lives and responsibilities spread across multiple jurisdictions, risk often appears through oversight, delegation, or structural gaps that no one noticed until the moment they mattered. Modern criminal systems treat certain administrative or regulatory failures as potential offenses, and the threshold for what triggers an investigation is lower—and more unpredictable—than most people expect.

In many countries, behavior that was considered minor or irrelevant a few years ago may now fall under stricter enforcement, not because the activity changed but because the political environment did. When authorities face pressure to demonstrate control, efficiency, or fairness, they often turn their attention to individuals who are visible, mobile, or perceived as influential. Criminal law then becomes a tool of signaling, not only a mechanism of justice.

For high-net-worth individuals, this creates a distinct challenge. It is rarely the conviction that causes damage; it is the accusation itself. Once a criminal process begins, the reputational impact moves faster than any procedural protection. Even when the facts are eventually clarified, the emotional, financial, and operational consequences remain.

Crimes born from negligence

Most exposure does not involve dramatic conduct. It arises from technical noncompliance, late filings, errors in reporting, improper delegation, or gaps in governance. A missed form, an unregistered transaction, or an administrative delay may be interpreted as intentional rather than accidental, especially when the individual involved has wealth or influence. Cases involving data protection, financial reporting, cross-border movements of assets, and digital infrastructure are increasingly common and often begin quietly, through automated alerts or routine verification.

Political prosecution

Some jurisdictions use criminal investigations to pursue objectives unrelated to the alleged offense. A wealthy individual may become a convenient example for demonstrating institutional strength, addressing public frustration, or pressuring a network of associates. In these environments, criminal law is less about the underlying facts and more about the narrative built around the case. Being adjacent to political actors, operating in sensitive industries, or maintaining visible international ties may increase this risk, even if your conduct is fully lawful.

Criminal accusation as reputational destruction

Long before any court reaches a verdict, the simple act of opening an investigation can affect business relationships, banking access, travel permissions, contract negotiations, and personal trust. Institutions tend to react defensively. Banks may temporarily freeze access. Corporate partners may distance themselves. Regulators may take interest in unrelated matters. These reactions are not necessarily punitive; they are operational responses designed to protect themselves from uncertainty. What damages you is not the conviction but the presumption that something may be wrong.

How wealth amplifies suspicion

Wealth often changes how authorities interpret behavior. Transactions that would be overlooked for an ordinary citizen may appear suspicious when carried out by someone with substantial resources. The same is true for mobility, private structures, or professional relationships. Complexity, even when justified and lawful, can be mistaken for concealment.

For this reason, transparency and internal coherence are essential. When your actions make sense on paper, in practice, and in context, institutions are less likely to reinterpret them. But when your structures are inconsistent or your explanations contradict your documented behavior, even simple events may escalate.

Criminal exposure is therefore not only about legality. It is about maintaining systems that remain calm, logical, and well-documented under scrutiny, and ensuring that your advisors, your structures, and your records support the version of events you know to be true.

Fiscal pressure: when you become a high-yield target

Taxation is often presented as a neutral obligation, a simple interaction between an individual and the state. In practice, it is one of the most strategic areas of exposure for anyone with significant assets, mobility, or visibility. Modern tax authorities operate in an environment shaped by political expectations, public opinion, international cooperation, and the increasing dependency on automated systems. As a result, wealthy individuals are not simply contributors; they are treated as high-yield profiles whose compliance carries symbolic weight.

Fiscal pressure today does not begin with a dispute. It begins with observation. Authorities analyze travel patterns, registry data, transactional flows, corporate filings, property ownership, lifestyle indicators, and digital footprints. Even before a question is asked, the system has already formed an impression of your behavior and the likelihood that further review will produce results. This is not about suspicion; it is about prioritization.

The psychology of tax authorities

Tax administrations are expected to demonstrate fairness, efficiency, and control. When public budgets tighten or political pressure rises, the focus often shifts to individuals whose cases can deliver revenue, deterrence, or public reassurance. Wealth amplifies this effect. A discrepancy that would be ignored in an ordinary case may attract immediate attention when the amounts involved are substantial.

Authorities also operate under the assumption that individuals with complex lives may inadvertently make mistakes. This assumption encourages proactive reviews. The more international your activity, the more likely it is to fall within a category monitored for inconsistencies.

Algorithmic suspicion

Much of the initial screening now happens through automated systems. Algorithms compare declarations with information from banks, registries, foreign authorities, and third-party databases. They identify inconsistencies such as:

- declared residence that does not match travel data
- spending patterns inconsistent with reported income
- company ownership structures that appear artificial
- abrupt changes in economic behavior
- missing, late, or duplicated filings

These systems do not decide guilt or innocence. They decide who merits a closer look. Once flagged, the human review that follows tends to be stricter, because the assumption is that something within the profile triggered the alert.

CRS, FATCA, and Beneficial Ownership Registers

International cooperation has transformed the notion of financial privacy. CRS and FATCA automatically transmit information about your accounts, corporate structures, and financial flows to the jurisdictions that claim you. Beneficial ownership registers reveal personal and corporate connections that once remained private. Even countries that historically protected discretion have adapted to global transparency standards.

The consequence is not only that authorities have more data, but that they expect your declarations to match this data perfectly. Any gap is interpreted as a potential misalignment. The burden shifts to you to demonstrate consistency.

The burden of proof shift

Once an inconsistency is identified, the dynamics change. You are no longer responding to routine questions; you are required to justify your decisions, your structure, your residency, and your reported activity in a way that withstands both legal and factual scrutiny.

In some regions, retrospective audits now span several years, and authorities may request explanations for transactions or movements that seemed irrelevant at the time.

This shift does not reflect hostility. It reflects a global trend toward greater control, driven by technology and international cooperation. For individuals with assets and mobility, the most effective way to reduce fiscal exposure is not by hiding or simplifying their lives, but by ensuring that the facts of their life, the documents that support them, and the legal structures they use all align under a coherent and lawful framework.

Fiscal pressure is not only financial. It affects trust, mobility, and long-term planning. Those who maintain clarity, consistency, and proper documentation rarely face lasting difficulties. Those who rely on assumptions or outdated habits often encounter challenges that could have been prevented through timely structure and discipline.

Transnational risk: how systems join forces

Cross-border life creates a landscape where multiple jurisdictions can interpret your actions at the same time. What happens in one country no longer stays confined to that country; it can influence how you are treated elsewhere, even if the systems involved operate independently and have different priorities. This interconnectedness is one of the most underestimated sources of exposure for individuals who live internationally or whose financial and personal affairs span several regions.

Transnational risk does not arise because you have done something wrong. It emerges because you are visible across systems that communicate, coordinate, or act based on their own internal logic. Some countries exchange information automatically, others respond to specific requests, and some take unilateral action based on what they perceive as their interest or responsibility. The result is a patchwork of procedures that can affect you unpredictably.

A civil dispute in one country may lead to financial restrictions elsewhere. A regulatory inquiry can trigger questions in jurisdictions that would otherwise have no connection to your case. An administrative misunderstanding in a place where you rarely spend time may create obstacles when you attempt to operate or travel in another region. Each system views your situation from its own perspective, but the combined effect can be significant.

Treaties and cooperative frameworks

International treaties play a central role in connecting jurisdictions. Agreements on taxation, criminal cooperation, asset tracing, and administrative assistance allow countries to request information, freeze assets, or coordinate investigations with varying degrees of formality. Some treaties require full due process, while others rely on simplified procedures or reciprocal trust. As a result, the same request can be treated with strict scrutiny in one country and with immediate compliance in another.

Understanding the network of treaties that applies to your life is important, because these agreements can extend your exposure far beyond what you might expect.

Extradition and cross-border enforcement

Extradition is one of the clearest examples of transnational cooperation. A person may face an investigation or accusation in one country and find themselves subject to detention or surrender in another, even if the underlying conduct is legal where it occurred. Extradition procedures vary widely in fairness and reliability. Some countries require strong evidence and judicial oversight. Others act quickly, placing the burden on the individual to challenge the process.

For someone with international mobility, the safest jurisdictions for travel are not always the most obvious ones.

Enforcement of foreign judgments

A judgment issued abroad can be recognized and enforced in another jurisdiction with surprising efficiency. Property can be frozen, bank accounts restricted, or contractual rights suspended based on a decision you may not have known existed.

Enforcement often happens before you are notified, because many treaties allow authorities to act proactively to preserve assets. This is not unusual; it is standard procedure.

The lesson is not to avoid international engagement, but to ensure that you always know where potential claims might arise and how they could interact with your presence in other regions.

Simultaneous audits and parallel procedures

It is increasingly common for different authorities to open independent procedures based on the same set of facts. A tax audit in one country may be accompanied by regulatory inquiries in another. A business dispute may trigger compliance checks elsewhere. These procedures do not have to be coordinated to produce cumulative pressure. Each authority acts in its own way and on its own timeline, but the combined effect can overwhelm even well-structured individuals if they are not prepared.

Conflicting legal cultures

Not all jurisdictions interpret law the same way. Some prioritize due process. Others prioritize efficiency. Some rely heavily on documentation; others on testimony. Some operate within clear legal frameworks; others leave broad discretion to authorities. When you live across borders, these differences shape your experience. A routine administrative question in one country might be treated as a compliance concern elsewhere. A delay in responding to an authority in one jurisdiction may be interpreted as evasion in another.

Understanding these cultural differences does not remove risk, but it helps you anticipate how your actions will be interpreted and how your decisions in one place may influence your position in another.

Transnational exposure is a natural consequence of global mobility. It becomes dangerous only when individuals assume that each jurisdiction will interpret their situation independently. In reality, these systems are increasingly interconnected, and their combined influence is what shapes the environment in which you operate.

Structural weakness: people, teams, environments

Exposure rarely comes from distant institutions or abstract systems. Most of the time, it begins in familiar places: the people you trust, the environments you frequent, and the structures you rely on to manage your life. Wealth and mobility expand your circle, and with that expansion comes a larger surface of vulnerability. Understanding where these weaknesses appear—and why—is essential to building a stable protective framework.

Structural weakness is not about blaming others. It is about recognizing how information travels, how conflicts escalate, and how ordinary interactions can unintentionally create openings that others may use. When you understand these dynamics, you can design better boundaries without isolating yourself or limiting your relationships.

Family, relationships, and conflict

The people closest to you generally have no intention of causing harm. Yet they often hold the most information, the deepest emotional access, and the greatest insight into your routines and vulnerabilities. Conflicts, divorces, financial disputes, or personal tension can turn this proximity into exposure. Even benign situations—comments made in passing, misunderstandings shared with friends, or frustrations expressed during difficult moments—can travel far beyond their original context.

Family members may also face their own external pressures. A problem unrelated to you can spill outward, connecting you indirectly to claims, publicity, or investigations.

The lesson is not to distance yourself from those you care about, but to understand how your personal environment interacts with your public and legal reality.

Advisors under pressure

Advisors play an important role in shaping your decisions and maintaining stability. Yet their ability to protect you depends heavily on their discipline, their professional integrity, and their ability to perform under stress. An advisor who excels in normal circumstances may struggle when confronted with media attention, regulatory inquiries, or high-stakes conflict.

Choosing advisors is not only about credentials; it is also about temperament. Some professionals rush under pressure, take shortcuts, or communicate informally when the situation demands structure. Others may prioritize their own reputation or interests over yours, even unintentionally.

This is why advisors should be evaluated not only for what they know, but for how they behave when the environment becomes difficult. Testing this early saves time and prevents exposure later.

Professional teams and institutional environments

Success expands your operational structure. Assistants, employees, consultants, accountants, fund managers, and external partners all interact with a different fragment of your world. Problems arise when: information circulates without control, responsibilities are not clearly defined, conflicts of interest go unnoticed, - or too much reliance is placed on a single person.

Weak internal processes can expose you even when everyone involved has good intentions. A small mistake—an email sent to the wrong person, a misplaced document, a shared login, a poorly drafted contract—can grow into a larger issue simply because it entered the wrong environment.

Strong teams are those that understand boundaries, follow protocols, and maintain professional distance even when they work closely with you.

Digital ecosystems

Much of your personal and professional life passes through digital platforms: cloud services, messaging apps, client portals, email systems, and social networks. Each of these environments carries its own risk. Data may be hosted in jurisdictions you have never visited. Encryption may not be configured correctly. Access may be shared more widely than intended. Even if the platform itself is secure, users are not always disciplined. Screenshots are taken, conversations are forwarded, and files are accessed from public networks. Every digital interaction creates a trace that can travel far beyond your control.

The issue is not technology; it is alignment. Systems must be chosen, configured, and used in a way that matches your level of exposure.

Social ecosystems

Clubs, charitable boards, events, schools, luxury service providers, real estate brokers, travel partners, and private communities all create networks of interaction. These environments are often friendly and informal, but they are not neutral.

Information circulates quickly. People draw conclusions from partial visibility. Competitors observe each other. Personal stories become material for discussion. Most reputational narratives start here, not in public spaces.

And your goal is not to withdraw from these environments but to understand how they operate and how they interpret presence, absence, behavior, and association. When you know how a social ecosystem works, you can participate without unintentionally creating stories that may later reach the wrong audience.

Structural weakness is part of life, especially for individuals who move across jurisdictions and interact with diverse groups. The purpose of understanding these weaknesses is not to eliminate them, but to ensure that they do not surprise you. When the people around you, the systems you use, and the environments you enter all align with your level of exposure, your risk becomes measurable, manageable, and far less likely to escalate.

Preventive defense architecture

Most people only think about defense once they are already under pressure. For individuals with complex lives, this timing is reversed. Effective protection is built long before anything goes wrong, while the environment is calm and you still control the pace. Preventive defense is not about anticipating every possible scenario; it is about creating a structure that can absorb shocks without collapsing.

A preventive architecture aligns your lifestyle, your documents, your advisors, your digital practices, and your mobility patterns into a coherent system. When each part of your life is consistent with the others, institutions interpret your behavior as stable and predictable. When your systems contradict each other, even minor issues can escalate.

Preventive defense is not about fear. It is about clarity, discipline, and designing a life that remains functional even when circumstances shift unexpectedly. The more international your activity, the more important it becomes to prepare before you need protection.

Why defense begins before the attack

A crisis rarely begins with an obvious signal. It often starts with a small inconsistency, an unexpected inquiry, or a misunderstanding that someone else may interpret in a way you did not anticipate. When your systems are not prepared, even a minor request can create stress, urgency, and confusion. But when the fundamentals are in place—structured files, organized entities, disciplined routines—the same request becomes manageable.

Preventive defense is essentially an investment in stability. It ensures that no single event, whether legal, personal, or administrative, has the power to destabilize you completely.

Compartmentalization

Compartmentalization is one of the strongest forms of structural discipline but with easy implementation. It does not depend on secrecy or complexity; it only depends on your organization.

Each part of your life should operate within its own boundary. Advisors should have access only to the information required for their work. Personal matters should be insulated from business matters. Sensitive assets should not depend on the same people or processes that manage your public activities.

Compartmentalization prevents chain reactions. If one area becomes vulnerable—because of a mistake, a dispute, or an external event—the impact remains contained. This approach requires regular maintenance. Boundaries can weaken over time, especially when routines evolve or when people become too familiar with your environment. Reviewing your structures periodically helps ensure that each area still stands on its own.

Layered protection

A strong defensive posture relies on multiple layers. Your public-facing information forms the outer layer. Behind it stands your professional and financial structure, and behind that, your private and personal world.

When the outer layer absorbs routine pressure—questions, public scrutiny, administrative requests—the deeper layers remain untouched. Many individuals inadvertently reverse this order by exposing their personal lives publicly while placing their financial or structural arrangements too close to the surface. This inversion makes them vulnerable.

And remember, layered protection does not hide your life; it only arranges it in a way that protects what matters most from unnecessary exposure.

Documentation as a shield

Documentation is one of the simplest yet most effective tools in preventive defense. Well-organized records—contracts, emails, explanations of decisions, internal protocols—provide clarity when questions arise.

When an authority or counterpart requests information, the ability to present complete, coherent documents reduces doubt and limits escalation.

This applies equally to digital documentation. Cloud systems, shared folders, messaging apps, and archives must be configured to match your level of exposure. A misplaced file or an unprotected device can create risks that are disproportionate to the underlying content.

Documentation is not an administrative formality. It is the foundation that allows you to demonstrate lawful intent and coherent behavior in situations where interpretation matters.

Mobility patterns as evidence

Your physical movement is often interpreted as a form of evidence. Travel records, hotel registrations, immigration stamps, flight manifests, and transaction locations create a continuous map of your real life. When your mobility reflects your declared circumstances, your profile appears consistent. When it contradicts them, it may raise questions.

Preventive defense means ensuring that your travel aligns with your legal identity, your fiscal position, and your structural choices. It also means understanding when a particular route, destination, or timing may inadvertently create exposure.

Mobility itself is not a risk. The risk arises when movement generates a picture that does not match the rest of your life. Preventive defense helps you maintain alignment so that your patterns reinforce rather than undermine your position.

Crisis protocols: what happens when pressure arrives

A crisis rarely announces itself clearly. It often begins with a letter, a sudden inquiry, a bank request, a complaint, or an unexpected notification. Sometimes it starts with silence—an application delayed, access restricted, or a system that suddenly responds differently than usual. When this happens, your reaction becomes as important as the underlying issue. How you handle the first hours and days of pressure shapes the entire trajectory that follows.

Crisis management is not about improvisation. It is about slowing the situation down, limiting movement, and making sure that the decisions you take under stress do not create additional exposure. Even strong cases can become vulnerable when handled impulsively, and even serious situations can be contained when approached with discipline and calm.

The purpose of crisis protocols is not to guarantee a favorable outcome; no system can offer that. Their purpose is to preserve options, protect your position, and avoid creating new weaknesses while the facts are being understood.

Containment

The first goal in any crisis is containment. This means bringing the situation under control by reducing unnecessary activity, centralizing communication, and ensuring that information does not move in unpredictable ways.

Containment is not defensive or evasive; it is responsible. It prevents misunderstandings, limits the spread of inaccurate details, and gives you the space to understand what is actually happening before reacting publicly or formally.

Once containment begins, only the essential people should continue handling the matter. Devices, documents, and records should be secured. Communication should shift to reliable and confidential channels. Internal conversations should be minimal and deliberate. Containment buys time, and time is what gives you the ability to make informed decisions.

Assembling the right perimeter

In moments of pressure, your existing team may not be enough. Crisis situations often require specialized expertise—regulatory defense lawyers, cross-border litigators, asset-protection strategists, or advisors with experience in enforcement procedures. Selecting these professionals must be done calmly and discreetly.

In smaller jurisdictions or niche industries, everyone knows each other. A single premature conversation can reveal your posture before you are ready. Sometimes it is safer to involve independent intermediaries or separate legal entities to manage the initial engagement with specialists. Your perimeter is not only legal; it is strategic and emotional, and logically, the people you bring close to you in a crisis will influence every step that follows.

Response strategy

Once the perimeter is in place, every response must be structured. No informal explanations. No personal clarifications. And no messages sent under stress, even if the intention is good.

Authorities and institutions rely on the tone and coherence of your responses to decide whether to escalate or stabilize a situation. Over-explaining invites new questions; under-explaining can appear uncooperative. The balance lies in delivering what is required by law, and only that. When handled correctly, a crisis response becomes a controlled process, not a negotiation under pressure.

Jurisdictional retreat vs. Legal standing

When pressure increases, many individuals are tempted to leave the jurisdiction or pause their presence until matters calm down. While this instinct is understandable, timing is crucial. Leaving at the wrong moment can trigger formal presumptions, asset freezes, restrictions on movement, or accusations of evasion. Remaining, however, can also be risky if the environment becomes unpredictable or if authorities decide to act quickly.

Retreat is not inherently harmful. In some cases, it is the safest long-term choice. The key is to plan it early, when the situation is still stable and your departure appears structured rather than reactive. Families can relocate in advance, assets can be reorganized, and the legal command structure can be moved to a jurisdiction with stronger guarantees. This approach allows for negotiation or resolution without the optics of escape.

Designing the defensive perimeter

Every individual with cross-border exposure needs more than a single line of defense. A well-designed perimeter has several layers that protect each other.

The outer layer includes what is public: filings, corporate information, social media presence, and visible activity. The middle layer contains your business structure, banking relationships, and operational routines. The inner layer holds what is most private: family, personal relationships, motivations, and vulnerabilities. When pressure begins, the outer layer absorbs the initial impact. The middle layer slows the momentum. The inner layer remains insulated.

Crises escalate when these layers are mixed—when personal matters become visible, when operational routines depend on emotional decisions, or when financial structures are exposed without protection. Of course, a defensive perimeter does not completely isolate you; it organizes your world in a way that prevents external events from reaching what matters most.

Final note

Understanding the legal landscape is not about memorizing rules, it is about recognizing how those rules interpret you. Every jurisdiction reads your presence through its own logic, and every system forms an opinion long before you speak.

The purpose of this chapter was not to overwhelm you with technicalities, but to show you the ground on which your life stands. When you understand the legal frame that surrounds you – residency, domicile, tax position, reporting duties, and institutional expectations – you stop floating in the dark. You move with intention, and the systems around you respond with clarity instead of suspicion.

Chapter III. Digital attack and media exposure

The logic of media systems

It is impossible to anticipate every attack, and no structure, no matter how well designed, can eliminate risk entirely. What you *can and must do* is control the surface you expose. You can shape your presence so that nothing significant can be used against you, and you can learn to see yourself the way the system sees you long before anyone attempts to weaponize that perception.

The purpose of this chapter is to show how exposure actually forms: where it starts, how it grows, who amplifies it, and at what point you must intervene to stop its momentum. Digital exposure is not a secondary threat sitting alongside others. It is the environment in which every other risk takes shape, accelerates, and becomes visible. Understanding that environment is the first step toward controlling it.

Why visibility is a currency

Visibility has become a modern form of capital, liquid, volatile, and traded in ways that resemble financial markets more than traditional journalism. You do not choose to participate in this economy; participation begins the moment someone takes interest in you. Once your name appears in a feed, a registry, or a headline, you enter a system that profits from attention and interprets your life according to its own incentives.

This shift carries profound consequences. Media outlets monetize visibility. Platforms reward it. Politicians exploit it. Adversaries manipulate it. Even silence becomes a form of participation, because refusing to speak does not keep you invisible; it merely leaves others free to define your meaning. In this world, visibility behaves like currency, speculated upon, inflated, suppressed, or weaponized according to the needs of those who find value in your presence.

For high-net-worth individuals, visibility is not a lifestyle choice, it is a structural reality that cannot be denied. You may avoid interviews, decline public appearances, or refuse to engage online, but the system still captures you. Your image, routines, travel, associations, and even your absences feed a machine that extracts stories the way financial markets extract price signals. Once your profile enters circulation, interpretation escapes your control. Your wealth, behaviors, and relationships become symbols that travel farther than your own words ever could.

Visibility, whether sought or resisted, becomes a resource that others use. Some amplify it to elevate themselves. Others distort it to damage you. Unless you learn to manage it as deliberately as you manage your assets, you will be subject to valuations that have nothing to do with who you are, yet determine how institutions and audiences treat you.

How narratives are selected, amplified, and recycled

Media systems operate not on accuracy but on narrative logic. Facts only gain traction when they fit into stories that resonate with existing cultural or political currents. A minor detail about your holdings may be irrelevant for years, then suddenly become central if it aligns with a broader narrative about inequality, corruption, privilege, or power. The frame determines the fate of the fact.

Amplification follows a familiar rhythm. An initial publication appears, sometimes in a fringe outlet, sometimes as a leak on a platform with no editorial oversight. Other outlets pick it up, often reducing context and sharpening emotion. Influencers add commentary that widens the audience. Opponents add insinuation. By the time institutions notice, the story has become a signal requiring response, not a claim requiring verification.

Once repeated often enough, even an inaccurate narrative becomes a form of metadata. It enters databases, compliance files, and OSINT tools. At that point, the truth matters less than the persistence of the story. Institutions act to manage optics, not to uncover substance. And what began as an interpretation becomes, through repetition, part of what others see, your official public profile.

The role of algorithms, aggregators, and incentives

Digital visibility is shaped far more by algorithms than by editors. These systems reward conflict, novelty, and emotional intensity. Content that performs well once is elevated again and again, regardless of fairness or context. A single negative story, if it gains traction, can remain visible for months simply because the system interprets it as "engaging."

Aggregators collect mentions of your name and link them to topics, locations, or other individuals. Monitoring tools used by journalists, regulators, and compliance officers rely on these same algorithms. As a result, your public identity becomes a cluster of associations that may have little to do with reality but are repeated because the system finds them useful.

Algorithms do not understand nuance; they understand momentum. Once your name acquires momentum, it circulates whether you participate or not.

Media gatekeepers: journalists, platforms, and shadow editors

The actors shaping your visibility extend far beyond journalists. Editorial teams frame stories according to impact, not balance. Headline writers optimize for clicks, they don't or cannot afford to care for responsible journalism. Corrections, when they appear, rarely reach the audience of the original.

Behind them stand other, less visible gatekeepers: platform moderators, algorithmic policy groups, automated filters, indexing systems, and compliance teams within large tech firms. These actors decide what surfaces, what disappears, what is flagged, and what remains searchable, not through legal standards but through internal rules that shift without notice.

Your reputation is influenced not only by what is said, but by which digital structures choose to highlight or suppress parts of your digital footprint. Accuracy becomes secondary to architecture.

How silence is interpreted, and sometimes provoked

Silence is often misread as admission. When a narrative spreads and you do not respond, audiences assume you cannot deny the claim. But in legal and strategic terms, silence may be the strongest defensive position you have. Speaking can trigger new liabilities. Clarifying can lock you into statements that adversaries reinterpret. Responding may amplify a story you are trying to contain.

Hostile actors understand this. They provoke, not to win an argument, but to pull you out of silence and force a misstep. Their goal is to move you from strategic restraint into reactive exposure.

Silence must therefore be intentional and controlled. In a media environment that thrives on reaction, choosing not to speak is not passivity, it is control.

Signal-reading: how others interpret your digital presence

People rarely judge you by what you say directly. They judge you by what they *think* they are seeing. Modern digital environments operate on interpretation rather than confirmation; they extract meaning from signals that were never meant to communicate anything at all.

Every gap is treated as intention. Every delay becomes a clue. Every mismatch between your public footprint and your private movements is interpreted as strategy. In this landscape, you are not only evaluated by your actions but also by the patterns others believe they can detect. And once a pattern is assumed, it becomes a filter through which all new information is interpreted.

Institutions do this systematically. Banks, regulators, compliance teams, and corporate intelligence services read your behavior the way analysts read financial markets, looking for shifts, anomalies, or inconsistencies. Journalists, on the other hand, read signals through narrative logic: they search for the detail that confirms a story they are already inclined to tell. Competitors interpret your signals through the lens of opportunity, deciding when to pressure, when to provoke, and when to remain silent.

Even individuals close to you, partners, advisors, employees, interpret your digital behavior unconsciously. A change in routine may be seen as instability. A sudden absence may be interpreted as conflict. A new travel pattern may suggest negotiation or retreat. None of these interpretations have to be correct to become influential. Once people believe they understand the underlying message, they will act based on that belief.

You do not control the conclusions others reach, but you can control the signals you emit. A consistent rhythm creates stability. A fragmented presence invites speculation. In environments where perception drives action, the way others read you becomes as important as the facts themselves. Understanding this process allows you to design your digital presence in a way that limits misinterpretation, reduces volatility, and prevents small signals from escalating into full narratives.

The architecture of unintentional exposure

Most people assume exposure happens when they say something publicly, make a mistake, or attract attention. But in high-visibility environments, the most damaging exposure rarely comes from deliberate actions. It comes from the architecture of your daily life, the silent systems that collect, synchronize, interpret, and distribute information without your involvement.

Your devices, accounts, and digital habits build a structure around you. Every app you install, every service you use, every identity you register creates another surface you do not fully control. Over time, this structure becomes a map that others can read even if you never intended to leave a trace. It reveals how you move, how you decide, who influences you, and what you care about. None of this requires a mistake; it only requires existence in a system designed to observe.

Exposure grows through routine: a calendar automatically syncing across platforms, a ride-sharing app that records every trip, a cloud backup that stores drafts you never meant to publish, a loyalty program that tracks your spending, or a device that logs your sleep, steps, or proximity to other devices. None of these data points reveal much on their own, but together they create a pattern, one detailed enough for others to interpret, model, or potentially exploit.

The danger is not that these systems malfunction. The danger is when they function perfectly. They record everything because that is their purpose. They share data because that is how they operate. They combine, mix, connect and track information because it makes the user experience smoother, at the cost of making your life legible to strangers, institutions, and adversaries.

You may believe that discretion protects you. In reality, discretion is only one layer. The architecture surrounding you continues to act even when you remain silent. If you do not shape this architecture intentionally, choosing what to reveal, what to separate, what to minimize, and what to isolate, it will shape itself around convenience, and convenience is rarely compatible with protection.

Unintentional exposure is not the result of carelessness. It is the result of an environment where every movement, preference, and interaction produces a record. Understanding this architecture is the first step in weakening its influence, while controlling it is the first step in reclaiming your privacy.

The cost of mismanaged exposure: institutional, financial, and personal consequences

Exposure becomes dangerous not when it begins, but when it stops being managed. Most people imagine that visibility becomes a threat only when a scandal breaks or when a narrative reaches the media, but the reality is far more subtle. Problems start long before the public sees anything. They begin inside systems - financial, institutional, legal, regulatory - that react to signals much earlier than the human eye does.

Institutions do not wait for certainty before responding. They react to indications, trends, unexplained movements, or inconsistencies that appear inside their own frameworks. A headline is rarely the trigger. Instead, the trigger is a pattern: an unusual transfer, a conflicting document, a mismatch between historical data and current behavior, or a cluster of online mentions that suggests the possibility of risk. What the public interprets as "sudden trouble" is usually the final stage of a sequence that began quietly months earlier.

The financial consequences of unmanaged exposure often appear first. Banks reduce limits, delay transfers, or request clarifications. A compliance officer flags a transaction that would have gone unnoticed weeks before. Credit slows. Partners hesitate. Deals stall because someone inside an institution wants to "wait for clarity." Most of the time, these reactions are not punitive, they are protective. Institutions move to shield themselves from whatever they think may be unfolding. And whether the concern is justified or not becomes irrelevant. Their response creates pressure that reshapes your options going forward.

The institutional consequences follow a similar logic. Regulators act when something in their field of vision becomes noticeable. A casual mention in a journalist's inquiry triggers a file review. A leaked document prompts a background check. An algorithmic alert inside a governmental database generates an internal note that you will never see, but that influences decisions months later. These reactions accumulate quietly, long before any formal action is taken. By the time a letter arrives, the process has already run through multiple stages without your participation.

The personal consequences are often the slowest to appear but the most lasting. Mismanaged exposure creates distance. People around you begin to behave differently, cautious, curious, protective of their own interests. A board member asks unexpected questions. An advisor becomes hesitant. A partner senses that something is shifting and prepares for the possibility of reputational risk. Relationships that once felt secure become conditional, shaped by the perception that you may be entering a period of instability. This perception alone can alter dynamics that took years to build.

What makes these consequences especially damaging is their cumulative nature. Each reaction, financial, institutional, personal, reinforces the next. A delayed bank transfer leads to additional scrutiny. Additional scrutiny triggers an internal review. Internal reviews fuel speculation among partners. Speculation creates behavioral changes. Behavioral changes produce more signals that something is wrong. Exposure becomes a self-reinforcing loop that grows simply because no one interrupted it early enough.

Mismanaged exposure is rarely about guilt, but momentum. Once visibility begins to move through systems faster than you can control it, even neutral information can be interpreted as risk. In environments that reward caution, no one wants to be the person who ignored the warning signs. The result is a slow tightening around you, procedural, administrative, interpersonal, until actions that once felt routine now require explanation, justification, and oversight.

Understanding this dynamic is essential. The true danger is not being seen; it is being seen before you have a structure prepared to handle the attention. The cost of unmanaged exposure is not a single event. It is a shift in how institutions, partners, and observers interpret your presence. And once that shift occurs, the effects are difficult to reverse. The only effective defense is anticipation: recognizing exposure early enough to prevent the system around you from making assumptions you can no longer influence.

When you become searchable

Beyond the name: email, metadata, registries, tags.

Searchability does not begin with fame, nope, it actually begins with identifiers such as email addresses, phone numbers, device signatures, IPs, usernames, etc., data that enter systems you cannot see. These fragments are bought, sold, indexed, and cross-referenced until your digital footprint becomes a map that others can navigate.

Metadata inside documents or images, timestamps, geolocation, device models, can reveal where you were, what device you used, and who might have been with you. Corporate registries, land records, procurement databases, and licensing files expose information across jurisdictions, even when you are not named directly. A single datapoint can open the door to a network of others.

Can you see it? Y are not searchable because you are public, you are searchable because you exist in systems already designed to catalogue you.

Digital patterns: travel, purchases, app usage

Behavior becomes identity long before your name is discovered. Travel patterns, luxury purchases, reservation habits, and even the way you use ride-sharing or banking apps all generate signals. These signals are anonymized in theory, but re-identifiable in practice, especially for high-value individuals.

Apps monitor location, device settings, and background activity. Payment processors track routines. Airlines track preferences and routes. Hospitality platforms detect patterns long before you appear in any media story. To a skilled analyst, your behavior forms a profile that is identifiable without ever seeing your face.

The system does not need to know who you are, it needs to recognize the pattern that only you generate, your profile, and even worse, that same system will sooner or later, be able to predict your choices. Who will this benefit?

The power of geolocation and cross-platform syncing

Location data is one of the most revealing forms of exposure because it collapses privacy with precision. Your phone emits your position even when apps appear closed. Wearables, vehicles, and household devices do the same. This information is stored across multiple systems - some commercial, some governmental, many opaque.

Cross-platform syncing deepens the risk. A reservation added to a calendar syncs with a travel app. The confirmation email syncs with cloud storage. The cloud syncs with devices. A single action in one system echoes across several others, creating a sequence that reveals not only what you do, but when and how you do it.

When your routine is known, any deviation becomes meaningful. And once deviations matter, exposure follows quickly.

Public registries and corporate disclosures

Public registries, land titles, beneficial ownership databases, professional licenses, political donations, expose information that can be assembled into a coherent portrait of your activities. Third-party platforms scrape and republish these registries, sometimes permanently. Even when your name does not appear directly, indirect associations do: a company, a trust, a directorship, a foundation.

In a fragmented system, opacity is an illusion; believe me, fragments can always connect themselves.

Who is actually searching, and why it matters

Searches are rarely neutral. Why would anyone randomly search your name in Google? Clients search for opinions, fans search for someone to love or hate, journalists search to build stories, regulators search to justify intervention, political actors search for leverage, competitors search for vulnerabilities, intelligence agencies search to build profiles even before you become interesting to the public... And sometimes some bad guys may search for your name too.

The risk is not simply that you can be found, the risk is that the motivations behind the search are invisible to you.

Understanding your searchability means understanding your value , not as a person, but as a target.

Managing existing and accessible information

Open source intelligence (OSINT) risks.

OSINT has become the default tool for constructing profiles. It relies entirely on public data, yet its effectiveness is devastating. In a few hours, a competent analyst can trace patterns you no longer remember: properties, investments, relationships, routines, digital associations, and archived traces from platforms you forgot you ever used.

OSINT does not require fame, it only requires someone's interest.

Hidden but accessible: what authorities see even if the public doesn't

Authorities operate with data the public never sees: financial intelligence reports, immigration logs, cross-border information exchange, bank compliance files, and internal alerts triggered by algorithms. You may never appear in a newspaper, yet still exist in databases that map your life with precision.

This silent visibility is often more dangerous than public exposure. Stories fade, but systems do not.

What social graphs reveal without your input

Maybe you never post, tag, comment or even press like. It does not matter. Social networks infer your connections from mutual contacts, device proximity, shared metadata, and even the behavior of others around you. A friend's post, a partner's tag, a colleague's photo, or a shared location can link you to people and places without your consent or awareness.

Your network speaks about you even when you remain silent. The system listens.

Platform memory and the illusion of deletion

Deletion is rarely real. Removing a post gives the comforting impression of control, but the digital system is designed to remember. What disappears from your screen continues to live in servers, backups, audit logs, and cached versions scattered across platforms you will never see. A comment you erased a decade ago may still exist inside a search engine snapshot. A photograph you removed from a social platform may remain preserved by crawlers that archive the internet in real time. Even private messages, deleted threads, or expired stories often survive inside backend systems used by regulators, data brokers, and adversarial actors.

The danger lies in the illusion. Believing that something is gone encourages the kind of confidence that leads to vulnerability: relaxed communication, careless posting, or emotional reactions shared online under the assumption that they can be undone later. But nothing digital truly disappears. What you "destroy" is merely removed from public display; its shadow remains available to anyone who knows where to look, and the people who will eventually look are often those whose intentions do not align with yours.

Digital memory is not built to forgive. It is built to store, classify, and retrieve. The system forgets nothing, you simply stop seeing what actually still exists somewhere.

Quiet audit of your own footprint

Before the world examines you, you must examine yourself. A quiet audit is not an attempt to rewrite your past; it is the discipline of seeing your digital and institutional presence the way an adversary, journalist, regulator, or political actor would see it. You cannot control what you have not mapped.

The audit begins with what is formally recorded: land registries, corporate filings, professional directories, ownership databases, and cross-jurisdiction records that reveal connections you may have forgotten. From there, it expands into the digital fragments that tie different versions of your identity together, old email addresses, dormant domains, reused phone numbers, backup accounts, and overlooked digital signatures that connect one part of your life to another.

Your social history must be treated with the same rigor. Posts you deleted years ago may still exist in screenshots or archives. Comments you made casually in professional forums may be preserved in cached versions of pages that no longer appear in search results. Interviews, panel appearances, articles, philanthropic contributions, and even minor mentions in newsletters can resurface out of context, forming a narrative you never intended.

The rule is simple: conduct the audit without emotion. Approach your own footprint with the cold distance of someone whose goal is to expose you. Every record must be categorized by sensitivity, accessibility, and the ease with which it could be reframed in a hostile narrative. Exposure is not created by the content itself, but by the way it can be interpreted and combined with other fragments.

A quiet audit gives you foresight. It transforms the unknown into a mapped landscape, one you can defend before someone else claims authority over it.

Third parties, echo chambers, and uncontrolled actors

Friends, family, and former employees posting without consent.

Exposure often begins with someone who never meant to harm you. A relative shares a photo from a private dinner. A friend posts the view from your new property without realizing what it reveals. A former employee alludes to "exciting times" at a company you quietly exited. These gestures feel benign to them, but they create ripples you must manage.

People close to you operate under assumptions of ordinary life. They believe that visibility is harmless because, for them, it is. They do not see the geopolitical, legal, financial, or reputational architecture surrounding your world. Their normalcy becomes your liability, not through malice but through mismatch of context.

Surrogates speaking out of loyalty or ego

Some exposures emerge not from carelessness, but from loyalty. Advisors, colleagues, or self-appointed defenders may speak publicly on your behalf, believing they are helping. In reality, they create contradictions, fuel speculation, and interfere with legal strategies already in motion. Their statements may reflect their own ego more than your interest. When you choose silence, others must not fill it for you.

Online communities amplifying without context

Once your name enters circulation, you lose control over who discusses you. Forums, group chats, private channels, and niche digital communities can recycle fragments of your life without any understanding of the full picture. These environments reward speculation, not truth. A false interpretation, repeated by enough people, becomes a version of reality that spreads outward until it touches mainstream platforms.

By the time you become aware of these conversations, they may already have created a shadow narrative, a story built from pieces of you, reassembled by strangers.

Competitors or adversaries seeding narratives

In high-stakes environments, exposure is sometimes engineered. Competitors plant stories. Political opponents leak documents. Disgruntled partners file complaints designed to create momentum, not justice. These tactics are rarely illegal; they are strategic. They exist to weaken you, distract you, or force your hand in negotiations. When you operate at a certain level, you are no longer a person, you are a pressure point.

The risk of digital projection and misattribution

You may be blamed for things you did not do, associated with causes you never endorsed, or quoted for statements you never made.

Once a narrative fits a preexisting expectation, it spreads faster than correction. Silence is interpreted as confirmation. Explanation is interpreted as defense. Denial is interpreted as guilt.

Projection is not an error of information. It is a flaw in perception. And you cannot control how others perceive what they want to believe.

Leaks, breaches, and exposed materials

Typical sources of breach: technical, human, and contractual.

Leaks rarely come from sophisticated hacking. More often, they arise from old habits and misplaced trust. A server misconfigured by a contractor. A personal device used casually by an assistant. A document forwarded through an unsecured email provider. A service provider that reuses passwords. Each small lapse creates an opening.

Human breaches are even more common: a former partner seeking leverage, an employee feeling slighted, an advisor overwhelmed by pressure, or someone simply unaware of the sensitivity of what they handle. Contractual breaches occur when nodes are poorly drafted, unenforceable across jurisdictions, or ignored by those who never feared consequences.

In every case, the breach is not merely the leak itself , it is the existence of material that should never have been accessible in the first place.

Data fragments that create bigger stories

Single documents rarely cause disasters. It is the combination that destroys. A casual email. A half-finished contract. A text message lacking context. A screenshot taken without permission. Adversaries connect these fragments into a storyline that "makes sense," even if it is false. Reconstruction is not about discovering truth, it is about creating coherence. What feels harmless in isolation can become explosive when assembled by someone who seeks to use it against you.

What happens after a leak: reaction chains

A leak triggers a cascade. Journalists ask questions. Regulators open files. Banks request explanations. Partners distance themselves. Board members panic. The reaction can be worse than the content. Your timing, silence, or hesitation becomes part of the story. Institutions act not because the leak is damning, but because they must be seen responding.

In other cases, the leak never becomes public at all, but is used quietly to pressure or destabilize you. Influence is exerted in darkness long before the light ever appears.

Containment strategies and legal tools

Total erasure is impossible, but containment is not. Immediate legal action may remove or restrict material. Platforms can be pressured. Hosting providers can be compelled. Silence can be negotiated. Sometimes the best course is non-action, especially when intervention would elevate the visibility of a leak that has not yet gained traction.

The goal is not to pretend the leak never happened. It is to prevent it from becoming a force that shapes your future.

Structural review triggered by breach events

A breach is a signal that your architecture has failed. Once initial containment is achieved, the entire system must be examined without sentimentality. Access privileges must be reviewed. Advisors re-evaluated. Jurisdictions reassessed. Digital infrastructures rebuilt. The assumption that the incident is isolated is a dangerous luxury.

One leak usually means others are waiting.

A breach is not the end of a chapter, it is the beginning of a warning. Treat it as rehearsal for the next attack, not as an anomaly.

Reputation engineering and strategic silence

Building for suppression, obfuscation, or positive control

Reputation is not accidental. It is constructed with the same precision as a legal structure. Before you act, you must decide what you want: to suppress damaging information, to bury it under complexity and volume, or to replace it with a stronger narrative that displaces hostile interpretations.

Suppression relies on force, legal action, injunctions, removal requests.

Obfuscation relies on volume, publishing neutral content until harmful material loses visibility.

Positive control relies on identity, curated narratives, verified records, institutional anchors that define what appears first when your name is searched.

These strategies must be aligned; mixing them without coherence produces contradictions that undermine you.

Deciding what must be removed vs. What must be replaced

Not everything deserves deletion. Sometimes erasing a record makes it louder. Sometimes leaving it buried, untouched, is the safest option. Other times, the only solution is replacement: adding context, publishing a deeper explanation, or releasing neutral documents that shift perception without engaging directly.

Your objective is not to sanitize the internet. It is to control what rises to the surface and what is forgotten through fatigue.

Active vs. Passive reputation defense models

Not every individual can afford the same posture. Some must engage. Others must disappear. The choice has nothing to do with temperament and everything to do with architecture.

Active defense belongs to people whose lives are already visible. They cannot rely on silence because silence becomes interpretation. Their protection comes from presence: publishing when necessary, clarifying when useful, contextualizing when risk appears. They intervene not to win influence, but to prevent others from shaping their identity for them.

Passive defense is the opposite discipline. It rests on a structure built for opacity, minimal information, limited indexing, and a rhythm of life that produces no exploitable signals. It is not withdrawal; it is deliberate underexposure. The less you appear, the less the system can assemble.

Both models are valid, and neither works if you try to combine them. If you attempt to be visible and invisible at the same time, contradictions appear, contradictions that attract attention and invite scrutiny.

The first step is choosing your model with precision. The second is sustaining it without fractures.

Tailoring strategy to the structure: public, private, hybrid

Your role determines your strategy. Public figures, owners of companies, political actors, institutional leaders, cannot operate like private citizens. Their decisions generate records, their presence creates documentation, and their absence raises questions. They must build a controlled narrative, one that exists before anyone else can impose one.

Private figures require the opposite approach. Their protection comes from ambiguity. They don't need statements or deliberate visibility. Their value lies in the absence of definition, in leaving no clear identity for others to interpret. When a private profile is well designed, curiosity dies quickly because there is nothing coherent to analyze.

Hybrid profiles are the most delicate. These individuals operate publicly in one sphere and privately in another. A philanthropist may need visibility for a foundation but complete opacity for their personal life. An investor may appear in corporate filings but nowhere else. For them, reputation is modular, a system in which each layer must be isolated from the others.

Reputation management is not a uniform craft. It adapts to your function, to the jurisdictions that touch you, and to the audiences that observe you.

It is not about being seen or hiding, it is about placing every fragment of your identity exactly where it serves you, and nowhere else.

When digital silence is not absence, but architecture

Digital silence is not a void, it is a structure carefully built over time.

The individuals who seem to have “no online presence” rarely arrived there by accident. Their lives are designed so that data exists only in fragments, scattered, incomplete, and impossible to assemble into a coherent story. They do not vanish by refusing to appear. They vanish because the system cannot interpret them.

Some maintain a minimal footprint: a brief institutional mention, a legal reference, a formal biography. Enough to appear real, but not enough to generate momentum. Others cultivate an absence so clean that it appears accidental. In both cases, the silence is not emptiness, it is engineering.

A well-designed silent profile blocks aggregation. It denies correlation, and discourages curiosity. You don’t really disappear by hiding, instead, you can disappear by becoming unresolvable.

Final note

You cannot control the digital system around you. It rewards noise, thrives on repetition, and reacts faster than truth. But you can control your position inside it. You can decide how you appear, what you reveal, what you leave untouched, and which parts of your identity are inaccessible by design.

Visibility has stopped being a sign of relevance. It has become a structural weakness. Every post, every archive, every tag, every leak, every informal reference contributes to a map that others can interpret, even when the interpretation is wrong.

Your responsibility is not to erase that map. It is to redesign it until no path leads somewhere dangerous.

The strength of your profile, your public one, your private one, or the hybrid that connects them, comes from coherence. A life constructed with intention can withstand the distortions that would destroy others: narratives built by strangers, misinterpretations amplified by algorithms, projections created by adversaries.

The question is no longer whether you exist online. The question is whether your existence has been architected to protect you, or to serve those who watch.

Chapter IV. Emotional warfare and psychological pressure

When the attack is personal, not legal

Emotional vulnerability in high-profile environments

The higher your visibility, the more others project onto you. Admiration, resentment, dependency, and expectation begin to replace genuine perception. What was once a personal bond slowly transforms into a symbolic relationship, where you are no longer seen as an individual but as an asset, a status marker, or in some cases, a threat.

For those who operate under constant scrutiny, this shift is inevitable. In private life, the boundary between affection and opportunism is fragile. A partner may unconsciously measure intimacy against material security. A friend may calculate loyalty against access. Even family members, driven by rivalry or need, may reframe you as a resource to be tapped, a shield to be used, or a name to be leveraged.

This creates a profound emotional asymmetry. You may continue to interpret the relationship in human terms, trust, love, familiarity, while the other party begins to interpret it in strategic ones, advantage, leverage, control. The imbalance is subtle at first, almost invisible. It does not erupt in dramatic betrayals, but accumulates slowly: in silences where once there was conversation, in subtle shifts of tone, in small violations of confidence too minor to alarm you individually but too frequent to ignore collectively.

The greatest risk is not the act itself, but the delay in recognition. Emotional warfare rarely begins with open hostility. It seeps into the fabric of intimacy, hiding within gestures and omissions until the structure of trust is already weakened. By the time you recognize the attack, it often carries collateral damage that cannot be contained without sacrifice. A relationship is fractured, a reputation compromised, or a secret exposed, long before you realize that the private has turned adversarial.

Emotional vulnerability, therefore, is not a side issue in high-profile environments. It is the frontline of exposure. Legal and financial structures may hold under pressure, but if emotional asymmetry is allowed to grow unchecked, it can dismantle the discipline that protects everything else. Recognizing the shift early, before the personal becomes weaponized, is not a matter of intuition. It is a matter of survival.

Intimate exposure: partners, children, parents, and siblings

Those who stand closest to you, partners, children, parents, siblings, often hold the keys to your most sensitive domains. Their access is rarely symbolic. It is tangible, concrete, and multidimensional. They may share financial authority through joint accounts or co-owned property. They may carry legal weight through decision-making rights or inheritance claims. They may possess practical access: passwords to devices, codes to residences, or the ear of household staff. In ordinary circumstances, these forms of access are signs of intimacy and trust. In moments of pressure, they transform into potential weapons.

Stress magnifies this vulnerability. A divorce can turn private correspondence into court exhibits. An inheritance dispute can convert family history into a battlefield of claims. Ideological divergence, over politics, values, or personal choices, can push relatives into alliances with adversaries or opportunistic intermediaries. A partner, disillusioned or betrayed, may choose to leak information. A parent, out of fear or manipulation, may reveal details unintentionally. A sibling may file litigation as a means of leverage. And children, perhaps the most painful vector, can be used indirectly as instruments of control, through custody, education, or even the threat of publicity.

What begins as a personal rupture almost never stays contained. Once documented or disclosed, intimate conflict crosses into the public sphere. It becomes media coverage, legal action, or reputational collapse. The intimacy that once protected you becomes the breach that dismantles you.

The core problem is not the existence of these relationships, family cannot and should not be eliminated. The problem is the absence of structural limits within them. Boundaries are rarely defined in advance because love, loyalty, and blood ties are assumed to be enough. Yet in high-visibility environments, assumption is not protection. Without structural frameworks, legal, contractual, procedural, even the strongest personal bond can be weaponized when pressure arrives.

To operate without acknowledging intimate exposure is to confuse affection with immunity. The risk lies not in the people themselves, but in the unchecked access they hold. Recognizing this reality is not cynicism. It is the first step toward survival.

The use of family and relationships as strategic pressure

In many legal and cultural contexts, family life is regarded as a private sphere, protected by tradition and assumed to be outside the reach of external interference. Yet in adversarial environments, whether legal, corporate, or political, that very assumption becomes the vulnerability. Personal ties are rarely fortified by formal safeguards, and it is precisely their informality that makes them exploitable.

Adversaries understand this. A business partner facing investigation may threaten to implicate your spouse in order to secure concessions. A former friend, embittered or opportunistic, may align with a journalist to feed narratives that you cannot easily disprove. An ex-partner may exploit the location, activities, or even education of your children to destabilize you emotionally and strategically. Even trusted advisors, if their loyalty rests more on familiarity than on clear structure, may shift allegiance under pressure and become conduits of exposure.

This is not speculation, nor is it paranoia. It is the operational logic of leverage in systems where formal authority is absent or insufficient. When institutions cannot reach you directly, they seek points of indirect pressure. And nothing is more accessible, or more destabilizing, than relationships that are presumed to be private.

Pressure is never applied randomly. It is directed toward the weakest point of resistance, and for most individuals, even those with the most sophisticated legal or financial architectures, that weak point is the emotional domain. Family, intimacy, and personal loyalty are the areas least reinforced by protective structure, yet they are the very levers most frequently pulled when strategic pressure is required.

Recognizing this reality is essential. Until personal ties are reframed as potential vectors of exposure, they remain the most effective instruments that others can use against you.

Psychological fallout: shame, fear, isolation, and panic

When the attack shifts from structures to the personal domain, the response is rarely calculated. It becomes emotional. Individuals who can withstand regulatory scrutiny, complex litigation, or financial disruption with composure often collapse when the threat comes from someone they once trusted. Emotional betrayal bypasses reason. It reaches deeper than legal exposure because it strikes at the very core of identity and belonging.

This collapse manifests in different forms. For some, it is explosive rage that alienates allies and accelerates exposure. For others, it is paralyzing panic or silent withdrawal, creating operational vacuums that adversaries are quick to exploit. Confusion and compulsive action are equally dangerous: the tendency to call, to confess, to explain, or to retaliate without a plan often dismantles carefully built defenses in a single moment. What was once coherent becomes fragmented. Decision-making loses hierarchy. Priorities shift irrationally, from measured survival to emotional retaliation, or worse, from disciplined containment to self-destructive disclosure.

This is precisely what adversaries count on. Their goal is not always to destroy you outright, but to introduce enough emotional noise that your other defenses, legal, financial, reputational, begin to weaken from within. Emotional disarray transforms strength into liability. Even the most sophisticated architecture collapses if the operator cannot function coherently under pressure.

Without a predefined protocol of emotional containment, no structure will hold. Systems depend on the discipline of the person at their center. If that discipline disintegrates, walls built over years can fall in days. The lesson is clear: survival is not only about defending against external threats. It is about mastering the internal battlefield, where shame, fear, isolation, and panic are as dangerous as any regulator, journalist, or adversary.

When personal crisis escalates into public risk

In high-visibility environments, personal problems rarely remain confined to the private sphere. What begins as a rupture within the walls of intimacy soon acquires a documentary form that pushes it into the public domain. A divorce filing becomes part of the public record, accessible to journalists, investigators, and anyone with an interest in your downfall. Custody disputes, no matter how private the intent, often find their way into headlines because they involve questions of morality, responsibility, and status. Domestic incidents, even minor, are converted into police reports that can be reframed as evidence of instability. Family betrayals, once whispered in private, resurface as court exhibits. Emotional messages, texts written in moments of anger, despair, or vulnerability, are transformed into screenshots that circulate far beyond their original context.

These events usually start quietly, almost invisibly. Yet the moment they are documented, they cease to belong to you. They become part of the legal and reputational system, where their meaning is no longer defined by truth but by perception. From that point onward, control slips away. Institutions, the media, and adversaries interpret, frame, and weaponize the fragments of your personal life according to their own incentives.

Your adversaries do not need to fabricate evidence when your own history supplies enough raw material. Their strategy is simpler and far more effective: they wait. They allow the private to cross the threshold into the public sphere, and once it does, they amplify it. A small legal filing becomes a headline. A single text becomes a symbol. A quarrel becomes a story of decline.

At that stage, the burden is no longer to explain what really happened. Explanations are drowned in speculation. The task is far harder: to survive the narrative that others construct around fragments of your reality. Once your crisis is in the public domain, you are no longer dealing with facts. You are dealing with interpretation, repetition, and the machinery of perception. And in that arena, truth alone is rarely enough.

Strategic manipulation and targeted destabilization

Emotional blackmail, threats, and leaks by inner circle

The most effective attacks do not begin in courtrooms or on front pages. They emerge in the most familiar spaces, kitchens, bedrooms, and late-night conversations where trust is assumed and defenses are lowered. Emotional blackmail is subtle, intimate, and corrosive. It undermines stability not with direct confrontation but with suggestion, hesitation, and silence charged with meaning.

A partner may not openly file a lawsuit, yet they may imply it with a single phrase: *"I could talk to someone."* A family member may never ask directly for money, but their behavior signals an expectation of compensation in exchange for their silence. An ex-friend, knowing what they once had access to, may begin dropping names in public settings, just often enough to remind you of the leverage they still hold. None of this is written, filed, or recorded. It exists in the realm of implication.

These threats are coded, and that is what makes them dangerous. They rarely arrive in explicit terms that can be confronted through legal mechanisms. Instead, they operate in the space between words, what is suggested rather than declared, what is withheld rather than revealed. This ambiguity makes them difficult to intercept, harder to disprove, and nearly impossible to neutralize without escalation.

The true manipulation does not lie in the statements made, but in the deliberate withholding of action. The silent suggestion that exposure could occur at any moment forces you into a posture of anticipation, constantly second-guessing your own moves. It corrodes emotional balance, leading to overreactions, concessions, or defensive actions that may be more damaging than the original threat.

By the time the manipulation becomes visible, it is often too late. The private has already been transformed into pressure, the silence into leverage, and the implication into a weapon that destabilizes your judgment. What makes this form of attack so effective is precisely what makes it so corrosive: it turns intimacy itself into a battlefield.

Litigation as a tool of intimate revenge (divorce, custody, allegations)

Few instruments are as powerful, or as widely misunderstood, as the legal system when it is repurposed for personal revenge. Proceedings that should serve justice, divorce petitions, custody battles, claims of domestic violence, or financial disputes between relatives, are often stripped of their original intent and used instead as mechanisms of control, humiliation, and symbolic destruction.

What makes these processes so dangerous is not their technical complexity but their nature: they are public, slow, and invasive. They demand the disclosure of sensitive assets, private correspondence, and personal behavior. They expose elements of your life that would otherwise remain shielded by discretion. And because they unfold in public or semi-public arenas, they attract the gaze of regulators, journalists, and opportunists eager to capitalize on your vulnerability.

Unlike commercial litigation, where disputes may be measured in contracts and numbers, intimate legal conflicts strike at the very center of personal identity. Those initiating them often know your soft points better than any external adversary ever could. They understand which disclosures will be most damaging, which insinuations will resonate most deeply, and which weaknesses, emotional or reputational, can be amplified in the courtroom and beyond.

In these contexts, victory in the legal sense does not guarantee protection. You may win the case on paper and yet lose your reputation in the process. You may clear your name formally, but in doing so, you expose documents, testimonies, or fragments of private life that permanently alter how you are perceived. The cost of visibility becomes greater than the technical dispute itself.

The true danger lies not in the lawsuit as a legal mechanism but in its emotional framing. When legal action is infused with personal betrayal, resentment, or symbolic motives, it becomes harder to contain. The attack is no longer limited to courtroom arguments, it spills into perception, narrative, and memory. Unlike commercial disputes, intimate litigation has no clear perimeter. Its battlefield is as much your private life as it is the law.

False allegiances: friends, spouses, and advisors aligned with others

In moments of crisis, loyalties shift. A spouse may feel abandoned and seek validation elsewhere. A close friend may feel threatened by your silence. An advisor, legal, financial, or strategic, may have divided loyalties, especially if they are tied to entities, institutions, or people outside your direct control.

False allegiance is not always betrayal. It can be slow drift. A friend starts sharing information without telling you. A partner voices concern to third parties. An advisor delays response times, hoping for clarity from someone else.

These fractures are often invisible until they are irreversible. And by then, your operational map includes actors who are no longer aligned with your interest.

The most effective destabilization happens through people who still have access, because they haven't declared themselves adversaries yet.

Manipulated children and generational leverage

Children occupy a unique and dangerous place in the architecture of exposure. They are not just vulnerable human beings; they are also powerful instruments of leverage. Their names, their locations, their daily schedules, and even their behavior can be converted into emotional weapons. In custody disputes, political struggles, or reputation attacks, the child ceases to be a protected figure and instead becomes the medium through which pressure is applied.

This leverage is not always direct. It often takes the form of narratives carefully constructed to destabilize you. Allegations of neglect, accusations of inappropriate parenting, claims of ideological manipulation, or suggestions that children are being exposed to excessive wealth or privilege, all of these can be deployed to frame you in ways that are difficult to contest without amplifying the narrative further. In many cases, extended family members or external actors are enlisted, consciously or unconsciously, to shape the child's perception or to influence their willingness to cooperate with you.

The true objective is rarely to punish the child. It is to unbalance you, to weaken your emotional stability, to push you into concessions that you would never otherwise make, or to provoke mistakes under the weight of personal anguish. A single accusation about a child can command more attention than years of commercial disputes, because it touches on the deepest layers of human instinct: protection, legacy, and responsibility.

In high-stakes environments, generational links are no longer sacred. What was once considered untouchable, the bond between parent and child, is now viewed as a point of entry, a pressure point that adversaries can exploit with devastating precision. To operate under the illusion that children will be spared from strategic conflict is to underestimate the ruthlessness of environments where perception and leverage outweigh morality.

How emotional warfare weakens legal and financial judgment

No amount of legal planning or financial engineering can function under emotional destabilization. When the source of stress is personal, your capacity to analyze, delegate, and decide degrades rapidly.

You may override advisors. You may delay urgent moves. You may disclose sensitive information out of frustration, or escalate unnecessarily out of fear.

This is not weakness. It is physics. Human systems under emotional load lose bandwidth for risk management.

Your adversaries know this. Whether they are internal or external, they count on the fact that emotional stress will weaken your other defenses, and that if they cannot win legally, they can win by making you collapse from within.

Isolation, paranoia, and the collapse of trust

The psychology of disbelief and delayed response

When betrayal originates from within, the first instinct is rarely decisive action, it is disbelief. You begin to doubt what you see, to reinterpret signals, to convince yourself that there must be an alternative explanation. The emotional cost of acknowledging that someone close has shifted into opposition often feels greater than the operational cost of doing nothing. Accepting the rupture means accepting that intimacy has been weaponized, and most individuals hesitate to face that reality.

This hesitation is precisely what manipulators rely on. They know your reaction will not be immediate. They know you will second-guess yourself, seek reassurance, or delay confrontation until you have clarity that never arrives. The time you spend rationalizing their behavior, telling yourself it is stress, misunderstanding, or coincidence, is the time they use to consolidate their advantage. Delay is not an accident of emotion; it is part of the design of the attack.

In high-pressure environments, hesitation is never neutral. It is exposure. Each day spent in disbelief is a day in which your adversary strengthens their position, builds their narrative, or prepares their next strike. By the time you allow yourself to accept the truth, they have already moved several steps ahead. What you experience as the moment of recognition is, in reality, the moment of confirmation that you are already late.

The collapse of trust accelerates isolation. You begin to question not only the betrayer but everyone around you. Paranoia emerges, not because you are irrational, but because you now understand that proximity itself can be dangerous. Yet paranoia is a double-edged weapon: it can sharpen awareness, but it can also corrode your capacity to act with balance. Left unchecked, it erodes alliances and replaces strategic discipline with defensive suspicion.

The critical lesson is this: in adversarial environments, disbelief is a liability. The refusal to recognize betrayal in time is often more destructive than the betrayal itself. Emotional reluctance to act can dismantle operational systems that would otherwise have held under external attack. Survival requires the discipline to accept harsh truths quickly, even when they contradict your instincts of loyalty and trust.

Social withdrawal and the risk of operational paralysis

As pressure intensifies, many high-net-worth individuals instinctively retreat. Meetings are quietly canceled. Travel plans are indefinitely postponed. Teams, once relied upon, are kept at a distance. What begins as a temporary shield quickly becomes a pattern of avoidance. You start doubting your ability to read people, to interpret tone, to distinguish loyalty from opportunism. The very skills that once sustained your influence are suspended under the weight of uncertainty.

This withdrawal often disguises itself as strategy. You tell yourself that silence is discipline, that reduced exposure is protection. Yet in practice, it becomes a slow erosion of function. Files remain unopened, correspondence unanswered, decisions indefinitely postponed. Delegation ceases because trust feels dangerous, and instead of engagement, you rely on surveillance, watching from a distance, collecting fragments of information without context, mistaking monitoring for control.

What follows is paralysis. Not because resources are lacking, but because your cognitive bandwidth has been consumed by emotional turbulence. Doubt takes precedence over analysis. Fear replaces initiative. The machinery of decision-making grinds to a halt even while the external world continues to move. In the absence of forward momentum, adversaries, opportunists, and even allies begin to shape the environment in your place.

Isolation does not freeze the environment around you; it only freezes your participation in it. The more you withdraw, the less you can influence outcomes, and the more others fill the vacuum with their own agendas. What begins as self-protection turns into abdication of control. The lesson is simple but unforgiving: in adversarial environments, withdrawal is not neutral, it is surrender by delay.

The role of loneliness in high-exposure profiles

Wealth, influence, and discretion often come at the cost of deep connection. The higher your profile, the smaller your trusted circle becomes, and the harder it is to know whether loyalty is real or rented.

This structural loneliness is not a failure. It is a side effect of sovereignty. But under stress, it becomes a strategic weakness. You have fewer people to consult, fewer to confide in, and fewer who can act without hesitation on your behalf.

In normal times, this distance preserves privacy. In moments of attack, it fuels despair. Even in full rooms, you may feel unreachable, and therefore unprotected.

Fear of delegation: when no one is trusted

Once internal trust erodes, every task becomes a risk. You begin to question the loyalty of your assistant, the judgment of your attorney, the competence of your financial manager. You review old conversations. You delay approvals. You create bottlenecks that weaken your own structure.

In some cases, this mistrust is justified. But the consequence is always the same: decentralized systems revert to central command, and that command is now emotionally compromised.

Without trusted delegation, even the best architectures falter. The more you try to regain control manually, the more errors accumulate, because you are now operating under pressure, with limited visibility, and diminishing trust. The collapse does not come from outside. It comes from trying to do everything yourself while under attack.

Recognizing when you are being slowly disassembled

Not all collapses are visible. Some happen gradually, one personal loss, one delayed response, one quiet betrayal at a time.

If you find yourself reviewing documents alone at night, avoiding communication, scanning for signs of disloyalty, or rewriting tasks that others once managed, you are likely already inside the disassembly phase.

The system has not failed. You have withdrawn from the system, and now it is decaying in your absence.

Recognition is critical. You must detect when strategic solitude has turned into tactical vulnerability, when your silence is no longer discipline, but erosion. The sooner you identify this shift, the more likely you are to reverse it before it becomes structural.

Emotional containment and structured discipline

Building emotional routines that do not depend on stability

Most individuals design their daily routines around conditions of comfort, time availability, personal mood, or the presence of supportive environments. In ordinary life, this works. In high-risk environments, these very variables are the first to collapse. Sleep is interrupted by stress, schedules are disrupted by crisis, and moods swing violently under pressure. If your functioning depends on stability, then instability itself becomes a weapon against you.

The solution is not to wait for balance to return, but to create routines that function in spite of instability. These are structures designed to operate under siege, to anchor your capacity for judgment when external reference points are disintegrating. They are not about wellness in the conventional sense; they are about survival of decision-making capacity.

Such routines must be non-negotiable, regardless of circumstance. A fixed waking hour establishes rhythm even when time zones, crises, or emergencies intrude. Physical movement, deliberate, simple, and without external stimulation, grounds the body and prevents paralysis. Mental calibration without screens or devices clears the cognitive field from intrusion, if only briefly, creating space for disciplined thought rather than reactive emotion. A short operational review, conducted at the same time each day, ensures that no matter the level of chaos, you remain connected to priorities and decisions that must move forward.

The value of these rituals is not their scale but their consistency. Even at moments of extreme disruption, they preserve a fragment of normalcy, a controlled corner of reality untouched by external noise. That fragment is more than symbolic. It is the platform from which control can be rebuilt. Without it, the risk is total absorption into chaos, where emotion dictates response and discipline evaporates.

To contain emotion is not to suppress it. It is to channel it through structures strong enough to survive turbulence. Structured discipline creates a perimeter inside the self. And within that perimeter lies the one resource that cannot be outsourced, delegated, or purchased: the ability to act with coherence when the world is trying to dismantle it.

The use of structure as antidote to emotional chaos

Emotional breakdown does not appear spontaneously. It thrives in ambiguity, in the spaces where nothing is defined, where tasks are left open, where deadlines are fluid, and where communication is unclear. Chaos grows in the absence of boundaries. It feeds on gaps, delays, and unstructured processes until the mind, already strained, collapses under the weight of uncertainty. The antidote to this erosion is not inspiration, but structure.

Structure, when properly designed, must extend across four essential domains: time, decision-making, communication, and responsibility. Time must be segmented so that every hour carries a boundary, preventing crises from stretching into endless, unproductive loops. Decisions must be anchored in triggers and deadlines, so that choices are made not when panic dictates but when pre-defined conditions demand. Communication requires a filter to prevent emotional messages, hostile narratives, or impulsive responses from bypassing discipline. Responsibility must always include not only an assignee but also a fallback plan, ensuring that no task collapses entirely when one person falters.

This may appear rigid. Yet under pressure, rigidity creates functional flexibility. By narrowing options in advance, you prevent panic from producing erratic choices. By predefining boundaries, you leave more room for strategic clarity. What looks like restriction in calm times becomes resilience in crisis.

When your emotional bandwidth is depleted, structure protects you from yourself. It stops you from making permanent decisions under temporary conditions, from burning alliances that could have been repaired, or from abandoning strategies that only needed time to mature. Structure does not eliminate chaos in the environment, but it neutralizes chaos within you. And in high-pressure environments, that difference can determine whether you endure or unravel.

Externalizing pressure without broadcasting weakness

In high-pressure environments, silence is rarely sustainable. Internalizing every form of stress leads to distortion, overreaction, and eventually collapse. It is therefore essential to externalize pressure, but to do so with precision. Expression without calibration does not provide relief; it amplifies exposure.

The instinct to broadcast distress across your team, your family, or public channels is dangerous. What feels like honesty to you can be interpreted as instability by others. A moment of unfiltered expression may invite scrutiny, escalate conflict, or embolden adversaries. Once distress becomes visible beyond your chosen perimeter, you cannot control how it will be repeated, framed, or weaponized.

Yet the alternative, total suppression, is equally destructive. Pressure must be released to preserve coherence. The solution lies in controlled discharge, not indiscriminate venting. This means identifying and maintaining designated channels of expression: therapists trained to absorb volatility, strategic advisors capable of contextualizing events, or discreet allies who are both aligned with your posture and disciplined in confidentiality. Their role is not casual support. It is structural containment.

The critical factor is the perimeter of containment: who hears what, when, and why. Each disclosure must be deliberate, limited in scope, and aligned with your strategic posture. You may share the emotional weight of events, but never in ways that compromise operational clarity or decision-making authority. In this way, pressure is externalized without eroding your position.

Venting is not a strategy. It is reactive, chaotic, and destabilizing. Controlled discharge, by contrast, is strategic hygiene. It transforms raw emotion into manageable fragments that can be processed without spilling into the arenas where adversaries or opportunists wait. By designing a system of calibrated release, you create a safety valve for yourself while maintaining the integrity of your role.

The paradox is that strength is not measured by silence alone, but by the ability to release pressure without displaying weakness. Mastering this balance ensures that you remain human without becoming vulnerable, expressive without being exposed.

Predefined crisis scripts for personal relationships

In moments of emotional warfare, the attacks rarely arrive from strangers. They come from those closest to you, partners, parents, children, friends, individuals who know your vulnerabilities and can provoke reactions that outsiders could never access. These provocations often take the form of messages, demands, or insinuations timed to catch you unprepared. The danger is not in the words themselves but in your instinct to respond from the moment, which almost always means responding from emotion. And that is precisely what adversaries, conscious or not, rely upon.

The antidote is preparation. By designing crisis scripts in advance, you create a protective barrier between impulse and response. These scripts are short, neutral, and deliberately non-reactive. They are not meant to resolve conflict in the moment but to pause the dynamic, to prevent escalation while preserving space for measured action.

A well-crafted script does three things simultaneously: it acknowledges receipt of the message, it defers engagement to a controlled setting, and it signals that you are not destabilized. Phrases such as *"I need time to respond properly"*, *"we will discuss this in a different setting"*, or *"legal counsel is reviewing everything, I cannot speak freely"* are not evasions. They are shields. They create space, and space is the most valuable resource in a crisis. Space buys clarity. Clarity preserves posture.

Without such scripts, you fall into one of two extremes: saying too much or saying nothing at all. Both are dangerous. Over-disclosure provides material that can be reframed or weaponized. Silence, if prolonged or misinterpreted, can be read as guilt, weakness, or abandonment. Scripts provide the middle path: controlled engagement that protects you from your own impulses while denying adversaries the emotional reaction they are seeking.

Predefined crisis scripts are not cosmetic techniques. They are instruments of discipline. They ensure that, even when your emotions are under attack, your words remain aligned with strategy rather than with fear, anger, or despair.

Digital and physical boundaries within intimate environments

Your greatest vulnerability often lies not in boardrooms or public arenas but within the spaces where emotional life and operational reality blur. These are the environments where trust and routine coexist with sensitive information, creating a setting in which exposure can happen without malice, without planning, and sometimes without awareness.

The risks emerge in ordinary habits: shared devices that carry confidential data, open calendars visible to people who do not need access, casual conversations conducted in spaces that are not secure, or late-night exchanges of messages when stress, fatigue, or emotion weaken judgment. In these moments, the boundary between private intimacy and strategic operation dissolves, and what feels harmless becomes material for exposure.

The antidote is the deliberate construction of boundaries, both digital and physical. Digitally, this means devices without shared access, encrypted channels for sensitive communication, and strict separation between professional and personal accounts. Workspaces must be clearly defined, with secure storage for files and systems that prevent cross-contamination of personal and operational spheres. Even the hours of discussion should be bounded, so that critical matters are not debated impulsively during moments of vulnerability.

The same discipline must be applied to the physical environment. Certain rooms, times of day, or entire zones must be kept free from negotiation, conflict, or crisis dialogue. This is not about emotional coldness, it is about ensuring that your environment actively supports containment. When physical and digital spaces are left undefined, even well-intentioned relationships can become sources of risk.

Discipline, in this context, is not the opposite of intimacy. It is its architecture. By building clear structures around when, where, and how sensitive matters are addressed, you protect both your relationships and your operational integrity. Without these boundaries, trust alone becomes insufficient, and exposure becomes inevitable.

Functional distance without dehumanization

How to maintain connection without exposure

In high-pressure environments, where trust is fragile and every interaction carries potential consequences, the instinct is often to withdraw completely. Yet total withdrawal fractures relationships and fuels narratives of abandonment. The alternative is not immersion but functional distance, a calibrated separation that preserves human connection while shielding the structures that keep you operational.

Distance is not abandonment. It is a form of architecture. It allows you to maintain ties without exposing sensitive plans, emotional weaknesses, or the details of your strategic intentions. This balance can be achieved by narrowing the scope of interaction rather than severing it. Limit discussions to defined topics, confine them to scheduled calls or public settings, or rely on written communication that follows predefined limits. In this way, connection is preserved, but exposure is reduced to near zero.

The essence of functional distance lies in signaling presence without granting access to your interior architecture. You remain available, but selectively. You remain in contact, but through structures designed to prevent intrusion. The people around you feel continuity, but they do not gain leverage. What they perceive as relationship, you maintain as boundary.

It is critical to remember that you are not obligated to explain everything. The expectation to justify or to disclose is often socially constructed, not strategically necessary. What you are obligated to protect are the elements that keep you functional, the clarity, stability, and privacy that allow you to make decisions under pressure.

Functional distance, when properly applied, is not coldness. It is containment with respect. It maintains the dignity of connection without sacrificing the sovereignty of control. In adversarial environments, this balance is not optional. It is the only way to remain human without becoming vulnerable.

The role of limited disclosure in high-risk bonds

Not every relationship must be severed in high-pressure environments, but almost all must be redefined. The redefinition does not lie in affection or loyalty, but in the discipline of disclosure management, the deliberate decision about who knows what, when, and why. Without this discipline, even the strongest personal bonds become vectors of exposure.

Disclosure management begins with restraint. Even those closest to you, partners, children, parents, lifelong friends, should not be granted automatic access to information about legal timelines, asset movements, emotional states, or strategic decisions. Access must be intentional and secured within a framework that considers both necessity and risk. To disclose out of habit, comfort, or the desire to feel understood is to confuse intimacy with immunity.

Every fragment of information you share must be treated as if it could be leaked, repeated, or distorted. This does not mean that those around you act with deliberate malice. More often, disclosure failures occur through stress, manipulation, or simple confusion. Words are repeated in the wrong setting, details are revealed under pressure, or narratives are subtly reshaped by third parties who intercept them.

The most difficult truth to accept is that the people who love you may still expose you. This is not necessarily betrayal. It is structure failing in a place where there was never a system. Affection without boundaries cannot withstand the mechanics of adversarial environments. What protects you is not trust alone, but the frameworks that define how information flows and where it stops.

Limited disclosure does not diminish love, respect, or loyalty. On the contrary, it protects them by preventing ordinary human error from becoming catastrophic exposure. In a world where information is currency, the discipline of disclosure is not a sign of distance. It is a condition of survival.

Legal and practical tools to redraw intimate boundaries

Boundaries within intimate environments do not need to be hostile or confrontational. They can be established quietly, through contracts, logistics, and procedures that preserve relationships while minimizing exposure. The objective is not to diminish affection but to prevent emotional proximity from mutating into structural vulnerability.

On the legal side, there are numerous instruments that can redefine the terms of closeness without breaking the bond. Post-nuptial agreements clarify financial expectations in ways that reduce the leverage of future disputes. Cohabitation contracts formalize living arrangements, delineating rights and responsibilities in case of rupture. Trustee rules can be drafted to separate family loyalty from the management of wealth. Parenting plans, negotiated in advance, impose order on one of the most contested areas of conflict, custody and decision-making, ensuring that ambiguity cannot be weaponized in times of disagreement. Even access to communications, property, or shared accounts can be limited through legally recognized structures, removing confusion before it becomes conflict.

Parallel to the legal framework, practical constraints are equally essential. Shared devices should be eliminated to prevent unintentional access to sensitive material. Passive tracking systems, such as location sharing or automatic backups, must be deactivated. Emergency access settings should be reviewed so that crises cannot be used as pretexts for intrusion. Passwords require periodic rotation, and sensitive operations should be shifted away from informal or emotionally charged channels into environments that are secure, monitored, and separate.

When these measures are in place, distance becomes survivable. Relationships are preserved, but they are redefined through structure rather than assumption. Without such systems, intimacy can disguise itself as trust while in reality functioning as a point of exposure. The absence of boundaries is not love, it is risk. Designed correctly, boundaries allow affection to continue without granting leverage. Neglected, they transform closeness into a threat in disguise.

Reconstructing loyalty on terms you define

Loyalty is not always a natural state. It is often an arrangement, sometimes implicit, sometimes explicit, that survives only as long as circumstances remain stable. When pressure arrives, what appeared to be loyalty may reveal itself as convenience, dependency, or mere habit. For those who operate under scrutiny, this ambiguity is dangerous. It must be corrected.

Reconstruction of loyalty requires deliberate architecture. It is not about testing affection or provoking sacrifice. It is about establishing rules of engagement that eliminate confusion and expose the true basis of each bond. Operational clarity is the foundation: every key relationship must be reframed according to what can be shared, what must remain private, what is open to negotiation, and what is permanently off-limits. Without this clarity, loyalty becomes a word without weight.

This redesign applies across all categories of proximity: spouses who may have access to sensitive financial or digital channels, adult children whose choices can impact public visibility, long-time advisors whose loyalties may be split, and business partners who once thrived on informal arrangements. Each of these circles must be recalibrated. Familiarity cannot be mistaken for alignment.

True loyalty is loyalty that functions under stress. It does not collapse when secrecy is required, when distance must be imposed, or when silence is the only rational posture. It does not resist boundaries, but respects them. Those who recoil from new rules were never loyal to your stability, they were loyal to your availability. And availability is the weakest currency you can offer in environments where exposure is fatal.

Reconstruction also requires testing. You do not need to wait for crisis to discover who will hold. Introduce structural constraints gradually: limit access, separate functions, document expectations, and observe the response. Genuine loyalty adapts to clarity. Conditional loyalty breaks when its privileges are reduced. Both outcomes are useful, because only one deserves to remain within your operational perimeter.

Finally, loyalty must never be romanticized. It is not eternal, not unconditional, and not immune to context. It is a living contract, renewed each time it is placed under pressure. By defining the terms, you remove illusion and replace it with structure. You do not destroy trust, you refine it. And in high-risk environments, refined trust is the only kind that endures.

When to walk away and how to do it without leaving traces

Not every relationship can be preserved. Some, no matter how carefully redefined, will continue to generate instability, legal, emotional, or operational. At that point, the only rational decision is exit. Walking away is not failure; it is recognition that survival requires subtraction as much as construction.

An exit must be designed, not improvised. It should be structured, gradual if possible, and invisible to outsiders. A financial settlement may be required to neutralize lingering claims. A staged separation, where access and communication diminish in controlled phases, can avoid the shock that provokes escalation. In other cases, compartmentalization of interaction into narrow, predefined channels will create natural distance until the connection dissolves. And sometimes, the cleanest option is silence: no further engagement, no explanation, no visible rupture.

Confrontation is rarely productive. If separation must occur in full view, the goal is to minimize narrative. No public framing, no defensive statements, no drama. Every justification you provide becomes part of someone else's story. By refusing to explain, you deny the raw material from which reputational attacks are built.

Walking away does not mean erasing a person. It means removing a vector of exposure from your operational map. The individual still exists, but they no longer exist within your perimeter of risk. This distinction is critical: elimination is emotional, but removal is architectural.

Letting go is not weakness. It is a reflect of inner strength and design. It demonstrates that you are willing to sacrifice proximity in order to preserve sovereignty. And in the logic of survival, sovereignty always outweighs sentiment. The strongest structures are not those that cling to every connection, but those that can detach without collapse and without leaving traces behind.

Final note

Emotional warfare is not an exception to strategic risk; it is its most subtle and corrosive form. Legal, financial, and digital threats strike openly, leaving traces that can be mapped and countered. Emotional threats, by contrast, infiltrate silently. They nest inside relationships, habits, and conversations that feel too familiar to question. They dismantle coherence not by attack, but by erosion, draining clarity before a single lawyer is called or a single asset is touched.

The purpose of this chapter was never to promote coldness or detachment. It was to remind you that emotional stability must be engineered with the same precision you devote to contracts, governance, or asset structures. Emotional containment is not an afterthought, it is the first perimeter of defense. Without it, every other system becomes vulnerable to the noise of betrayal, fear, or panic.

Discipline over self is the only antidote to chaos. Functional distance, carefully designed, allows you to maintain connection without surrendering control. Silence, when intentional, becomes not absence but strength. These are not gestures of isolation, they are architecture.

Sovereignty cannot exist without mastery of the emotional domain. And legacy cannot endure if it fractures from within. What determines survival is not the wealth you preserve, the structures you build, or the narratives you control. It is the ability to withstand pressure in silence, without breaking, without leaking, without surrendering the coherence that holds everything else together.

In the end, emotional control is not a luxury. It is the foundation of endurance. Without it, every other defense is temporary. With it, you become untouchable from within, and therefore far harder to dismantle from without.

Chapter V. Asset preservation under siege

When access to your assets is targeted

Understanding how visibility triggers asset scrutiny

Wealth does not draw attention merely by existing. It attracts intervention when it becomes visible, when the fact of possession crosses into the field of perception. Visibility does not always require a headline or a scandal. It can emerge from the most ordinary events: a lawsuit filed in open court, a high-profile divorce where disclosures become public, a political reshuffle that alters the landscape of alliances, or a digital breach that releases fragments of information. Any of these can act as a switch, transforming private wealth into public target.

Once your name or structures are captured inside institutional systems, regulatory filings, journalistic databases, compliance platforms, you cease to be anonymous capital. You become a beacon for scrutiny. The act of being searchable is enough to invite mapping. Banks will model your exposure. Tax authorities will cross-reference your filings. Adversaries will reconstruct your holdings from fragments. None of them require complete information; the signal itself is enough to activate the process.

Visibility multiplies. A single mention in a registry can cascade into algorithmic alerts, media indexing, or compliance escalations across borders. What felt like private control yesterday becomes a dossier tomorrow. And once you are inside these systems, the question is no longer whether you own an asset, it is whether you can access it freely. Ownership without unhindered access is an illusion of security.

Access is the real vulnerability. A property frozen by precautionary order, an account suspended by a compliance department, or a transfer delayed under "review" can paralyze your ability to act precisely when mobility is most needed. Even without seizure, the mere interruption of access can weaken your negotiating position, signal instability, and invite further demands.

The lesson is simple but rarely absorbed: the risk does not begin when wealth is questioned. It begins when wealth is seen. Visibility is not neutral, it is the trigger that transforms assets into liabilities in the eyes of systems designed to regulate, extract, or exploit. To survive, you must treat visibility itself as the first threat vector, and build architectures that separate what you hold from what others can interrupt.

Frozen accounts, legal seizures, and blocked transfers

The interruption of access to assets is one of the most destabilizing forms of pressure. It rarely begins with conviction or judgment. More often, it begins with precaution, an administrative order, a civil injunction, or an internal review triggered by suspicion rather than proof. In this way, financial paralysis functions less as a conclusion and more as a tactical opening move.

Civil courts can immobilize accounts before litigation is resolved, effectively punishing long before any ruling is delivered. Tax authorities often impose precautionary liens or initiate collection measures based on contested assessments, shifting the burden onto the individual to prove solvency or compliance. Banks, operating under the shadow of regulatory liability, may freeze transactions without external order at all, relying solely on internal compliance reviews. These suspensions are usually framed as "temporary," yet in practice they can stretch for weeks or months, neutralizing critical liquidity when it is most needed.

Blocked transfers represent another layer of disruption. They may arise from mismatches between jurisdictions: an aml algorithm flagging unusual activity, a transfer entangled in dual nationality conflicts, or the absence of clarity around beneficial ownership. In some cases, the blockage is not punitive but procedural, yet the effect is the same. Even assets held within compliant structures can be paralyzed if their visibility exceeds what the system is comfortable accommodating.

What matters in such scenarios is not the legal form of ownership, but the ability to exercise use. A frozen account in your name is no different, operationally, than an account you never had. A transfer delayed for "review" can be as strategically damaging as a seizure, especially when timing defines leverage.

This is the critical shift: wealth under scrutiny ceases to be a store of value and becomes a point of vulnerability. In an environment where institutions act to protect themselves first, the individual's access becomes conditional, fragile, and subject to forces outside their control. The challenge, therefore, is not only to hold assets, but to design systems that ensure usability under pressure, without triggering the very mechanisms built to restrict them.

Institutional overreaction: banks, regulators, and intermediaries

Institutions are not built to protect you. They are built to protect themselves. Their loyalty is not to clients, but to survival within the regulatory environment that governs them. In moments of perceived risk, this priority becomes visible with brutal clarity.

When your name, company, or structures appear linked to reputational signals, an investigation, a media headline, an unexplained transaction, the reaction of banks, trustees, and even family offices is rarely measured. It is defensive, immediate, and often disproportionate. Accounts may be frozen without prior notice. Credit facilities are quietly retracted. Promised services dissolve into silence. Requests for clarification are met with vague references to “compliance review,” leaving you functionally paralyzed while essential assets remain out of reach.

This overreaction is not rooted in fact. Institutions do not wait for courts to decide or for evidence to mature. They react to perception, because perception is what determines their own vulnerability. Regulators operate under the same logic. An inquiry in one jurisdiction can trigger parallel inquiries elsewhere, not because of any substantive link, but because no authority wishes to be accused of negligence. In this environment, risk spreads virally across systems that imitate one another, amplifying suspicion into operational paralysis.

The critical point is that none of this is personal. The bank manager may value your business, the trustee may believe your integrity, and the advisor may sympathize with your situation. But at the institutional level, self-preservation overrides relationship. The institution acts not as an ally, but as a firewall, cutting you off to protect itself from association.

For you, however, the consequences are immediate and personal. Liquidity vanishes at the exact moment it is needed most. Communication channels collapse into silence. Options shrink, not because of wrongdoing, but because systems have decided that neutrality is safer than service.

This asymmetry must be anticipated. Institutions are stable in appearance, but their loyalty is conditional and their reactions are often extreme. To operate in such an environment, you must assume that overreaction is not the exception but the default response once visibility crosses a certain threshold. The challenge is not to demand loyalty from structures incapable of it, it is to design your own architecture so that institutional overreaction does not equate to personal collapse.

Informal restrictions: reputational freezes, "soft" refusals, and silent denials

Not all barriers come with formal notice. Some of the most effective restrictions are invisible, enforced not by law or contract but by silence. In high-net-worth ecosystems, where reputation and risk perception shape decisions as much as statutes, the most decisive judgments are delivered behind closed doors and never written down.

You may encounter what appear to be delays: a loan application placed "under review" indefinitely, an investment opportunity that is repeatedly "under consideration" but never confirmed, or an advisor who gradually shifts from engagement to hesitation. These are not coincidences. They are reputational freezes, silent signals that, for the institution or counterpart, proximity to you has become a liability.

Family offices, private banks, and specialized intermediaries often use disengagement as their first line of defense. They will not declare you unwelcome. They will not accuse you directly. Instead, they will allow the relationship to wither through unanswered calls, vague acknowledgments, and non-committal replies. To the outsider, nothing appears broken. To you, the message is unmistakable: you have crossed from asset to risk.

The power of silent denial lies in its deniability. Unlike a court order, there is no document to challenge, no procedure to contest. The refusal leaves no trace. Yet the effect is identical to formal sanction: your access to capital, networks, or opportunities is blocked. Worse, because the mechanism is informal, it can spread quickly through whispers and unstated consensus. Once one institution quietly distances itself, others follow, not through evidence, but through imitation of caution.

This dynamic is among the most dangerous because it is impossible to fight head-on. You cannot litigate silence. You cannot compel enthusiasm. And you cannot demand loyalty from entities whose very survival depends on avoiding reputational exposure. The only viable response is anticipation: designing structures that minimize dependency on single institutions, maintaining diversified channels of access, and recognizing that silence is itself a form of verdict.

To ignore soft refusals is to misread the system. To overreact is to confirm suspicion. Survival requires a third path: to interpret these signals early, to reconfigure quietly, and to ensure that silent denials never have the power to immobilize your architecture.

How asset disruption is used to weaken your negotiating power

The interruption of access to assets is rarely framed as punishment. More often, it functions as leverage, a silent tool designed to reduce your capacity to maneuver when decisions matter most. Unlike outright confiscation, which is visible and politically costly, disruption operates in the shadows: freezing accounts, delaying transfers, questioning compliance, or creating administrative bottlenecks. The result is the same, you cannot act with speed or autonomy.

This tactic is particularly effective during periods of litigation, regulatory scrutiny, or political transition. In such environments, time is a weapon. Your inability to mobilize funds, secure liquidity, or complete transactions forces you into reliance on others: co-signers who may demand concessions, family members whose cooperation may be conditional, legal teams who now control your options, or counterparties who sense weakness and renegotiate from a position of advantage. Dependency replaces sovereignty, and once dependency is established, pressure multiplies.

Asset disruption is not random. It is engineered to weaken resistance. The longer the paralysis lasts, the more you are incentivized to accept terms you would normally reject: premature settlements, intrusive disclosures, or lopsided agreements. The adversary does not need to defeat you in court or seize your property outright. They only need to make you unable to deploy your resources at the precise moment they are required.

The logic is simple: wealth that cannot move is wealth that cannot defend. Once your resistance is compromised by enforced immobility, control shifts to those dictating the pace of access. They hold the key to restoration, and in that imbalance, leverage becomes domination.

The ultimate objective is not to strip you of ownership. It is to neutralize your capacity to use what you own when it matters most, turning assets from instruments of freedom into instruments of pressure.

Strategic vulnerabilities in asset ownership

The illusion of control in name-only ownership structures

One of the most persistent myths among high-net-worth individuals is that the absence of their name on registries or contracts equates to protection. Assets are placed under the names of nominees, relatives, or layers of legal entities. On paper, exposure seems distant. The illusion is comforting: the belief that invisibility in official records equals immunity from scrutiny.

But true control is not defined by signatures on documents. It is defined by behavior, benefit, and operational linkage. If you occupy a property, direct its maintenance, or make decisions about its use, the system will treat you as its owner regardless of who holds the title. If you direct the flow of funds in an account, approve transactions, or derive the benefits of its existence, your fingerprints are there, visible to auditors, regulators, and investigators who are trained not to follow names, but to follow patterns.

Legal discovery, forensic accounting, and cross-jurisdictional cooperation have made name-only distance obsolete. Banking systems are designed to identify beneficial ownership, not just formal signatories. Tax authorities evaluate substance over form, asking who lives where, who benefits how, and who exercises decision-making authority. Courts are empowered to pierce structures that exist only to obscure, especially in contexts of divorce, litigation, or fraud investigation.

The danger of name-only ownership is not just that it fails to protect, it fails precisely when protection is most needed. At the moment of dispute, audit, or seizure, the façade collapses. What seemed like a safe shield is revealed as a liability, because the very separation that was supposed to protect you now complicates your defense. You cannot claim control when convenient and deny it when challenged. Systems will reconcile your benefits with your denials, and the contradiction will expose you further.

The most damaging element of this illusion is timing. The collapse rarely occurs during stability. It occurs at the point of maximum vulnerability, when the asset becomes critical to defend. In that moment, structures built for appearance provide no leverage, and what was designed to protect becomes evidence against you.

Illusion is not protection. It is delay. And in environments where scrutiny is inevitable, delay is not strategy, it is self-sabotage disguised as discretion.

Weak links in layered holdings: trusts, foundations, nominee accounts

Layered structures, trusts, foundations, nominee accounts, are often presented as fortresses. They project an image of complexity, sophistication, and immunity. To the uninitiated, they suggest opacity so dense that no adversary could penetrate it. But the strength of such structures is never absolute. They depend on compliance frameworks, governance quality, and, most fragile of all, human discretion. Every additional layer does not always mean more protection; it can also mean more points of failure.

Consider the trustee who quietly disagrees with your strategy, or who interprets fiduciary duty in a way that diverges from your intent. Their hesitation alone can delay critical decisions or trigger disclosures. A nominee, selected for convenience, may fold under regulatory pressure, handing over documents or testimony to protect themselves. A board member carrying unrelated legal troubles may become compromised, exposing the entire structure to scrutiny that had nothing to do with your own conduct. Each of these represents not theoretical risk, but practical collapse vectors embedded inside the very system designed to shield you.

Jurisdictional conflicts further weaken the illusion of invulnerability. A trust recognized under common law may be disregarded in a civil law jurisdiction, treated as fiction rather than substance. A foundation legally protected in one country may be forced into disclosure in another. What survives comfortably in one legal order may be frozen, pierced, or disregarded entirely when adversaries exploit cross-border inconsistencies. The very diversity that once appeared to provide insulation can, under coordinated attack, create cracks through which visibility pours in.

Perhaps most dangerous is the false sense of confidence these structures create. Because they look fortified, you assume they are secure. But adversaries, whether regulators, litigants, or investigative journalists, map them patiently. They identify the human nodes, the jurisdictional overlaps, the governance gaps. By the time you become aware of the threat, your fortress may already be charted in detail, its weak points marked, its sequence of failure predicted.

Complexity without coherence is not protection, it is exposure disguised as sophistication. True resilience does not come from the number of layers, but from the strength of each link and the consistency of the logic that binds them. Without that, the structure designed to protect you may in fact be the most elaborate invitation to attack.

How tax compliance can be weaponized in audits or litigation

Tax compliance is often presented as the highest form of protection: the proof that you have acted transparently, fulfilled obligations, and aligned your conduct with the law. But this belief is misleading. Compliance is not a shield, it is a record. And when adversaries seek leverage, records are the most convenient weapon. What you file in good faith becomes an archive of your movements, decisions, and structures, preserved in your own handwriting or stamped with your advisors' authority.

In litigation, opposing counsel can demand years of declarations, transforming tax filings into an investigative blueprint. Line by line, they can be dissected to reconstruct ownership, identify cash flows, or expose indirect control. Even when correct, these documents are rarely neutral. They invite interpretation. They allow narrative. They provide the architecture upon which suspicion can be built.

The danger multiplies in cross-border disputes. Mutual assistance treaties, automatic exchange frameworks, and intergovernmental data-sharing agreements ensure that filings submitted in one jurisdiction may surface in another. A declaration prepared under one country's standards can look evasive elsewhere, especially when filtered through divergent accounting rules or legal doctrines. What was compliant in Paris may be suspicious in New York. What was ordinary in Singapore may be weaponized in Madrid.

Even flawless compliance does not insulate you. A valuation based on outdated criteria, a timing difference produced by local conventions, or an omission aligned with one jurisdiction's law but irrelevant to another's can all be reframed as concealment. The context in which you filed will rarely survive the review. Intention becomes irrelevant. Interpretation is everything.

The most dangerous aspect is how easily your own records can justify coercive measures. Freezing orders, precautionary reassessments, or new investigations often cite prior filings as their foundation. The transparency designed to prove good faith becomes the raw material from which regulators or litigants construct leverage. You are judged not only on what you filed, but on how it can be reinterpreted under pressure, years after the fact.

This is not an argument against compliance. Non-compliance is indefensible. But it is a warning against complacency. Filing correctly is not enough. Tax records are not passive archives; they are loaded weapons, waiting for whoever has authority or incentive to use them.

Survival requires more than accuracy. It requires anticipation. You must assume that everything you disclose will one day be read by someone whose objective is not to understand, but to accuse. Compliance is necessary, but only when paired with foresight, context management, and structures designed to resist hostile reinterpretation does it become part of defense, rather than the beginning of exposure.

Multi-jurisdictional frictions: conflicting claims and cooperation requests

To own and operate across borders is to live inside multiple legal logics at once. Each jurisdiction carries its own definition of ownership, disclosure, and liability. But these logics do not coexist peacefully. They collide. And in the friction between them, exposure is created.

A trust recognized in London may be treated as legal fiction in Madrid. A foundation respected under civil law in Liechtenstein may be disregarded under U.S. common law standards. One jurisdiction obliges you to disclose every beneficial link, while another assumes secrecy unless disclosure is forced. These contradictions are not anomalies, they are systemic. And they leave you caught between mutually exclusive obligations: reveal in one country, conceal in another; defend in one forum, admit in another.

The problem escalates under modern cooperation regimes. Information that once remained local is now global by default. CRS (common reporting standard), FATCA, and AML frameworks ensure that banking, tax, and ownership data travel faster than you do. A holding that quietly existed in Switzerland can be flagged in Spain without any movement on your part. A dormant company in Dubai may suddenly surface in a French file because of a single cross-referenced request. Distance no longer guarantees obscurity. Protocols erase borders faster than law can protect them.

This creates a paradox: the very structures once designed to fragment visibility now amplify it. Multiple jurisdictions no longer provide insulation, but multipliers of scrutiny. Adversaries, regulators, or litigants can select the jurisdiction most hostile to your position and use cooperation requests to drag other countries into alignment. What is legal in one arena may be criminalized in another through selective framing.

What you thought was safe by geography is now vulnerable by protocol. The fortress of distance has been replaced by the network of automatic exchange. Survival requires recognizing that friction is not temporary, it is permanent. And in this environment, the strongest architecture is not the most complex, but the most coherent across borders. Contradictions invite exposure. Coherence resists it.

Personal guarantees and pledges: the hidden liabilities in wealth

Not all assets are held purely as stores of value. Many are entangled, pledged as collateral for loans, credit facilities, or strategic partnerships. On paper, these arrangements may seem harmless, even advantageous, when liquidity is abundant and confidence high. But in moments of stress, these same instruments become accelerators of vulnerability.

Personal guarantees, often signed years earlier with little attention, can reappear without warning. What once seemed a symbolic clause in a negotiation becomes a binding obligation the moment an adversary or institution decides to enforce it. Dormant debts, thought irrelevant or long settled, can suddenly resurface, calling on property once considered untouchable. Credit facilities that once fueled opportunity can demand forced liquidation of shares, often at the exact point when markets are least favorable and your position is most fragile.

The danger lies in invisibility. These instruments rarely appear in surface-level audits or simplified financial overviews. They are buried in contracts, annexes, or personal undertakings that do not show up in standard asset maps. Yet they are fully enforceable, and institutions never forget them. They may lie dormant for years, waiting not for breach but for weakness, because enforcement is most effective when resistance is lowest.

The strategic risk is compounded by the psychological dimension: you may not even remember signing them. Negotiations conducted in another context, under different assumptions, resurface in a legal environment that has shifted against you. What you regarded as routine paperwork is suddenly leveraged as binding evidence. In that moment, your memory is irrelevant. The institution's records define reality.

These hidden liabilities transform wealth from an anchor into a lever for others. What you believed safeguarded becomes extractable. What you thought stable becomes negotiable. And because guarantees and pledges rarely attract attention until enforcement, they represent one of the most dangerous blind spots in high-net-worth architecture.

The lesson is clear: wealth is not only what you hold, but what you have promised. And promises, unlike assets, are designed to resurface precisely when you can least afford them.

First principles of defensive structuring

Control without exposure: balancing legal authority and operational invisibility

The first principle of defensive structuring is deceptively simple: you must retain control without creating visibility. Control, in this context, is not about formal titles or public signatures. It is about the ability to influence outcomes, direct flows, and halt actions, without positioning yourself as the single point of attribution. Visibility, conversely, is the enemy of resilience. Once your authority is identifiable and traceable, it becomes a lever for regulators, litigants, or adversaries to apply pressure.

This does not mean concealment through illegality. It means deliberate architecture, systems that preserve your ability to act while dispersing the appearance of command. Legal ownership should be distinct from beneficial control, and beneficial control should be further separated from operational execution. Each layer reduces the clarity with which outsiders can map your influence, while still ensuring that your intent shapes the system.

In practice, this separation is achieved through design rather than decoration. Timing mechanisms that delay or condition actions prevent impulsive seizures. Veto rights embedded in governance documents allow you to halt movements without appearing as the originator. Liquidity traps can preserve value within a structure while restricting external access. Embedded protocols, automatic triggers, conditional mandates, and multi-signature requirements, ensure that no single event or actor can override the system without your indirect consent.

True control is not exercised by holding every key yourself. It is exercised by ensuring that every key operates in alignment with your architecture. Authority is distributed in form but concentrated in effect. When done correctly, you remain indispensable to function but peripheral to form. Outsiders see a coherent structure, boards, trustees, committees, or delegated officers, but the rhythm of that structure answers to your design, not to your name.

This balance, authority without attribution, is the essence of defensive structuring. It denies adversaries the ability to collapse your system by targeting you directly, while ensuring that the system still reflects your strategic intent. Sovereignty is not about being visible as the owner. It is about being irreplaceable in practice, while leaving no single signature that can be weaponized against you.

Distributed holding patterns across risk-weighted jurisdictions

Concentrating wealth in a single jurisdiction may provide simplicity, but it also creates fragility. A system that relies on one legal order, one regulatory culture, or one political environment is exposed to single-point failure. When the rules change, through legislation, crisis, or external pressure, the entirety of your position is at risk.

True resilience requires distribution across jurisdictions with different logics, vulnerabilities, and incentives. A bank account in Singapore is not governed by the same reporting culture as one in Switzerland. A trust under cayman common law does not function like a foundation under Liechtenstein civil law. Each environment interprets ownership, disclosure, and enforcement differently. These differences are not obstacles, they are buffers.

But distribution must follow logic, not convenience. Placing assets wherever fees are lowest or where a banker is most persuasive creates incoherence. Effective structuring demands alignment between asset type and jurisdictional protection. Intellectual property may find strength in one environment, while liquid financial holdings demand another. Real estate, operating companies, and reserve capital each require a jurisdiction tailored to their vulnerabilities and intended use.

This approach transforms diversification into strategy. Instead of scattering wealth randomly, you construct a portfolio of legal ecosystems calibrated to absorb different forms of pressure. Some jurisdictions provide creditor resistance, others fiscal predictability, others reputational neutrality, and still others enforcement complexity. Together, they form a lattice in which no single attack, inquiry, or political shift can compromise the whole.

Diversification across legal logics is more than a defensive tactic, it is a form of sovereignty. It neutralizes harmonization efforts, where states coordinate to close perceived loopholes, and resists unilateral aggression, where one jurisdiction attempts to extend its reach beyond its borders. By ensuring that assets live under multiple legal realities, you deny adversaries the simplicity they seek.

The goal is not dispersal for its own sake, but coherent resistance. A well-distributed structure does not look improvised. It looks inevitable: each asset located where it makes the most sense to exist, each jurisdiction chosen for its capacity to protect against a specific category of threat. Simplicity sacrifices resilience. Strategic distribution creates it.

Using time, geography, and substance to protect continuity

Time is one of the most underappreciated defensive assets. In the legal arena, chronology matters as much as compliance. An entity or holding created today, under pressure, will be interpreted as concealment. The same entity, if established years before the crisis, appears natural, embedded, and legitimate. Assets moved at the moment of scrutiny attract suspicion; assets that have been in place for years are harder to contest, harder to freeze, and harder to portray as evasive.

Continuity begins long before pressure arrives. Structures must be built in advance, not as reactions to attack. They must carry the weight of economic substance: real operations, functioning governance, documented decision-making, professional oversight, and consistent rationale. A shell that exists only for convenience is fragile, it collapses the first time someone asks “why.” A structure that operates under its own internal logic can withstand scrutiny because its reason to exist is clear, visible, and defensible.

Geography is equally strategic. It cannot be guided by tax rates alone. Jurisdictions must be chosen for their political neutrality, the complexity of their enforcement systems, and their recognition in international law. A jurisdiction that resists political interference is more valuable than one that simply offers low fees. A country that has established a reputation for honoring due process protects more than one that markets secrecy but folds under diplomatic pressure. Geography defines not just the fiscal cost of holding assets, but the survivability of those assets under external attack.

Substance, too, is often misunderstood. It does not mean renting offices or hiring token staff. It means creating a credible reason for the structure to exist beyond your personal convenience. Substance is demonstrated through economic activity, documented decision-making, audited records, and governance that reflects more than paper logic. The more a structure can be defended on its own merits, the less it depends on your personal explanations, and the less vulnerable it becomes when you are targeted.

Continuity is not built in moments of crisis. It is built quietly, in advance, through time, geography, and substance working together. Time makes structures harder to challenge. Geography makes them harder to reach. Substance makes them harder to dismiss. Combined, they create a perimeter that endures beyond events, beyond pressure, and beyond you.

Firewalls between personal, operational, and strategic assets

Wealth that remains mixed is wealth that remains vulnerable. The absence of separation creates single points of failure: if one element is attacked, the rest becomes accessible by association. The discipline of survival requires firewalls, clear, deliberate, and multi-layered barriers between categories of assets.

Personal wealth must never be entangled with operational capital. Your living space, family accounts, and private reserves should not sit in the same vehicles that fund companies, finance ventures, or absorb commercial risks. Intellectual property must be isolated from the flows of cash that sustain daily operations. Strategic reserves or family endowments must not be co-mingled with the liquidity needed to meet payroll or finance transactions. Each class of asset must serve a distinct purpose and must be protected by the firewall appropriate to that function.

Firewalls are more than technical separations. They are narrative, legal, and operational. Narrative firewalls create a story that outsiders can understand: this is private, this is commercial, this is philanthropic. Legal firewalls ensure that contracts, governance documents, and ownership titles reflect these divisions in ways that can withstand scrutiny. Operational firewalls make separation real in practice: distinct accounts, boards, signatories, and decision-making processes. Without all three dimensions, the firewall is cosmetic, not functional.

The test of a firewall is collapse. If one part of your map is seized, frozen, or attacked through litigation or regulation, the rest must remain untouched. The firewall ensures that contagion does not spread, that a targeted measure does not cascade into total paralysis. In environments where overreaction is the norm and suspicion spreads across networks, this insulation is not luxury, it is survival.

True resilience does not come from holding assets everywhere. It comes from ensuring that no single failure, no matter how severe, can compromise the whole. Firewalls enforce that discipline. They preserve continuity by ensuring that your architecture does not exist as one vulnerable mass, but as separate systems, each designed to survive even if another falls.

Avoiding red flags: how not to over-engineer your defense

In asset defense, complexity is often mistaken for strength. The instinct to add more layers, more nominee directors, more entities across more jurisdictions creates the appearance of sophistication. But in practice, overengineering is one of the most dangerous errors. It does not conceal, it illuminates. A structure that looks unnatural, incoherent, or excessively layered becomes a red flag. Instead of shielding you, it signals to regulators, auditors, or litigants that concealment is the primary objective.

Credibility is as important as complexity. Simplicity, coherence, and lawful plausibility are not weaknesses; they are shields in themselves. A structure that is rational, purposeful, and proportionate to the wealth it protects will often survive scrutiny because it looks defensible. By contrast, an architecture that exists only on paper, filled with dormant shells or recycled entities, collapses the moment someone asks “why.” The more artificial it appears, the faster it is dismantled.

The most common error is designing systems that mimic the patterns of money laundering. Moving assets without functional reason, fragmenting ownership in ways that lack operational justification, or replicating entities that perform no real role, all of these behaviors mirror the very models compliance systems are programmed to detect. Once your structure fits the pattern, technical legality is irrelevant. It will be treated as deception because it looks like deception.

A strong defensive system is not a labyrinth. It is disciplined architecture. Each entity has a reason to exist. Each layer serves a distinct function. Each jurisdiction aligns with the nature of the asset it holds. There are no unnecessary replications, no unexplained movements, no paper logic without operational substance. The system survives because it is rational, not because it is hidden.

The principle is clear: protection must not come at the cost of plausibility. When your defense looks like evasion, you have already lost. Resilience comes not from invisibility, but from coherence, structures that withstand pressure precisely because they make sense.

What not to do under pressure

Common panic reactions that increase visibility and risk

Pressure distorts judgment. When scrutiny intensifies, through investigation, litigation, regulatory inquiry, or media exposure, even the most disciplined individuals can lose strategic perspective. Survival instincts narrow clarity and push toward impulsive action. But these reactions, though intended to protect, often create the very evidence adversaries require.

The most common panic responses are also the most visible: sudden restructurings that appear reactive, abrupt transfers of funds with no underlying rationale, unexplained cash movements that mirror laundering typologies, or emergency formations of trusts and entities established precisely when pressure begins. None of these actions suggest resilience. They suggest concealment. And concealment, when aligned with timing, becomes a narrative of guilt.

Regulators, investigators, and adversaries do not need direct proof of intent. They infer it from sequence. If the creation of a holding company follows a media leak, the assumption is obvious. If an unexplained transfer occurs days after a subpoena, intent will be presumed. Timing itself becomes evidence, and the reactive pattern speaks louder than the documents you present.

This is why stillness is often stronger than speed. In crisis, the instinct to act immediately must be restrained. Moving assets after the trigger event is rarely strategic, it is self-incriminating. The correct sequence is pause, assess, and only then rebuild within a deliberate framework. Structure, not improvisation, is what survives scrutiny.

The paradox of defensive structuring is that the moment of maximum pressure is the worst time to improvise. What protects is not reaction under stress, but preparation in advance. Once pressure arrives, the safest posture is discipline: silence, stillness, and adherence to pre-existing design. Crisis exposes weakness; it should never dictate architecture.

Attempted concealment: why last-minute moves backfire

Once risk has materialized, concealment is no longer strategy, it is evidence. The instinct to protect wealth by moving it suddenly, disguising it on paper, or inserting intermediaries at the last moment does not shield assets. It highlights vulnerability. These actions are interpreted not as foresight but as panic, and panic is the easiest state to exploit.

The patterns are predictable. Properties are transferred to relatives in haste, as if kinship could provide insulation. Corporate minutes are backdated to manufacture legitimacy after the fact. New nominees are appointed with no operational relevance, their only role being to serve as a name on record. Each of these maneuvers collapses under scrutiny. Courts are adept at unwinding fraudulent conveyances, invalidating retroactive documentation, and disregarding nominees who provide no real function. What was meant as protection becomes proof of intent to deceive.

The consequences extend beyond failure of the tactic. Such moves often erase defenses that might otherwise have been available. Courts interpret concealment as implicit admission: why hide if there was nothing to fear? Banks treat it as violation of compliance obligations, triggering freezes and exits that might never have occurred otherwise. Governments interpret it as guilt, expanding investigations and reframing cases as deliberate misconduct rather than administrative oversight. In one gesture, the defensive position shifts from arguable to indefensible.

The critical principle is this: asset preservation must occur before exposure, not as a reaction to it. Structures created under calm conditions, with coherent logic and demonstrable substance, can withstand review because they appear consistent with normal governance. Structures improvised under duress collapse because they appear designed for concealment. Timing does not only influence perception, it defines legality.

Last-minute moves backfire because they are not invisible. They are luminous. And once illuminated, they serve as the adversary's narrative: that wealth was hidden, that intent was corrupt, that defense was an afterthought. The lesson is absolute: protection is preparation. Anything built after the threat emerges is not protection, it is confession.

Overreaction through excessive compliance or forced disclosures

Fear distorts judgment not only toward concealment but also toward overexposure. Under investigation or pressure, many individuals and their advisors fall into the trap of excessive transparency, delivering entire asset maps without being asked, volunteering explanations that no authority required, or drafting narratives that exceed legal obligations in the hope that eagerness will be rewarded with leniency.

This strategy rarely produces the intended outcome. Instead of projecting cooperation, it provides ammunition. Every disclosure becomes a new path of inquiry. Each detail offered can be cross-checked, reinterpreted, or framed against alternative data sources. What was revealed to demonstrate good faith becomes a roadmap for attack.

Authorities and adversaries do not reward excess disclosure. They exploit it. A document volunteered without request is treated as an admission that more exists. A timeline presented too comprehensively is combed for inconsistencies. A narrative drafted by counsel that goes beyond statutory requirements is dissected for contradictions or omissions. The act of giving more than necessary does not close inquiries, it expands them.

The danger is compounded by sequence. Over disclosure under pressure is read as reaction. If you present information spontaneously during scrutiny, it is assumed you were concealing until forced. Even details that confirm compliance are reframed as defensive maneuvers. Timing again becomes evidence, and intent is inferred not from content but from behavior.

Strategic silence is often more protective than unsolicited honesty. Silence does not mean obstruction. It means responding strictly within the bounds of law, providing only what is required, and resisting the instinct to prove innocence by volunteering excess. In adversarial contexts, every word beyond necessity becomes liability.

True compliance is precise, not performative. It satisfies legal obligations without building new vulnerabilities. Excessive compliance does not shield, it erodes. The discipline lies in knowing that in hostile processes, the less you say, the stronger your position remains.

Misusing offshore tools: when bad execution destroys good structure

Offshore structures in themselves are not inherently problematic. Trusts, foundations, and companies incorporated in international financial centers are neutral instruments, legal frameworks designed to provide flexibility, estate planning, and multi-jurisdictional efficiency. What turns them into liabilities is not their existence, but their misuse. And misuse is most common when these tools are deployed hastily, without substance, or under visible pressure.

A company created offshore with no operational logic, no governance, and no real function is not a shield. It is a signal. To regulators, auditors, and courts, it represents evasion dressed as formality. Similarly, a trust that lacks properly executed letters of wishes, or where the governance between trustee and settlor is incoherent, will collapse under scrutiny. It does not demonstrate foresight; it demonstrates theater. A foundation administered by unqualified nominees, often chosen for convenience rather than competence, will disintegrate at the first request for compliance. In each case, the weakness lies not in the tool, but in the execution.

The critical misunderstanding is the belief that "offshore" means invisible. It does not. Offshore means extra-jurisdictional, assets or entities placed within a legal order different from your own. That status can provide strategic advantages, but only if managed with professionalism, continuity, and demonstrable rationale. Improvised incorporations, paper-only entities, or reliance on nominees without substance undermine the very logic of cross-border structuring.

When offshore tools are badly executed, they betray intent. Instead of offering diversification, they announce concealment. Instead of insulating wealth, they expose the individual to suspicion, reversal, and reputational damage. Courts, regulators, and financial institutions do not need to prove fraud; they only need to demonstrate that form lacked substance. Once that case is made, the structure collapses, often taking credibility, and assets, with it.

Neutral instruments become liabilities when they are treated as shortcuts. Offshore must not be improvisation. It must be architecture: designed deliberately, executed competently, and sustained with governance that demonstrates substance. Anything less is not strategy. It is evidence waiting to be used against you.

How emotional decisions damage long-term asset stability

Wealth does not exist in a vacuum. It is shaped not only by law, regulation, and markets, but also by emotion. Under pressure, litigation, investigation, betrayal, or public scrutiny, the line between rational structuring and emotional reaction becomes dangerously thin. In such moments, fear, pride, or anger can drive decisions that unravel years of careful architecture.

The patterns are familiar. Assets are sold abruptly, not for strategic liquidity but to feel "in control." Holdings are reallocated impulsively, to punish a relative or reward an ally, regardless of long-term coherence. Entire entities are dissolved out of frustration, as if closure could substitute for stability. Each of these moves sacrifices continuity. They destroy the very systems designed to absorb pressure by replacing discipline with reaction.

The danger is compounded by timing. Emotional decisions occur at the precise moment when adversaries are watching most closely. A sudden sale, transfer, or dissolution during litigation or investigation is never interpreted as coincidence. It is seen as concealment, vulnerability, or disorganization. In this way, emotional reactions not only weaken structures internally, but also provide ammunition externally.

The paradox is that in moments of vulnerability, the urge to act immediately feels strongest. Doing something, anything, seems like proof of agency. Yet real strength lies in the opposite posture: stillness. The power to resist reaction, to preserve existing structures, and to reinforce them quietly is far greater than any visible gesture. Stability is not created in the heat of crisis; it is preserved by refusing to let emotion dictate movement.

Defense, at its core, requires patience. Patience allows scrutiny to pass without unnecessary signals. Patience preserves coherence by letting pre-existing architecture speak for itself. Patience prevents the erosion of credibility that follows erratic or impulsive moves.

Preservation begins with rejecting the reflex to act reactively. Emotional restraint is not passivity, it is strategy. In environments where every move is scrutinized, the ability to do nothing visible while reinforcing silently from within is not weakness. It is the highest form of control.

Adaptive resistance: how to withstand while under attack

Strategic inaction: deliberate delay as a shield

In moments of attack, the instinct to react is overwhelming. Pressure provokes movement. But in adversarial environments, immediate reaction is often the very trap set for you. Strategic inaction, the discipline of waiting deliberately, is not passivity. It is an active decision to deny the adversary the confirmation, the momentum, or the evidence they are seeking.

Inaction, when designed, creates asymmetry. By refusing to move first, you force the opposing side, regulator, litigant, or institution, to reveal its intent. They must commit resources, define their claims, and expose their procedural limits without yet knowing how you will respond. Delay does not weaken you; it weakens them by obliging action without feedback. Each step they take prematurely is one they cannot retract.

A deliberate pause provides clarity. It gives your legal and strategic teams the time to map options, identify vulnerabilities, and test potential countermeasures without the distraction of firefighting. It allows external systems to overextend, to make errors in haste, or to contradict themselves. Time itself becomes a filter: adversaries who act recklessly reveal weaknesses, while those who act slowly confirm that pressure may be less urgent than it appears.

But not all inaction is protective. To be a weapon, it must be structured, intentional, and timed. It must be communicated internally so that advisors, counsel, and key stakeholders remain aligned, preventing gaps or inconsistent signals. It must also be bounded, long enough to gather clarity, but not so long that silence is interpreted as default or negligence. Strategic inaction is measured resistance, not paralysis.

The paradox is that stillness under pressure often projects more stability than frantic motion. A system designed in advance to withstand scrutiny does not need to be reshaped in panic. Its strength is demonstrated by its capacity to hold. Inaction, when deliberate, signals discipline. It demonstrates that pressure has not dictated your pace. And in adversarial settings, control over pace is often the decisive advantage.

Controlled liquidity: managing access without exposing sources

In environments of scrutiny, liquidity is both a safeguard and a vulnerability. It ensures continuity of daily life and essential obligations, but it also serves as a pressure valve that adversaries attempt to close first. The critical principle is this: liquidity must be accessible without exposing the architecture behind it. The ability to act should exist, but the source must remain insulated from unnecessary visibility.

This requires advance preparation. Prearranged credit lines that can be drawn upon quietly are more resilient than emergency withdrawals. Multi-jurisdictional reserves, held in stable environments with predictable access protocols, reduce dependency on any single institution's goodwill. Delegated payment mechanisms, trusted intermediaries or structured accounts with defined mandates, allow for continuity of expenses without constant personal intervention. The key is not to conceal everything, but to ensure that every action has a plausible, documented narrative consistent with normal financial life.

By contrast, emergency moves are fatal. Appearing at a bank unannounced, tapping dormant or unusual accounts, or initiating high-value transfers without context are all red flags. They signal stress. They suggest concealment. And they provide institutions or regulators the justification to escalate oversight. Liquidity that appears improvised under pressure does not calm scrutiny, it amplifies it.

Controlled liquidity means designing buffers that allow function without improvisation. It is discretion combined with predictability. Funds must be accessible for legitimate needs, but always through channels that look intentional, proportionate, and consistent with established patterns. The narrative must align: tuition payments, household expenses, professional fees, all mapped in a way that does not trigger questions about source or timing.

The paradox of liquidity is that it must exist without being seen. You must be liquid without being seen trying to liquidate. True resilience lies not in the volume of cash available, but in the invisibility of its movement. Liquidity that flows quietly, within coherent structures, preserves both access and discretion, ensuring that continuity of life remains intact while scrutiny is deflected elsewhere.

Compartmentalized communications and operational channels

In moments of crisis, exposure rarely comes from outside systems alone. It often originates internally, through careless conversations, misused devices, or advisors operating beyond their competence. Phones can be traced, emails subpoenaed, encrypted platforms compromised, and spoken words misinterpreted. The weakness is not always in the technology. It is in the lack of separation between channels, contexts, and audiences.

Compartmentalization is the discipline of dividing communications by function. Sensitive strategy must never coexist with emotional reaction. The channel used to coordinate legal defense should not be the same as the one used to argue with family members or exchange routine updates with business partners. Each context requires its own perimeter, its own logic, and its own safeguards. Blurring them creates leakage points where stress transforms private discussions into public liabilities.

Legal coordination, for instance, must occur on channels that are jurisdictionally protected, auditable in a controlled way, and consistent with attorney-client privilege. Operational instructions, by contrast, may require secure but practical platforms accessible to multiple stakeholders. Emotional or personal exchanges must be isolated entirely, kept far from the systems that could later be scrutinized by regulators or courts. Mixing them collapses privilege, confuses narratives, and exposes strategy to misinterpretation.

Equally important is scope. Advisors must only know what they need to perform their role. Oversharing is not cooperation, it is contamination. Every extra piece of information provided outside of context multiplies the risk of leaks, mismanagement, or betrayal under pressure. By isolating knowledge, you reduce the damage that any single compromised node can cause.

The essence of compartmentalization is not mistrust, it is architecture. You cannot control how others will respond under scrutiny, or how they will act when pressured by regulators, adversaries, or fear. But you can control what they know, and therefore what they can expose. By separating channels, segmenting information, and aligning communication with function, you ensure that no single breach collapses the entire system.

In defense, silence is powerful. But structured silence, applied through compartmentalization, is stronger still.

Narrative engineering: controlling perception without provocation

In adversarial environments, silence is not neutral. It can be interpreted as fear, concealment, or instability. Similarly, open defense, explaining, justifying, or protesting, rarely produces clarity. It creates material for speculation and narrative distortion. The challenge, therefore, is not whether to speak or stay silent, but how to control what is perceived without revealing what is protected. This is the discipline of narrative engineering.

Adaptive resistance requires shaping posture as carefully as structure. The perception you project must balance opposites: confident but not arrogant, responsive but not exposed, protected but not panicked. This balance is not cosmetic, it determines how regulators, courts, adversaries, and even allies interpret your stability. In an environment where perception often precedes judgment, posture itself becomes a defensive tool.

Public actions play a critical role. Routine filings completed on schedule, quiet appearances at expected venues, predictable financial behavior aligned with prior patterns, all these create continuity. They signal normalcy. They provide a counterweight to narratives of crisis or collapse without disclosing strategy. To the adversary, they deny the illusion of victory. To institutions, they reinforce plausibility. To allies, they prevent panic.

Importantly, narrative engineering does not mean manufacturing explanations. It is not about persuasion. It is about framing what is already observable so that it aligns with stability. You cannot prevent speculation. But you can ensure that speculation collides with consistent, credible signals. A posture of coherence undermines attempts to cast you as unstable, evasive, or reckless.

The goal is not to explain yourself. Explanation invites interrogation. The goal is to remain operational without becoming the subject. The more predictable your outward behavior, the less incentive adversaries have to invent chaos. Narrative engineering makes you visible enough to appear stable, but never exposed enough to become vulnerable.

Perception, like structure, must be designed. Without it, silence and defense both betray you. With it, you control the space in which speculation operates, and deny adversaries the power to define you.

Endurance planning: what to do if the siege lasts months or years

Not all forms of pressure arrive like a sudden strike. Some unfold slowly, stretching across months or years. Regulatory inquiries that begin as routine reviews can expand into prolonged investigations. Litigation may drag through appeals for a decade. Political repression can convert temporary obstacles into a permanent state of uncertainty. In such environments, the question is not how to resist for a week, it is how to survive for the long horizon.

Endurance demands structures that function without constant intervention. Legal mandates must be preconfigured to persist autonomously, ensuring that essential actions continue even if you are unavailable. Liquidity flows must be governed by rules, automatic payments, programmed distributions, delegated authorizations, rather than ad hoc requests that require your signature at moments when you may be restricted. Relationships, too, must be designed for duration: alliances and advisors who can operate consistently without needing constant reassurance, and who remain loyal through distance and silence.

The human element is central. Fatigue is inevitable. Under prolonged pressure, you will be exhausted, isolated, or emotionally compromised. The risk is not collapse of the structure, it is collapse of your capacity to direct it. Endurance planning means assuming that weakness will come and building fallback mechanisms in advance: secondary signatories with limited mandates, escalation protocols for counsel, and pre-decided strategies for scenarios you may be too drained to analyze when they arrive. In effect, you preconfigure your decisions so that discipline holds even when willpower falters.

Adaptive resistance, in this context, is not about fighting harder. Escalation burns energy and resources that must be preserved. The aim is to outlast, to stretch beyond the timeline of the threat without consuming the very infrastructure designed to protect you. Systems must run quietly in the background, carrying your continuity forward while the external environment exhausts itself.

Survival, when pressure is prolonged, is not a temporary phase. It is an operating system. One that sustains itself, resists fatigue, and ensures that you remain intact long enough to watch the siege collapse under its own weight.

Final note

Preserving assets under siege is not about hiding, it is about designing resilience that does not depend on your ability to react in real time.

The moment of attack is not when protection begins. It is when protection is tested. If the structure must be created after the pressure appears, it is already too late. But if the system anticipates pressure, it absorbs it without noise, without contradiction, and without unnecessary exposure.

You are not defending a bank account or a property. You are defending a system of life. And that system must survive long enough to be reconfigured, not just legally, but mentally, emotionally, and structurally. What matters is not just what you hold, but how it holds when you're not there to defend it.

Chapter VI. Operating during crisis without losing status

Functional paralysis, when crisis halts decision-making

Executive fatigue and fear of exposure

Even the most experienced leaders encounter moments when pressure immobilizes them. In environments of litigation, investigation, or political targeting, the sheer weight of potential exposure can render decision-making inert. The fear is not abstract, it is precise. Every move may carry legal risk, reputational cost, or personal consequence. In that climate, the instinctive response is hesitation.

Fatigue compounds this paralysis. It is not simply the exhaustion of workload, but the deeper erosion that comes from sustained scrutiny: the knowledge that each decision will be dissected, reinterpreted, and possibly weaponized. The emotional burden of constant defense drains clarity, and the reputational anxiety of being misread corrodes confidence. What follows is silence, indecision, and the quiet breakdown of systems that depend on continuous and decisive leadership.

This state is not weakness. It is human reaction to sustained uncertainty under surveillance. But in the realm of high-net-worth operations, paralysis is dangerous. Complex structures, financial, legal, and operational, require timely action to preserve coherence. Deadlines pass, opportunities dissolve, and adversaries gain leverage when leaders hesitate. What begins as self-protection against error becomes, in practice, a sequence of unmade decisions that dismantle resilience from within.

The answer is not impulsive action disguised as courage. Leadership under pressure must be internalized as discipline. Discipline is the ability to continue executing preconfigured structures even when instinct demands withdrawal. It means adhering to systems and protocols established in calmer times, so that fatigue and fear cannot override design. It is less about improvisation than about fidelity, holding to rules when willpower is weakest.

In high-pressure contexts, decisiveness must never be emotional. Emotion creates noise, not strategy. True decisiveness is adherence to structure, applied with consistency, even when the self feels uncertain. Resilience lies not in acting boldly, but in ensuring that systems continue to function when the individual at the center momentarily cannot.

Institutional reluctance to follow instructions

In moments of crisis, institutions that once served faithfully often shift posture. Banks, trustees, directors, and advisors move from execution to self-protection. Their priority ceases to be your continuity and becomes their own regulatory survival. The result is not outright refusal, but hesitation, a quiet inertia that slows even the simplest commands.

Compliance departments extend reviews indefinitely, citing "standard procedure." Board members avoid votes, preferring delay over accountability. Trustees and nominees who once acted on instruction begin requesting unnecessary confirmations, or worse, retreat into silence to minimize liability. Transactions that would normally clear in hours, wire transfers, liquidations, procedural filings, stall without explanation. The obstacle is not illegality; it is fear of association. Once your name or structures trigger risk signals, every action is filtered through the institution's defensive instinct.

This paralysis is structural, not personal. The banker may value your relationship. The advisor may believe in your integrity. But at the institutional level, the logic changes. Executing your instructions is secondary to avoiding reputational or regulatory exposure. In effect, the institution reclassifies you: from client to potential liability. From that moment, efficiency is sacrificed to caution, and routine operations collapse into endless deferral.

The danger lies in timing. Crisis is when execution must be fastest, when liquidity must move, filings must be made, and governance must function seamlessly. Yet it is precisely then that institutional reluctance is strongest. The system you thought dependable becomes an obstacle, and your vulnerability is multiplied not by adversaries but by inertia.

Anticipation is the only defense. You cannot eliminate institutional caution, but you can design structures that depend less on discretion and more on preconfigured logic. Automated mechanisms, standing instructions, conditional mandates, pre-authorized distributions, reduce reliance on human decision-making under pressure. Delegated authority, distributed across jurisdictions and actors, minimizes the impact of any single institution's reluctance.

The principle is clear: do not assume loyalty from systems whose survival depends on avoiding you. Build architectures where essential functions continue, not because someone chooses to act, but because the system is already programmed to act.

Delays in legal decisions, authorizations, or bank access

Legal protections are only as strong as your ability to access them. Rights, contracts, and authorizations exist on paper, but in practice they are mediated by processes, courts, banks, notaries, agents. In moments of crisis, these processes slow down, turning formal protections into empty promises. What appears as delay is often denial in disguise.

Attorneys, under pressure, hesitate to issue decisive advice. Courts, burdened or cautious, defer rulings indefinitely. Banks invoke compliance to request endless rounds of documentation. Notarized authorizations, valid when issued, expire mid-process as bureaucracies stall. Powers of attorney, critical to execution under stress, are questioned, restricted, or outright rejected. Local agents who once ensured fluidity suddenly become unavailable, on leave or unwilling to engage. None of this is accidental. These are systemic slowdowns triggered by uncertainty, where every participant protects themselves first.

The effect is paralyzing. Crisis does not only limit what you can do; it extends the time required to do anything at all. Days become weeks, weeks become months. In adversarial contexts, delay benefits the system, not the individual. Regulators gain leverage while you wait. Opponents exploit time as an asymmetrical weapon, forcing you into fatigue, dependency, or premature concessions.

The discipline, therefore, is anticipation. Timelines must be recalibrated to account for obstruction, not efficiency. Expectations must be lowered: what normally clears in hours may require weeks. Structures must include fallback paths, redundant authorizations, preconfigured mandates, multi-jurisdictional signatories, so that no single bottleneck can immobilize continuity.

In high-risk environments, speed is not a given. It is an asset that must be engineered. Delays are not neutral, they are tactics. To survive them, you must assume them. By embedding redundancy and time awareness into your architecture, you transform delay from a fatal surprise into a predictable variable.

The hidden cost of pausing operations

When crisis or paralysis strikes, the instinctive response is to pause. Freeze transactions. Delay decisions. Cancel appearances. The logic feels sound: if movement creates risk, then stillness must create safety. Yet this reflex overlooks a critical truth, pausing operations is not neutral. It carries hidden costs that accumulate quietly until they become irreversible.

Businesses do not remain static when frozen. Clients drift. Contracts expire. Supply chains adapt to other providers. The market does not wait for your stability to return; it evolves in your absence. What was paused in theory often collapses in practice.

The same applies to reputation. Silence intended as protection begins to signal instability. Partners, competitors, and observers interpret absence not as discipline but as weakness. Each delay feeds narratives that you are under strain. Each unanswered call or postponed meeting creates a vacuum, and vacuums are always filled by speculation, rumor, or adversarial framing.

The danger is compounded by time. A single pause may be recoverable. Repeated pauses form a pattern, and patterns are treated as truth. A business seen as unreliable is not easily restored. Once credibility is questioned, continuity is doubted, and doubt spreads faster than clarification.

The discipline, therefore, is not to reject pausing entirely but to design it intelligently. You must determine in advance which functions are too critical to suspend and which can safely go dormant. Essential flows, payments to employees, regulatory filings, visible signs of activity, must be insulated from crisis and preserved at all costs. Secondary or symbolic functions may be slowed, but always within a framework that maintains narrative coherence.

This decision cannot be improvised after paralysis begins. It must be embedded into your system before pressure arrives, coded into mandates, automated processes, and fallback protocols. Pausing must itself be structured, targeted, limited, and reversible.

Survival is not about freezing entirely. It is about ensuring that when you do pause, the pause does not destroy the very infrastructure it was meant to protect.

Building continuity protocols to maintain flow

Paralysis cannot be overcome by force of will. In crisis, determination alone is insufficient. What preserves resilience is not improvisation but redundancy, the deliberate creation of systems that continue to function when leadership cannot. Continuity protocols transform vulnerability into endurance by ensuring that essential operations persist regardless of personal presence or capacity.

These protocols must be embedded into structure, not drafted in theory. Pre-signed mandates allow transactions to be executed even if direct authorization is delayed. Rotating signatories ensure that no single absence immobilizes decision-making. Multi-key approvals balance security with flexibility, permitting movement only when a pre-agreed combination of actors acts together. Decentralized execution channels distribute responsibility so that critical functions, liquidity, compliance, communications, do not collapse into silence when one node fails.

The principle is simple: intent must be translated into systems. A plan that exists only in memory or on paper dissolves under pressure. A system that is automated, pre-authorized, or delegated with precision survives because it requires no emotional energy or improvised courage in the moment of crisis. Continuity becomes operational, not aspirational.

It is essential to distinguish continuity from blind persistence. Not everything must move at all times. Certain operations can pause strategically. The discipline lies in predefining which functions must never stop, core liquidity flows, legal filings, regulatory obligations, reputational signals of activity, and which can safely go dormant. By deciding in advance who moves what, how, and when, you prevent chaos from dictating priorities when judgment is clouded.

Continuity is not about resisting pauses; it is about making pauses survivable. It ensures that silence at the leadership level does not translate into collapse at the structural level. Properly designed, continuity protocols do more than protect wealth, they preserve credibility, trust, and operational coherence long enough for recovery to become possible.

Silent command, leading without direct presence

Delegation systems that do not reveal hierarchy

Leadership in high-risk environments is not about visibility. It is about influence without exposure. Traditional hierarchies, signing authorities, email records, organizational charts, may function in normal times, but under scrutiny they become liabilities. They map your presence directly to decisions, leaving you identifiable as the single point of command. In adversarial contexts, that visibility is a vulnerability.

Silent command is the art of delegating authority without leaving identifiable fingerprints. The objective is not to erase leadership, but to reassign its footprint, dispersing execution so that control is exercised through design, not through direct presence. Properly engineered, delegation creates protective ambiguity. Outsiders see movement, but they cannot map its origin.

This requires more than appointing proxies or issuing powers of attorney. It demands structural design. Decision rights can be fragmented across multiple actors, each holding only part of the authority, so that no single signature reveals control. Instructions can be embedded in protocols, financial, legal, or operational, that trigger automatically without visible initiation. Communications can be layered so that guidance flows through intermediaries or coded routines rather than direct correspondence. In such systems, the role of the leader is preserved, but hidden in form.

The protective power of silent command lies in its opacity. Regulators, litigants, or adversaries may see outcomes, transfers made, entities managed, policies executed, but they cannot easily establish the line of authorship. Control exists, but attribution is blurred. This ambiguity reduces the ability of external systems to target you directly, while maintaining coherence within your own architecture.

Delegation that exposes hierarchy is a risk. Delegation that masks hierarchy is resilience. The goal is not abdication. It is the redistribution of visible authority so that the system functions with your intent, but without your name attached to every act. In this way, leadership persists quietly, ensuring that operations remain aligned while the leader remains insulated.

The power of protocol over personality

In many families, businesses, and high-net-worth structures, decision-making gravitates toward a single figure. Authority flows from personality, charisma, experience, or central presence. This may feel efficient, even natural, in stable times. But under scrutiny, this model collapses. A system that depends on one individual becomes fragile the moment that individual is targeted, exhausted, or removed.

Protocol is the antidote to fragility. A protocol-based system ensures that decisions are not improvisations but sequences. Authority flows through predetermined pathways. Choices are not dependent on personal will but on rules, triggers, and thresholds. Discretion is not concentrated in one person but distributed across roles, documents, and mechanisms. In such systems, continuity survives the absence, or the silence, of the figurehead.

The strength of protocol lies in its neutrality. A bank transfer executed under standing instruction does not draw attention to who ordered it. A board resolution triggered automatically by financial thresholds cannot be accused of bias. A governance process that delegates authority in rotation cannot be paralyzed by the hesitation of one actor. The more the system operates mechanically, the less it can be disrupted by external attack or internal fatigue.

Protocolization does not eliminate leadership, it redefines it. The leader's role shifts from being the visible origin of every decision to being the architect of the system that decides. Influence is embedded in design, not in signature. In this way, the leader remains central in intent but peripheral in form. Adversaries cannot destabilize the system by targeting the individual, because the system is programmed to function without constant intervention.

The principle becomes sharper as complexity increases. The more layered the assets, the more cross-border the risks, the more essential it is that leadership becomes mechanical. Personality cannot withstand multi-jurisdictional pressure, reputational attack, or institutional inertia. Protocol can, because it reduces exposure to human variability and enforces discipline even when individuals falter.

Dependency is vulnerability. Logic is resilience. The shift from personality to protocol transforms fragile structures into enduring ones. The more complex the risk, the more mechanical leadership must become, not because humanity is irrelevant, but because discipline must prevail where personality cannot.

Predefined fallback structures: mandates, tiers, guardians

Resilience requires more than a primary system. It requires the certainty that if one element fails, another is ready to take its place without hesitation. In high-net-worth operations, every role must have a fallback, every process a secondary path, and every critical function a designated guardian. Without these, even small interruptions cascade into systemic paralysis.

Fallback structures are not simple backups. A backup waits passively, often untested, and is rarely sufficient in moments of crisis. A true fallback is a parallel system, predefined, preauthorized, and designed to activate seamlessly when the primary is compromised. This is not contingency by improvisation; it is continuity by architecture.

The most effective designs use tiers of responsibility. Authority is distributed across levels, with clear thresholds that trigger delegation. If the primary decision-maker is unavailable, authority flows automatically to the next tier, not by negotiation but by design. Mandates, whether legal, financial, or operational, predefine who acts under which conditions, eliminating hesitation and dispute at the moment of pressure. Guardianship, too, must be explicit: individuals or committees tasked with safeguarding specific assets, functions, or relationships, prepared to act without delay when the system demands it.

Testing is essential. Fallback systems that exist only on paper are fragile illusions. They must be rehearsed, simulated, and validated under realistic conditions. Powers of attorney must be confirmed as executable across jurisdictions. Delegated authorities must be stress-tested to ensure institutions honor them. Guardians must be briefed and drilled so that activation is seamless, not experimental. Redundancy is not resilience unless it works under pressure.

The goal of fallback structures is not merely duplication. It is substitution that feels continuous, where the system functions as though no interruption occurred. By embedding mandates, tiers, and guardians into the architecture, you remove reliance on emergency improvisation. Continuity is preserved not because you are present, but because the system is programmed to survive your absence.

Decision latency vs. Operational consistency

In stable environments, decisions can be made quickly, often in real time. Leadership is present, information is clear, and actions follow almost instantly. But crisis alters the rhythm. Pressure, legal scrutiny, and reputational risk slow decision-making. Each choice requires verification, consultation, and hesitation. Latency increases just as the external environment accelerates. The illusion of control dissolves in the gap between events and responses.

The instinct is to fight latency with speed, to force decisions, to react as quickly as events unfold. But this response is flawed. In crisis, speed creates errors, and errors under scrutiny become liabilities. The correct response is not to chase events but to enforce consistency. Systems must be designed to function predictably without the constant injection of personal decisions. Your absence, hesitation, or silence must not cause hesitation in the architecture itself.

Consistency is engineered through predefined outcomes. Scenario-based instructions provide clarity: if one trigger occurs, the system responds in a programmed way. Conditional execution frameworks, mandates that activate under specific thresholds or signals, allow operations to continue without waiting for your confirmation. Multi-level signatory systems, automatic financial flows, or tiered escalation processes reduce dependency on individual judgment at the moment of pressure.

This discipline shifts the objective. You are not trying to keep up with events, you are trying to maintain alignment. Operational rhythm, preserved through predictability, reassures institutions, counterparties, and allies that the system remains coherent. Even if leadership is delayed, the structure appears seamless. Consistency absorbs latency.

Trust is not built on speed. It is built on rhythm, on the ability of systems to act reliably, even when leaders hesitate. By embedding decision logic into structure, you transform moments of paralysis into demonstrations of stability. In adversarial contexts, this rhythm becomes one of the most valuable assets you can project.

Invisible leadership in sensitive contexts

In high-risk environments, regulatory, political, or reputational, visibility is liability. The more directly leadership can be traced, the more easily it can be targeted, pressured, or discredited. Survival in such contexts requires a redefinition of leadership itself: authority must shift from presence to influence, from signatures to systems, from exposure to invisibility.

Invisible leadership does not mean abdication. You do not need to appear to be in charge to be in charge. Control is exercised indirectly, through the architecture of processes, the discipline of delegation, the framing of narratives, and the calibration of timing. When design governs action, the individual behind the design remains insulated. The structure moves, the system executes, but the origin is blurred.

This model allows you to remain functionally central while appearing externally peripheral. To outsiders, you are present but not decisive, visible but not exposed. To insiders, the system still reflects your intent, because you designed the rules, the flows, and the triggers that guide it. Leadership is no longer about intervention at every step. It is about embedding control into form so that the system aligns even in your absence.

Far from being weakness, this form of leadership is refinement. It minimizes attack vectors by leaving no singular point of command to target. It denies adversaries the satisfaction of identifying a "head of command." And it resists institutional overreaction by presenting decision-making as distributed, procedural, and logical rather than personal.

Invisible leadership is command without trace. It is the ability to remain indispensable in function while optional in form. In environments where scrutiny is weaponized, this refinement is not only strategic, it is essential.

Managing public and institutional perception

What visible silence says , and what it hides

Silence is never neutral. In high-profile contexts, absence communicates as loudly as words. The longer you remain quiet, the more meaning others assign to your silence. And meaning, once invented, often becomes reality in the minds of institutions, adversaries, and the public.

Interpretations diverge. To some, silence signals discipline, evidence of restraint, planning, or negotiation behind the scenes. To others, it suggests weakness, guilt, or collapse. Regulators may interpret it as lack of cooperation. Media may frame it as proof of disarray. Silence, therefore, is not emptiness. It is a canvas onto which every observer projects their own narrative.

The difference lies in posture. Visible silence, when improvised, invites speculation and destabilizes confidence. But silence that is staged, that carries the appearance of being deliberate, can project control. A pause presented as preparation suggests foresight. A temporary disappearance framed as maneuver looks tactical, not accidental. Institutions and adversaries respond differently to silence when it feels like a decision rather than a vacuum.

This requires careful design. If you withdraw, maintain external signals of continuity, routine filings, stable operations, or predictable financial flows. These quiet signals assure observers that systems remain intact even if the figurehead is absent. If you pause communication, do so with timing and context that suggest strategy: silence during negotiation appears protective; silence after victory appears dignified.

Perception fills the vacuum you leave. You cannot prevent others from assigning meaning to your silence. But you can shape the range of meanings available. Silence framed as collapse weakens you. Silence framed as calculation strengthens you. The discipline lies in making absence look intentional, never accidental.

In adversarial environments, what you do not say may be more decisive than what you do. Silence, when staged correctly, becomes not exposure but armor, a shield that conceals intent while projecting stability.

Public filings, corporate communications, and strategic absence

Even when you remain silent, your entities continue to speak. Public filings, regulatory submissions, shareholder updates, procedural documents, and internal communications form a narrative independent of your voice. They are read not only by regulators and counterparties, but also by adversaries and observers searching for signals. In environments of scrutiny, these signals matter as much as any public statement you might make.

Every act of compliance is a message. A tax filing delivered on time communicates discipline. A shareholder update issued regularly conveys continuity. Routine minutes of board meetings, notarized mandates, or procedural documentation, though seemingly administrative, serve as external proof that systems remain intact. Each silent motion reassures the observer: the structure is functional, the architecture is alive, and the absence of noise is not collapse but continuity.

Corporate communications amplify this effect when used with precision. Press releases or official notices do not need to explain crises or defend actions, that would invite interpretation. Instead, they anchor perception by maintaining rhythm. Predictable updates, neutral in tone and consistent in form, remind stakeholders that the organization is operating normally. They frame absence not as instability, but as recalibration within an ongoing system.

This is the essence of strategic absence. Your personal silence becomes less alarming, less exploitable, when your infrastructure continues to move visibly and predictably. Institutions, markets, and partners draw reassurance not from what you say, but from what your systems show. Stability is not declared, it is demonstrated.

The discipline lies in ensuring that infrastructure is designed to signal continuity even without your intervention. Filings must be automated, communications preprogrammed, and governance protocols resilient. When absence is supported by visible rhythm, it ceases to appear as weakness and instead projects control. In high-risk contexts, this distinction is decisive.

The role of lawyers, proxies, and formal statements

In high-risk contexts, direct response is one of the most dangerous mistakes an individual can make. Every word you say is preserved, dissected, and reinterpreted. Every tone, pause, or expression can be weaponized. What was intended as clarification may become contradiction. What was spoken in defense may be reframed as confession. Visibility turns language into liability.

This is why proxies are indispensable. Lawyers, corporate representatives, and formal filings act as narrative firewalls. They allow you to communicate without exposing yourself personally. A statement delivered through counsel is interpreted differently than one delivered in your own voice, it is procedural, not emotional; professional, not personal. Institutions, media, and adversaries understand this distinction. They expect lawyers to speak, and they treat such speech as part of process rather than performance.

The form of these communications is critical. Statements must be brief, factual, and unprovocative. Their function is not to persuade or fight speculation, but to deprive it of fuel. Each unnecessary detail multiplies paths for scrutiny. Each emotional inflection invites interpretation. Precision, neutrality, and restraint are the weapons of choice.

Proxies also manage expectation. When you speak directly, others expect explanation and justification. When your lawyer speaks, the expectation is reduced to minimal clarity. The shield is twofold: they deflect direct risk while simultaneously lowering the demand for disclosure. Silence from you, balanced by limited words from them, becomes plausible rather than suspicious.

The less emotion, the better. The less detail, the safer. The purpose of proxies is not to tell your story, but to prevent others from inventing it in your absence. They are not negotiators of truth; they are guardians of narrative discipline. Properly used, they create distance between you and the storm, absorbing its noise while leaving you insulated.

A shield is strongest when it is used sparingly. Proxies should speak only when necessary, and always in forms that reinforce continuity, not conflict. In this way, they convert the burden of speech into a protective mechanism, ensuring that the narrative moves forward without ever placing you directly in its path.

Financial behavior that signals continuity

In environments of uncertainty, financial behavior is read as signal. Numbers are not only technical, they are narrative. Every transfer, every payroll, every settlement contributes to the external perception of whether a system is stable or collapsing. Observers, regulators, banks, adversaries, even employees, interpret financial flows as indicators of control. In this sense, finance becomes a language, and what it communicates matters as much as the balance sheets themselves.

Continuity is conveyed through rhythm. Stable transactions, predictable salaries, timely payments, and routine corporate activity all suggest discipline and coherence. They project the impression that governance is intact and operations remain functional. These actions do not eliminate scrutiny, but they slow its momentum. They deny adversaries the visual cues of collapse. They make institutions hesitate before escalating, because the narrative of failure is contradicted by the data of continuity.

The opposite is also true. Sudden changes in financial flows, halts in payments, unexplained surges in activity, emergency restructurings, trigger questions. Disruption, even when technically justified, is interpreted as weakness. The timing of movements is as important as their content. An emergency transfer during litigation, a payroll delay during investigation, or a liquidation during negotiation all provide adversaries with leverage. To the external eye, disruption looks like vulnerability.

This is why continuity must be designed, not improvised. Financial flows should be preprogrammed to remain steady even under pressure. Salaries should clear on schedule, suppliers should be paid predictably, and recurring obligations must never be neglected. Where adjustments are necessary, they must follow a narrative logic that appears consistent with long-term planning rather than crisis management.

Finance, at its core, is not just numbers, it is story. Stable patterns write calm into the record, even if beneath the surface turbulence persists. Properly managed, financial behavior becomes a defensive tool: it reassures allies, denies adversaries evidence, and sustains credibility when words would be dangerous.

Continuity is not perfection. It is rhythm. And in the eyes of those watching, rhythm signals survival.

Avoiding the trap of over-justification or media exposure

One of the most dangerous impulses under scrutiny is the urge to explain. Pressure creates the instinct to clarify, defend, or correct the record. But each attempt to respond adds new material to the very narrative you are trying to escape. Every explanation becomes evidence. Every denial becomes a headline. Every effort to "set the record straight" makes the record real.

Over-justification transforms silence into visibility and visibility into entrapment. The more you explain, the more you feed speculation. Instead of closing narratives, you expand them. Each word introduces a timeline that can be dissected, a phrase that can be misinterpreted, or a position that can later be contradicted. Once you start speaking, silence becomes suspicious. You are locked into a cycle where presence is demanded endlessly and absence is condemned as guilt.

Media exposure compounds the risk. Interviews, even when carefully managed, give adversaries content to distort. Clarifications, however factual, will be excerpted selectively. Attempts at self-defense will be reframed as admissions of instability. The media's logic is not truth, it is story. And by stepping into that arena, you become the story.

Discipline requires rejecting the illusion that the public must be corrected. You are not obligated to provide explanations to satisfy curiosity or speculation. Your only obligation is to protect yourself, your structures, and your continuity. The record you need to preserve is not the one in headlines but the one in courts, contracts, and systems of governance.

Invisibility is not denial. It is strategy. It is the decision to operate above the noise rather than inside it. The absence of commentary does not mean absence of control, it means refusal to legitimize speculation by engaging with it. By remaining outside the narrative cycle, you deny adversaries the raw material they need to sustain attack.

Silence, when designed, is not weakness. It is armor. And in hostile environments, the refusal to explain can preserve more than the most carefully worded justification ever could.

Managing strategic appearances and retreats

When to reduce public footprint

There are moments when visibility ceases to be an asset and becomes a liability. Investigations, conflicts, or volatile narratives can turn public presence into a magnet for scrutiny. In such contexts, maintaining the same level of exposure is not resilience, it is risk. Strategic leadership requires knowing when to scale down your footprint in order to neutralize attention before it escalates.

Reducing presence does not mean vanishing. Total disappearance often raises more questions than it answers. Instead, it means removing unnecessary signals, social media activity, interviews, public events, or filings in your personal name, that contribute nothing to your defense but offer adversaries material to exploit. The principle is subtraction: eliminate what is nonessential so that what remains visible appears intentional, stable, and coherent.

This recalibration is not an act of fear. It is an act of discipline. Retreat is not surrender; it is reduction of surface area. What cannot be seen cannot be targeted. By limiting exposure points, you deny adversaries opportunities to build narratives against you, while keeping control over the few signals you choose to maintain.

Timing is decisive. The decision to reduce footprint must be made early, while you still appear in control, not late, when reaction looks like retreat. If you wait until exposure causes visible damage, withdrawal will be framed as defeat. If you recalibrate preemptively, it is seen as strategy, a maneuver rather than a collapse.

Strategic absence, like strategic presence, is part of narrative management. Appear where it strengthens your position, retreat where visibility invites attack. The rhythm between the two defines stability. The strongest posture is not permanent exposure, but the ability to appear and withdraw with precision, always on your terms.

How to re-enter without questions or suspicion

Retreat may protect, but re-entry is the true test. If managed poorly, the act of returning to visibility can reignite scrutiny, attract speculation, or undo the stability gained through absence. The challenge is to re-emerge without appearing to reappear, seamlessly, naturally, as if continuity was never broken.

Re-entry must be subtle. It should not announce itself, nor carry the tone of justification. No apology. No explanation. No public framing. Each of these signals disruption, and disruption invites questions. Instead, re-entry must look like routine, the quiet resumption of systems already in place, not the dramatic unveiling of something newly begun.

The method is gradual. A quiet reactivation of operations: filings made on time, routine transactions executed, scheduled communications delivered as if nothing had paused. A passive presence at neutral events, industry gatherings, cultural venues, predictable forums, where attendance looks ordinary, not calculated. Routine emails or updates that project normalcy without commentary. Each signal is small, but together they reinforce the perception that continuity was never lost.

The narrative must explain itself without words. Observers should conclude, on their own, that the absence was part of a cycle, not a collapse. The less you shape this conclusion directly, the more credible it becomes. A system that appears to run without interruption is stronger than a leader who tries to persuade that it never faltered.

The key distinction is this: you are not "returning." To return implies absence, rupture, and vulnerability. You are resuming, resuming what was always operational, even if invisible. The external world sees activity again, but you know it never truly stopped. That continuity is your shield.

In hostile environments, survival is not about dramatic exits or triumphant comebacks. It is about rhythm. When re-entry is staged as seamless continuity, scrutiny has nothing to grasp, and speculation has no oxygen. You have not returned. You have simply continued.

Timing and choreography of return

In high-risk environments, timing is not neutral. It is perception. Returning too early projects arrogance, as if pressure never existed or consequences do not matter. Returning too late suggests weakness, guilt, collapse, or hesitation. The art of return lies in choreography: aligning re-entry with external signals so that presence feels inevitable rather than strategic.

The environment must set the stage. Re-entry should coincide with the resolution of key disputes, the calming of media cycles, or the stabilization of institutional partners. When turbulence subsides, return appears logical, even expected. If you force reappearance against the current of events, it reads as provocation. If you wait until relevance fades, it reads as defeat. Precision in timing ensures that the act of return harmonizes with context rather than colliding with it.

Choreography is equally decisive. The return should not be dramatic or defensive but embedded in ordinary function. Symbolic acts carry more weight than speeches: chairing a routine meeting, signing a document, appearing in a benign or neutral setting where your presence is natural. These gestures convey stability without demanding attention. They show continuity without forcing narrative.

The key is subtle inevitability. The return must feel less like a maneuver and more like the natural continuation of what always existed. Calculated steps must appear uncalculated, deliberate choices must appear routine. Observers must see not a comeback but a presence that resumes seamlessly.

In this way, the return projects control without confrontation. It avoids the trap of over-justification while restoring visibility at a pace that reassures rather than provokes. Presence becomes rhythm again, expected, unremarkable, yet unmistakably intact.

Creating plausible narratives for disappearance

Absence does not exist in a vacuum. In high-profile environments, every withdrawal demands explanation, if you do not provide one, others will. And when others invent explanations, they rarely serve your interests. Speculation fills silence with stories of collapse, guilt, or instability. The discipline, therefore, is to frame your absence before others do.

These narratives must be plausible, restrained, and aligned with your established behavior. They must sound like natural extensions of your life or professional rhythm, not abrupt departures from it. A sabbatical for study or reflection. Attention to family health matters. A strategic retreat for long-term planning. Internal restructuring that requires focus away from external visibility. Each of these narratives is ordinary enough to be accepted, neutral enough to avoid provocation, and consistent enough to reduce curiosity.

The purpose is not deception. It is framing. You are not inventing elaborate stories but offering context, an explanation that closes the gap between presence and absence without inviting further inquiry. The narrative should not ignite interest or open new questions; it should extinguish them.

Timing is essential. The narrative must be positioned before speculation gains momentum, so that it feels like a planned choice rather than a defensive excuse. Once established, it must be repeated consistently across all signals, corporate communications, personal references, institutional filings, so that coherence reinforces credibility.

Most importantly, the chosen narrative must carry closure. It must provide enough reason for absence to appear sensible while leaving no hooks for outsiders to dig deeper. A sabbatical requires no follow-up. Family matters require privacy. Strategic retreats imply discipline, not scandal. Internal restructuring suggests process, not crisis.

The principle is simple: absence must never appear accidental or unexplained. A plausible narrative transforms disappearance from suspicion into continuity. It ensures that withdrawal is seen not as collapse but as design.

Repositioning without explaining

Crisis often forces evolution. Exposure, litigation, or reputational strain may make it necessary to shift roles, restructure companies, or even change geography. But the act of repositioning carries its own risks. If handled poorly, it signals rupture, an implicit admission that something broke. If handled with discipline, it becomes seamless, an organic adjustment that requires no explanation.

The temptation is to verbalize change: to say "I'm starting over" or "I've changed directions." Yet such statements undermine stability. They create a narrative of discontinuity, framing your transformation as reaction rather than design. In adversarial environments, rupture is weakness. It confirms the suspicion that pressure dictated your movement.

The correct approach is quiet repositioning through action, not declaration. Accept a new board seat in a domain that projects continuity. Engage in a different category of project, allowing activity itself to signal recalibration. Shift communication style, less exposure, more precision, without ever acknowledging the reason. Each action is subtle, but collectively they reposition your profile. Observers absorb the change not through what you say, but through what they see.

The strength of this method lies in its elegance. Transformation becomes visible without being announced. It feels natural because it unfolds consistently, step by step, across time and context. Adversaries have little to frame as disruption, because no explicit rupture has been acknowledged. Institutions interpret it as evolution, not evasion. Allies see adjustment, not collapse.

Repositioning is not denial of change, it is its refinement. You do not need to explain transformation to make it credible. You only need to embody it, quietly, consistently, and with discipline. The less you justify, the more authority you retain. And in environments of scrutiny, authority is not what you claim, it is what your posture makes undeniable.

Staying operational without becoming the story

Avoiding personal identification with corporate issues

In high-net-worth ecosystems, identity and entity are often fused. The individual's reputation drives credibility, and the entity's performance reinforces personal stature. In normal times, this entanglement creates efficiency and influence. But under crisis, it becomes lethal. When your name is synonymous with the issue, every movement of your companies is framed as a personal maneuver. Investigations expand to target you, media attention sharpens its lens, and institutional trust fractures. The system begins to read your presence not as strength but as contamination.

To survive, operations must be reframed as procedural rather than personal. Decisions must appear embedded in governance, not dictated by personality. Compliance actions must look routine, not reactive. Financial flows must align with institutional logic, not individual preference. This shift requires more than cosmetic distance. It demands architecture: boundaries between you and your companies, you and your teams, you and your money.

The less you appear as the protagonist, the more resilient the operation becomes. A shareholder meeting chaired by others. A public filing signed by professional officers. A restructuring announced as strategic review rather than personal retreat. Each signal shifts perception from "this person is acting to protect themselves" to "this organization is functioning as designed." That distinction is decisive: it insulates assets from being read as extensions of your vulnerability.

This is not abdication of control. It is transformation of posture. True leadership is embedded invisibly, in the processes, protocols, and narratives that carry the organization forward without constant reference to you. Influence flows through structure, not through spotlight. The more impersonal the surface, the stronger the continuity beneath it.

Resilience in hostile environments is not achieved by being seen to fight. It is achieved by ensuring that the fight never looks personal. Systems survive because they appear mechanical, logical, and institutional. By refusing to become the story, you allow your structures to keep writing theirs, calm, predictable, and untouchable.

Compartmentalization of reputation, performance, and presence

Reputation is one of the most volatile currencies in high-net-worth ecosystems. It can amplify influence, but it can also accelerate collapse if left uncontained. The error many make is allowing reputation to travel unfiltered across every function, personal, corporate, and private. In such a configuration, a single failure contaminates the whole system. A dispute in one domain becomes a crisis in all others.

Compartmentalization is the discipline that prevents this cascade. It is not about secrecy. It is about stability through isolation. Each sphere, your public image, your corporate activity, and your private interests, must operate on distinct rails, with firewalls that prevent contamination. If one derails, the others must remain intact.

This separation requires deliberate architecture. Public reputation must be curated independently of operational performance. A company can withstand volatility if its leader's image remains untarnished, and a leader can survive scrutiny if the company's processes are insulated from their personal profile. Private interests, family, philanthropy, lifestyle, must be walled off from both. In this way, loss in one arena is contained rather than multiplied.

The tools of compartmentalization are varied. Leadership must be differentiated, roles distributed so that no single individual is visibly central to all functions. Communication styles must vary across domains: personal messaging may project discretion, corporate communication routine competence, and private activity complete opacity. Legal architectures must reinforce these separations: distinct entities, trustees, and governance structures for each layer of life. The stronger the walls, the harder it becomes for adversaries to draw lines of connection that justify expanded attacks.

The principle is simple: you are one mind, but not one surface. To present as a single, undivided identity may feel powerful in calm times, but it becomes fragile in turbulence. By designing compartments, you ensure that pressure applied to one surface does not shatter the whole. Stability is not the absence of crisis; it is the ability to absorb crisis without systemic collapse.

Using advisors to deflect attention while maintaining function

Advisors are not only instruments of expertise, they are instruments of protection. In high-risk environments, their value extends beyond strategy into shielding. Properly positioned, they absorb visibility, standing between you and the scrutiny that would otherwise be directed at your name. In doing so, they allow systems to remain active while keeping your leadership insulated.

During sensitive periods, advisors become the visible surface of the structure. Legal counsel provides statements that neutralize speculation. Board members execute resolutions that appear procedural rather than personal. Operational leads maintain daily continuity, signaling stability to employees, partners, and institutions. Spokespersons project clarity without exposing the individual behind the design. Each advisor, when calibrated correctly, becomes a buffer, maintaining flow while reducing the risk of direct association.

This configuration allows the machine to run without revealing the mechanic. Outsiders see decisions, actions, and continuity, but they cannot easily trace them back to a single command point. The architecture functions as though leadership is distributed, when in reality, intent remains centralized and embedded within the system you designed.

However, delegation of visibility requires discipline. Advisors cannot be placeholders improvised under pressure. They must be trained in the narrative, briefed in the strategy, and trusted to execute without deviation. Their authority must be sufficient to act credibly in their domain, signing, deciding, communicating, yet limited enough to prevent capture or hijack. The balance between empowerment and containment is what keeps advisors effective as shields rather than risks.

Your absence protects only if the structure continues to operate predictably. If advisors improvise, contradict one another, or act outside defined boundaries, absence becomes instability rather than insulation.

Continuity is preserved not by silence alone, but by a disciplined system in which advisors project order, coherence, and reliability.

Advisors, when properly embedded, are not substitutes for leadership. They are extensions of design. They ensure that visibility is deflected while function continues. In this way, leadership is preserved invisibly, while the surface reflects only stability.

Turning exposure into institutional, not personal, challenges

Exposure is inevitable in high-net-worth environments. Structures attract scrutiny, transactions trigger reviews, and visibility invites questions. The critical discipline is not to eliminate exposure, an impossible task, but to redirect it. The target must shift from the individual to the institution, from personality to procedure. When scrutiny lands on systems rather than on self, its force diminishes.

Regulators respond differently to complexity than to narrative. An inquiry framed as "a compliance review" is treated procedurally, with rules and checklists. The same inquiry framed as "a scandal" is treated aggressively, with urgency and reputational stakes. Media behave the same way: once the issue becomes a matter of systems and processes, the story loses drama. Headlines about audits fade faster than headlines about personal misconduct.

The posture must be deliberate. Every attack should be positioned as procedural, not existential. A regulatory inquiry is "an audit." A delay in execution is "a process requirement." An accusation becomes "a point for clarification." This reframing shifts perception from crisis to routine. The narrative becomes one of systems under review, not of individuals under suspicion.

This is not deception. It is framing. The facts remain the same, but their interpretation changes. You are not the event to be judged, you are the environment in which the event occurred. The focus is diverted toward compliance departments, governance processes, or institutional protocols, rather than toward your name.

The benefit is twofold. First, it reduces personal exposure: adversaries find less traction when the story is about systems rather than personalities. Second, it preserves continuity: institutions are expected to adjust, recalibrate, and improve under scrutiny, but individuals are often destroyed by it. By placing the weight on the institutional side, you absorb pressure without collapse.

The principle is simple: when exposure comes, let it strike the surface of structure, not the core of self. Systems can be repaired, audited, or adjusted. Personal credibility, once fractured, rarely recovers.

Building a reputation for resilience, not defense

Defense is magnetic. The moment you adopt a posture of defense, you signal that you are under threat. Each counterpunch, no matter how justified, validates the attack by acknowledging it. Defense invites continuation. It sustains the conflict because it shows that you are engaged in it.

Resilience operates differently. Resilience does not meet attack with attack; it absorbs pressure without visible disruption. Systems continue to function, obligations are met, financial flows remain steady, and governance persists. In such an environment, aggressors lose momentum. Their narrative collapses when the expected reaction never arrives. Their energy drains into silence.

This is why reputation must be built not around defense, but around resilience. To be known for consistency rather than confrontation. For silence rather than noise. For outcomes rather than performance. When you are perceived as unshakable, not because you fight back, but because you do not need to, your adversaries begin to look disproportionate. Each attempt to provoke you highlights their instability rather than yours.

The mechanics of resilience are systemic. Automated compliance prevents allegations of concealment. Continuity protocols ensure that operations persist. Narrative engineering frames pauses as preparation, not panic. The external world sees rhythm, not rupture. Over time, this rhythm becomes your reputation: not combative, not evasive, but enduring.

The paradox is that by not defending your name, you protect it more effectively. You allow outcomes to serve as proof. Salaries paid on time, obligations fulfilled, institutions satisfied, these are reputational anchors stronger than any public statement. You demonstrate that the crisis is not about you because nothing in your system acknowledges it.

Resilience proves irrelevance. Not irrelevance of your structures, but of your name to the narrative of the crisis. When your presence ceases to be the center of the storm, the storm dissipates. In high-risk environments, this is the ultimate reputation: not a fighter of battles, but a figure who renders battles meaningless.

Final note

Crisis does not erase value. It distorts perception, delays execution, and tests continuity, but it does not eliminate the essence of what you've built. The mistake most HNW individuals make is confusing momentary exposure with structural collapse.

The strength of your leadership lies not in how loudly you speak during disruption, but in how little your systems depend on noise to function. Operating silently, without losing coherence, is not retreat, it is discipline. You are not required to convince the world. You are only required to remain in control of your architecture.

Power that survives visibility is strength. Power that survives invisibility is mastery.

Chapter VII. Long-term strategy, from survival to sovereignty

From victim to player, reclaiming the initiative

Ending the reactive mindset

For most individuals under sustained threat, survival begins with reaction. Each move is determined by the last attack. Each choice is defined by the pressure of external agendas. Weeks turn into months, and months into years, with life reduced to a cycle of defense: filing responses, absorbing scrutiny, neutralizing accusations, explaining instead of deciding.

This mindset, while understandable, is corrosive. It keeps you alive but erodes your capacity to live. Anxiety becomes the governing force. Vision narrows to the horizon of the next confrontation. Long-term planning is sacrificed to the tyranny of immediate risk. In such a posture, protection may be achieved, but evolution is impossible. You survive the storm, but you never sail beyond it.

Reclaiming initiative requires breaking this loop. It begins by recognizing that reaction is not strategy, it is surrender of agenda. The longer you remain in purely defensive mode, the more you reinforce the power of those who set the tempo of attack. To move from victim to player, you must reclaim rhythm, rules, and battlefield. You are no longer defined by the fire incoming. You choose the ground on which engagements occur, and you decide which confrontations are even acknowledged.

This transition is not structural at first, it is psychological. The decisive shift occurs when the central question changes. Instead of asking, "how do i protect myself from this?" You begin asking, "what do i want to build now?" Protection remains relevant, but it is no longer the whole story. It becomes a component of sovereignty, not its definition.

Once this mindset is internalized, structures follow. Defensive systems evolve into offensive platforms: networks that expand influence, assets that generate leverage, and architectures that create optionality rather than mere shelter. The horizon extends. You cease being the object of attack and begin shaping the environment in which attacks occur.

Survival is necessary, but it is not sufficient. Sovereignty begins the moment you stop existing in reaction and start designing in freedom.

Understanding when defense becomes stagnation

Defense is essential in moments of crisis. It buys time, absorbs pressure, and prevents collapse. But defense, if left unchecked, carries its own danger. There comes a point when defensive systems stop functioning as strategy and start functioning as paralysis. What once preserved your sovereignty can, over time, erode it.

Structures designed to shield you, legal shells, filtered communication, restricted presence, and operational firewalls, are powerful when deployed in response to immediate risk. Yet if left unreviewed, they harden into cages. Silence becomes absence. Barriers become walls you cannot step beyond. Systems meant to conceal vulnerability begin to broadcast it, signaling to adversaries, institutions, and even allies that you are stuck in survival rather than moving forward.

The discipline is evaluation. Every protective measure must be periodically tested against its purpose. Does this firewall still preserve continuity, or does it now prevent growth? Does this communication filter protect, or has it silenced influence? Does this restrictive presence neutralize exposure, or has it created irrelevance? What once saved you may no longer serve you.

Protection must never become weight. True resilience is defined by mobility, the ability to adapt, reposition, and act when opportunity emerges. If a structure no longer permits movement, it is no longer protection. It is liability disguised as security.

Initiative requires the courage to trim what no longer serves, even if it once saved you. Letting go of obsolete defenses is not recklessness, it is refinement. It is the acknowledgment that strategy is alive, that it evolves, and that survival is only the foundation for sovereignty.

Defense buys time. Initiative decides what to do with it. The moment defense becomes stagnation, it ceases to protect. And the moment you shed what has become weight, you reclaim freedom to move.

Reasserting control through strategic silence and asymmetry

True power is rarely visible. It does not shout, it does not react, it does not reveal its rhythm. It operates in ways that are unreadable to those who attempt to measure it. Reasserting control after crisis does not demand confrontation or spectacle. It requires opacity, discipline, and the deliberate use of asymmetry.

Strategic silence becomes the primary language of this posture. You do not respond on demand. You do not explain to satisfy curiosity. You allow others to expend energy creating narratives, while you preserve energy by withholding confirmation. Each unanswered question denies adversaries the feedback they seek. Each unspoken word becomes a barrier against manipulation. In this way, silence is not absence, it is resistance.

Asymmetry strengthens this posture. You never fight on the same ground as your opponents. Others escalate in public; you adjust quietly in private. Others make accusations; you alter systems. Others seek to provoke visible defense; you respond with invisibility. By refusing to play on their terrain, you exhaust their tactics. Their weapons are designed for open battle. You survive by denying battle altogether.

This asymmetry also shifts time itself. While others act impulsively in the immediacy of headlines and investigations, you act on a different time scale. Your systems are designed to outlast news cycles, to remain functional while storms burn themselves out. To those watching, your rhythm seems detached from the noise, as though you are governed by a logic they cannot decipher. That opacity is power.

Reasserting control, therefore, is not about attack. It is about becoming untraceable. You are not the story. You are not the event. You are the architect of an environment where attempts to target you find no fixed point of reference. In such a system, adversaries cannot land blows because they cannot find you in the space they are fighting.

Control is not reclaimed through confrontation. It is reclaimed through design, silence as language, asymmetry as shield, and unreadability as deterrent. When others cannot predict your moves, cannot measure your responses, and cannot fix your presence, you cease being vulnerable. You become untouchable, not by dominating the field, but by removing yourself from it.

Shifting from fear to game theory: becoming unreadable

Fear narrows the field of action. It produces rituals, predictable choices repeated in the hope of minimizing risk. Under pressure, individuals return to patterns they believe to be safe: contacting the same advisors, relying on the same accounts, issuing the same responses, repeating the same rhythms. What feels like control is, in fact, exposure. Predictability is the map your adversaries use to track, anticipate, and exploit you.

Institutions, litigants, and even personal rivals learn quickly. They study your tempo, your triggers, your tolerances. They know how long it takes you to answer a letter, how you respond to public leaks, which concessions you offer under stress. Once you are readable, you are governable. They dictate the game because they already know your moves.

The transition from victim to player begins with breaking this cycle. You must leave the predictable frame and enter the logic of game theory. Here, strength lies not in repetition but in variability, altering moves, timing, and presence so that no adversary can calculate your response with certainty.

Unreadability is not chaos. It is designed ambiguity. A system that never gives the same answer twice, but always within the bounds of coherence. Change your habits. Alter your visibility. Withdraw from routines. Vary the rhythm of responses. Sometimes act immediately, sometimes delay. Sometimes appear personally, sometimes act only through proxies. Each adjustment complicates the adversary's models, forcing them to expend resources against uncertainty rather than against you.

This does not mean confusion for its own sake. Randomness erodes trust. Strategic unpredictability, by contrast, creates advantage. It signals that you are not reactive but calculated, that you move on terms inaccessible to those attempting to frame you. Adversaries are disarmed not by your explanations, but by their inability to anticipate your rules.

Control is not regained by fighting harder. It is regained by shifting the board. By becoming unreadable, you stop being the piece that is moved and become the one who sets the rhythm of the game.

Rewriting your architecture after exposure

Identifying what cracked, and what held

Every episode of exposure, no matter how destabilizing, contains information. Pressure reveals the architecture of your system in ways that normal conditions cannot. Some structures bend and hold. Others fracture instantly. But survival in itself is not proof of strength. What remains intact must be interrogated as rigorously as what collapsed.

The first task after exposure is diagnostic. This is not about apportioning blame or punishing weakness, it is about establishing truth. Which systems absorbed pressure as designed? Which mechanisms failed silently? Which relationships transformed from assets into liabilities? Which assumptions proved naïve when tested? Without this clarity, the risk of rebuilding fragility into the next cycle is inevitable.

It is critical to distinguish between resistance by design and resistance by accident. Some companies, people, or platforms may have endured, but only because adversaries overlooked them or pressure did not reach them in time. Their survival was incidental, not structural. Others may have fractured under weight, yet revealed clarity, integrity, or discipline in the process of breaking. That difference matters: an accidental survivor cannot be trusted to withstand the next test, while a controlled failure may still contain lessons worth preserving.

Emotional loyalty is the greatest obstacle to accurate diagnosis. Advisors who appeared loyal may have done nothing more than freeze in fear, survival through inaction, not strategy. Platforms that resisted exposure may have held not from strength but from irrelevance. Clinging to them out of gratitude, habit, or sentiment only embeds weakness deeper into your future design.

What must be preserved is only that which resisted by architecture: systems that absorbed pressure without rupture, protocols that activated as intended, structures that maintained continuity without improvisation. These are the foundations of sovereignty. Everything else, whether cracked or apparently intact, must be evaluated without sentiment and discarded if it cannot prove intentional resilience.

Rewriting architecture after exposure is not repair. It is refinement. You are not returning to what was, you are building on what revealed itself as strong, stripping away what survived by accident, and discarding what collapsed under truth. The difference between the next collapse and the next evolution lies in that clarity.

Removing symbolic liabilities and obsolete structures

After exposure, the map of your environment is altered. What once appeared neutral, or even useful, may now carry weight it cannot sustain. Certain elements, people, titles, companies, digital traces, become radioactive. They are not necessarily dangerous because of what they contain, but because of what they signal. Their presence alone invites scrutiny, speculation, or attack.

The principle is not erasure of history. History cannot be erased, and attempts to do so only draw attention. The objective is neutralization, removing magnets for unwanted attention so they no longer attract observers or adversaries. Symbolic liabilities must be retired discreetly, without announcement or justification. A firm that no longer serves purpose should be closed quietly. A dormant foundation should be dissolved without commentary. A name that has become too closely linked to controversy can be replaced through natural administrative transition. Personal or institutional disassociations should occur silently, as though they were logistical adjustments rather than defensive maneuvers.

Equally important is the dismantling of obsolete structures. Many entities, trusts, or vehicles are created for contexts that no longer exist: tax regimes that have shifted, relationships that have dissolved, or strategies that are now irrelevant. Even if such structures still function, their logic may no longer align with the perimeter you now require. Obsolescence becomes vulnerability when adversaries exploit the gap between past design and current reality. Retiring these systems quietly is an act of refinement, not retreat.

This process requires discipline in perception management. The removal must not signal collapse or panic. It must look like natural evolution: restructuring, simplification, modernization. The less explanation, the more credibility. Every word of justification invites speculation. Every silence reinforced by continuity closes curiosity.

The rule is absolute: symbolic liabilities and obsolete structures must not remain simply because they once carried value. Their persistence sends signals that outweigh their utility. You do not need to explain their disappearance. You only need to ensure that they no longer exist as points of vulnerability within your architecture.

Introducing slow logic: designing for stability over speed

Systems created in moments of crisis are rarely elegant. They are fast, improvised, and brittle, assembled to absorb immediate pressure rather than to endure over time. They keep you alive, but they rarely let you live. Their opacity, urgency, and dependence on constant intervention make them fragile the moment calm is restored. What was built for survival cannot be mistaken for permanence.

Post-crisis architecture demands the opposite orientation. It must shift from speed to stability, from improvisation to intention, from fragile protection to antifragile resilience. This requires embracing *slow logic*: systems designed not to react instantly but to endure consistently, regardless of pressure.

Slow logic begins with legal entities built for long-term compliance viability, not short-term concealment. It favors structures that regulators respect and courts recognize, reducing the need for constant defense. Operational processes must be designed so they function autonomously, running on rules, protocols, and distributed responsibility rather than urgent personal intervention. Networks, too, must evolve: trust distributed across actors and jurisdictions rather than concentrated in single points of failure, so that no individual absence or institutional hesitation can immobilize continuity.

The essence of slow logic is intentional design. Each decision asks not "how does this shield me now?" But "will this remain credible and functional in ten years?" Stability does not mean stasis. It means movement at a rhythm that does not depend on constant reaction or personal energy.

You are not preparing for the next attack. You are preparing to live without needing to expect one. Systems built under slow logic make defense implicit rather than constant, allowing you to shift focus from reaction to creation.

Stability is not the absence of motion. It is motion that continues independently of you, deliberate, predictable, and durable. In this lies the true transition from survival to sovereignty: the freedom to exist without perpetual vigilance, because your architecture itself has learned how to endure.

Creating modular systems that can be retired without collapse

The culmination of resilient architecture is modularity. A system is only as strong as its ability to shed parts without jeopardizing the whole. When a single company, property, advisor, brand, or even identity becomes indispensable, fragility is introduced. Pressure applied to that one element can cascade into systemic collapse. True sovereignty demands structures that are divisible, replaceable, and expendable.

Modularity means designing every component with the possibility of retirement in mind. A company must be able to close without dismantling your operating capacity. A property must be disposable without eroding your liquidity base. An advisor must be replaceable without disorienting strategy. Even brands and public identities, those most tied to reputation, must be capable of being paused, rebranded, or abandoned without leaving you exposed.

This design discipline reduces emotional dependence. You cease tying your sense of security or status to the permanence of external forms. Instead, you recognize them as tools, temporary, functional, and ultimately expendable. The system serves you, but it does not define you. In this way, identity becomes layered rather than singular, and authority flows from design rather than attachment.

Importantly, modularity is not detachment for its own sake. It is not about indifference or instability. It is about sovereignty. The ability to retire a component without collapse demonstrates control at the highest level. It signals that your architecture evolves faster than the eyes watching it. By the time adversaries or institutions map your structure, parts of it may already be obsolete, replaced, or reconfigured.

You are not building an empire, static and monumental, vulnerable to siege. You are building a system, fluid, adaptable, and modular. An architecture that can sacrifice parts without losing coherence. An organism that regenerates rather than resists. In this lies the true logic of long-term resilience: survival not through permanence, but through the freedom to evolve continuously, faster than the forces seeking to contain you.

Radical selection, circles, advisors, and environments

Evaluating relationships under pressure

Crisis reveals more than systems. It reveals people. Legal shells, financial structures, and governance models can be tested on paper, but human behavior under stress is tested only in real time. Pressure exposes not only the architecture you designed, but also the character of those around you.

The distinctions become clear. Some individuals support you only when conditions are favorable, when association is effortless and risk is low. Others remain calm when turbulence strikes, absorbing instability without multiplying it. And then there are those who see disruption not as a threat, but as an opportunity, to renegotiate proximity, to extract influence, or to recast themselves as indispensable. These distinctions are not theoretical; they become visible only when the system is under siege.

Every relationship must therefore be evaluated through the lens of pressure. Who added complexity when simplicity was needed? Who remained functional when others panicked? Who, without consent, silently recalibrated your trust, speaking on your behalf, making decisions, or shifting alliances without mandate? These are not minor details. They are diagnostic signals.

Radical selection is the discipline of acting on these signals. It is not moral judgment, nor personal condemnation. It is recalibration. The purpose is not to isolate yourself but to remove illusions, false stability, hollow loyalty, or dependencies that crumble when tested. By stripping away what only appeared solid, you uncover the relationships and environments that can truly sustain sovereignty.

This process is uncomfortable, but essential. Pressure does not just reveal weakness in structures; it reveals weakness in circles. Advisors, partners, even family roles may need to be reassessed. Radical selection ensures that the next iteration of your system is not built on the same invisible fragilities.

You are not isolating yourself. You are redefining the perimeter of trust. And in high-net-worth environments, trust is not sentiment, it is infrastructure.

Dismantling toxic loyalty systems

High-net-worth individuals rarely suffer only from external threats. Often, the most corrosive risks come from within: loyalty systems that have outlived their purpose. Mentors, advisors, family members, or legacy associates may remain embedded in the architecture of decision-making long after their value has expired. Their presence is not sustained by alignment but by inertia, by history, emotion, or symbolism.

These dysfunctional systems generate friction. They slow clarity by introducing voices rooted in sentiment rather than strategy. They delay decisions by demanding consultation out of habit rather than necessity. They create invisible vetoes, unspoken pressures that punish innovation, reconfiguration, or independence. Over time, what began as trust becomes constraint.

Toxic loyalty is sustained not by merit, but by guilt. It resists evaluation because it cloaks itself in the language of obligation: *you owe me, you cannot move without me, you must not change without my blessing*. It punishes evolution by framing it as betrayal. And in doing so, it traps individuals in outdated contracts, written, oral, or entirely unspoken, that no longer serve the architecture of resilience.

Breaking these ties does not require confrontation. Drama feeds toxicity. Moral battles entangle you in narratives that only strengthen dependency. The method is silent precision: a quiet redesign of who enters, who remains, and who no longer belongs. Responsibilities are reassigned, access is reduced, and structures are reconfigured until the toxic element no longer occupies a decisive place.

This process is not about deleting people from your life. It is about dissolving contracts that no longer have legitimacy. A mentor who guided you in one phase may not be fit for the next. An advisor who once served faithfully may now be compromised. A family member who was once stabilizing may now destabilize. Their past contribution does not entitle them to permanent authority.

Sovereignty requires the courage to refine loyalty without apology. True alignment survives evaluation; only toxic loyalty resists it. And in high-stakes environments, removing these outdated anchors is not betrayal, it is survival.

Choosing environments with strategic value (geographic, legal, psychological)

Environment is not background, it is leverage. The jurisdiction where you reside, the legal system that governs your interactions, and the social culture that frames your visibility are not passive conditions. They are active variables that either shield or expose you. After a crisis, these elements must be reconsidered deliberately. What once felt like context must now be treated as design.

Geography defines more than climate or lifestyle. It dictates the proximity of regulators, the aggressiveness of enforcement, and the neutrality of institutions. Some jurisdictions reward discretion; they honor privacy, allow silence to coexist with legitimacy, and respect boundaries between personal wealth and public narrative. Others treat silence as guilt, demanding explanations for every act and punishing those who resist disclosure.

Legal frameworks are equally decisive. A country with robust due process and predictable enforcement timelines absorbs pressure differently than one where discretion collapses under political or diplomatic influence. Courts in some jurisdictions interpret complexity as sophistication; in others, the same structures are portrayed as concealment. Your architecture of sovereignty must be placed where its logic is understood and defensible, not where it is automatically reframed as evasion.

Culture, too, exerts pressure. Some societies normalize success, treating wealth as a signal of achievement. Others attach a moral tax to prosperity, framing it as exploitation or excess. The environment in which you operate determines not only legal exposure, but reputational resonance. A strategy that thrives in one cultural frame may collapse in another.

The principle is selection. You must now choose where you operate not solely on tax efficiency, but on compatibility with your entire architecture of sovereignty. The wrong environment amplifies exposure by framing every act as suspect. The right environment absorbs pressure, contextualizing your presence as natural and unremarkable.

This is not exile. It is territorial alignment. By situating yourself where geography, law, and culture reinforce your structure rather than undermine it, you convert environment from vulnerability into shield. Sovereignty is not only about what you build, it is also about where you place it.

Constructing a low-friction life: less narrative, more control

Friction is the hidden enemy of sovereignty. Every additional moving part in your daily existence, social obligations, institutional expectations, overlapping agendas, creates surface area. Each demand, ritual, or dependency becomes a vector through which pressure can be applied. Complexity, once a symbol of influence, transforms into vulnerability when tested.

The path forward is not accumulation but compression. Your new architecture must run lean: low-narrative, quiet, and designed for continuity without unnecessary exposure. This does not mean isolation from people or institutions. It means stripping away excess, eliminating the stories, activities, and dependencies that generate visibility without producing resilience. What remains is functional, intentional, and resistant to disruption.

A low-friction life replaces performance with discipline. You no longer need to demonstrate complexity through constant travel, public engagements, or visible expansion. Influence is not measured by how many moving parts surround you, but by how little slows you down. Every asset, relationship, and system must be evaluated by a single test: can it be maintained, repaired, or replaced without spectacle? If not, it introduces drag rather than strength.

Friction is also narrative. The more explanations your life requires, the less control you retain over how others interpret it. A lean existence minimizes storylines. Predictable flows, consistent patterns, and quiet systems project coherence without inviting questions. By reducing narrative noise, you preserve energy for the decisions that matter.

Freedom, at this level, is not expansion. Expansion increases surface, multiplies dependencies, and attracts scrutiny. True freedom is silence between necessary actions: the ability to move without resistance, to act without explanation, to pause without suspicion.

A low-friction life is not smaller. It is sharper. It is sovereignty expressed as efficiency: less narrative, more control.

The new code, operating with sovereignty and elegance

Ruling without empire: silent influence over visible power

Power that must be declared is already compromised. The most enduring forms of influence do not rely on visibility, titles, or formal acknowledgment. They work in silence, shaping environments without becoming their center. They operate through systems, not through spectacle.

In this new code of sovereignty, you no longer need to *own* the structure in order to direct it. Legal titles and public association are optional, sometimes even counterproductive. Control is exercised through architecture, not recognition. You do not need credit to set the terms of engagement. You do not need direct access to be the one who decides outcomes. The mechanics of authority have shifted from possession to orchestration.

Sovereignty is no longer tied to empire. The old model of power, visible holdings, monumental institutions, personal branding, creates surface for attack and dependency on recognition. By contrast, sovereignty in its refined form is tied to function. If systems answer to you, even when your name does not appear, you are sovereign. If outcomes bend to your intent, regardless of who receives attribution, you are in command.

This posture transforms leadership into elegance. You do not dominate by volume; you govern by rhythm. The world sees entities moving on their own, yet their choreography traces back to your design. Decisions flow as if inevitable, while your hand remains invisible. Influence is embedded in form, not announced in performance.

The paradox is that the less you are seen, the more untouchable you become. Systems that do not carry your signature cannot be frozen in your name. Institutions that move without your direct command cannot be accused of obedience. Yet, when pressure comes, it is these same systems that continue to serve you, proof that power resides not in ownership but in alignment.

To rule without empire is to embrace silent sovereignty. Your strength is no longer measured by how much you display, but by how little you need to display to achieve total effect. Elegance replaces spectacle. Function replaces title. What remains is influence that cannot be revoked, because it is not visible enough to be contested.

Managing exposure as currency

Exposure is no longer simply a risk to be avoided. In the new code of sovereignty, visibility itself becomes a form of currency, intangible but valuable, volatile but usable. Like capital, it can be managed, allocated, and protected. The question is not whether to be exposed, but how much, where, and under what terms.

The old paradigm operated in absolutes: either full visibility, with names and reputations tied to every act, or full secrecy, with attempts to disappear entirely from the record. Both extremes are fragile. Full exposure creates vulnerability; complete invisibility creates suspicion. The refined approach is surgical. You expose what strengthens you, and you conceal what slows you down.

In this architecture, visibility is always by design, never by accident. What others see is not the whole, but the surface, calibrated, intentional, and modular. A corporate filing, a public appearance, a controlled communication may be real, but they are never complete. They are fragments presented for effect, supported by deeper systems that remain untouched. To outsiders, this surface appears sufficient. To you, it is insulation.

The discipline is to treat exposure as something to be priced. Just as capital is deployed where returns justify the risk, visibility is allowed where it creates advantage, credibility with institutions, stability for markets, reassurance for allies. Where exposure generates only volatility, it is reduced. Where it creates leverage, it is allocated strategically.

And like any currency, exposure must be hedged. When it becomes too volatile, when narratives shift too fast, when scrutiny rises without proportional benefit, you hold less of it. You withdraw surface signals, retreat into opacity, and let stability reset the balance. Then, when conditions normalize, you reallocate visibility at levels you control.

In this model, exposure is not feared. It is managed. It becomes one more instrument in your architecture of sovereignty: scarce when dangerous, abundant when advantageous, always intentional, never accidental.

Practicing high-value discretion: how not to signal status

In an environment defined by oversharing, the rarest and most valuable form of wealth is discretion. Visibility has become cheap; silence has become scarce. But discretion must not be mistaken for secrecy. Secrecy implies concealment born of fear. Discretion is different. It is intention. It is the deliberate act of editing your footprint, choosing carefully what leaves a trace and what does not.

You are not hiding. You are curating. The discipline lies in eliminating signals that trigger unnecessary curiosity, whether from institutions, the media, or society at large. A visible purchase may invite regulatory attention. A poorly timed statement may feed speculation. A public association may attract narratives you did not choose. Discretion avoids these traps by ensuring that nothing visible can be reframed into liability.

Success, luxury, movement, and connection do not need to be broadcast to be real. Their value lies in being lived, not performed. By removing the urge to display, you deny adversaries raw material for interpretation. You also insulate yourself from the moral taxes of societies that punish wealth when it becomes ostentatious. The strongest posture is to be undeniable in substance but invisible in signal.

True power does not leak. It does not brag. It does not ask for validation. It operates without performance, because it does not depend on external confirmation. The structures you control, the systems you design, and the outcomes you generate speak more convincingly than any announcement. The less you signal, the more you are insulated. The silence around your actions becomes part of your strength.

In high-value discretion, what you do not say becomes your most powerful signature. The absence of noise is not absence of influence, it is proof that influence is embedded so deeply in systems that it requires no proclamation.

Living without justification: autonomy through structure

The highest expression of sovereignty is not wealth, visibility, or even control. It is the absence of justification. The ability to move, decide, and exist without explanation. In adversarial environments, justification is a trap. Every defense becomes evidence. Every rationale becomes a timeline. Every attempt to prove legitimacy creates material for others to reinterpret.

Living without justification does not mean living above accountability. It means designing systems so coherent, so self-reinforcing, that they require no external defense. Your structures answer for you. Legal frameworks that align across jurisdictions, financial flows that withstand scrutiny, governance that appears predictable and disciplined, these do not invite questions. They neutralize them before they are asked.

In this posture, you do not explain your choices. You do not defend your movements. You do not rationalize your architecture. Not because you refuse, but because refusal is unnecessary. The system itself demonstrates consistency. The very absence of contradiction becomes your defense. What you built sustains what you do.

This is not arrogance. It is precision. Arrogance resists questions with defiance. Precision prevents questions from arising at all. To live without justification is to accept that your design is your argument, your continuity is your proof, and your silence is your authority.

The outcome is elegance. A life in which explanation is redundant, because structure has already preempted the demand for it. You do not need to claim sovereignty, you demonstrate it in the way your systems persist, unshaken, regardless of scrutiny.

Living without justification is not withdrawal. It is refinement. It is the final stage of architecture: when the life you have built no longer requires narrative to validate it. A life that answers itself. And that is the most elegant outcome of all.

Legacy beyond presence, designing systems that survive you

Structural continuity: designing systems that do not depend on your name

Legacy is often confused with memory, with how you are remembered, with stories told after your departure, with monuments built to preserve your image. But in the architecture of sovereignty, legacy is not about remembrance. It is about function. It is measured not by what people say of you, but by what continues to operate without you.

If the systems you have built collapse the moment you withdraw, they were never sovereign. They were extensions of you, dependent on your presence, your decisions, your signature. True architecture proves itself only in absence. Continuity is the test of sovereignty. If the machinery keeps turning without the hand of its builder, then the system has become more than the individual, it has become independent reality.

The goal is not immortality. It is not the illusion of eternal relevance, which is itself another form of dependence. The goal is continuity without attachment. Businesses must be structured to function through governance, not personality. Vehicles and trusts must operate under rules and triggers, not under constant personal command. Relationships, professional and institutional, must be rooted in logic, benefit, and shared purpose rather than in loyalty to a single figure. Even identities, public or private, must be layered enough to outlast the disappearance of their originator.

This requires a shift in design philosophy. Instead of asking, *what can I control today?* You ask, *what can survive without me tomorrow?* The emphasis moves from direction to architecture, from personal intervention to systemic logic. The most powerful proof of influence is not in how tightly you hold the system, but in how long it runs after you let go.

The architecture must survive the architect. That is the only legacy that cannot be erased.

Reputation as infrastructure, not ornament

Reputation is often misunderstood. Too many treat it as ornament, an accessory to be polished, displayed, or performed. They cultivate charisma, lifestyle, and visibility, mistaking attention for authority. Yet attention is volatile. It fades, shifts, and turns against those who depend on it. True reputation is not a decorative layer, it is infrastructure. It is the invisible foundation on which sovereignty rests.

Your reputation is not a trophy. It is a shield. It deflects suspicion before it hardens into accusation. It is a passport, opening jurisdictions, institutions, and opportunities that would otherwise remain closed. It is a silent negotiator, working in every room where your presence is absent.

Long before you speak, long after you leave, reputation continues to transact on your behalf.

This is why reputation must be managed like infrastructure, not performance. It cannot be left to improvisation, publicity, or the volatility of spectacle. It must be cultivated quietly, consistently, and with depth. Infrastructure functions best when it is invisible but reliable. The same applies here: reputation is not what you show, but what others come to trust through patterns of precision, discretion, and endurance.

The danger lies in building reputation on charisma, lifestyle, or excess visibility. These may create immediate recognition, but they do not endure. They collapse the moment scrutiny rises or circumstances shift. A reputation built on substance, measured action, disciplined silence, resilience under pressure, cannot be undone by gossip or speculation. It holds because it is not dependent on display.

Reputation that survives you is not memory. It is not the stories told when you are gone. It is the operational residue of trust and continuity, the fact that doors still open, calls are still returned, and systems still associate your name with credibility even when no one actively invokes it. It is the afterlife of influence, embedded in institutions and processes, rather than in anecdotes.

To treat reputation as infrastructure is to strip it of vanity and anchor it in utility. It is no longer about how you are seen but about how effectively your name continues to function in your absence. In this way, reputation ceases to be decoration and becomes sovereignty's most resilient instrument.

Strategic withdrawal: preparing for relevance without dependence

You will not always want, or be able, to remain fully active. Circumstances shift, pressures accumulate, and priorities evolve. In such contexts, survival and sovereignty require the ability to withdraw strategically, dissolving presence without triggering collapse. Strategic withdrawal is not retirement. It is not abandonment. It is the deliberate process of detaching visibility from functionality, ensuring that continuity persists even when you recede from the forefront.

The essence of this discipline lies in reducing operational dependencies. If your presence is required for every signature, every negotiation, every adjustment, then your system is not sovereign, it is hostage to your availability. Withdrawal becomes impossible because the architecture collapses the moment you step aside. Strategic withdrawal requires the opposite: structures that move on their own momentum, guided by protocols, mandates, and design rather than constant intervention.

This does not mean surrendering control. It means reshaping control into forms that are less visible and less fragile. Delegation must be precise: empowering advisors, boards, and systems to act within clear parameters, while embedding safeguards that preserve alignment with your intent. Visibility can diminish while leverage remains. Influence need not be exercised through direct command; it can be embedded in processes that continue to answer to you even when your name is absent.

A properly executed withdrawal ensures resilience. If tomorrow you were to step away, whether by choice or necessity, the systems continue, the outcomes remain aligned, and the center holds. Operations remain coherent because they are anchored in design, not in personality.

Partners, regulators, and institutions perceive continuity rather than disruption. Silence does not equal vacuum; absence does not equal collapse.

Presence, in this model, becomes a choice, not an obligation. You can engage when you wish, withdraw when you must, and return without destabilizing the whole. Sovereignty is demonstrated not by constant performance, but by the freedom to move in and out of visibility without threatening the stability of your architecture.

Strategic withdrawal is therefore not an end, but an evolution. It transforms presence from necessity into option. It proves that what you built is not only effective because you lead it, but because it has matured into a system capable of enduring beyond you.

Ending well: how to leave power without creating vacuum

The final act of sovereignty is not accumulation, expansion, or even survival. It is departure. To know when to step back, and, more importantly, how to do so without leaving noise, vacuum, or fragmentation. Authority is tested not only by how it is exercised, but by how it is relinquished. Leaving badly creates chaos. Leaving well proves mastery.

Departure must never be improvised. You do not exit with statements, declarations, or ceremonies. Words invite speculation; they spark narratives that live long after your presence has ended. You exit with systems. Structures designed to continue operating without your constant weight. Processes that require no new explanations. Outcomes that unfold predictably, regardless of whether you are present to oversee them.

Every exit must be planned with the same precision as an entry. Timing is decisive: too early, and withdrawal is read as weakness; too late, and it appears as collapse. Narrative control is essential: silence framed as discipline, absence framed as continuity. Collateral impact must be contained so that no stakeholder, institution, or ally interprets your withdrawal as abandonment.

The principle is clarity. You leave behind no confusion, only coherence. No speculation, only stability. The architecture must remain upright on its own internal logic, not on the illusion of your permanent presence. If continuity collapses when you step aside, then you were never sovereign, only central. True sovereignty means that the system holds even when the sovereign departs.

To end well is not to vanish. It is to embed yourself invisibly into the design so that the structures continue to reflect your intent, even in your absence. You leave power without relinquishing influence. You step back without creating a void. You remove your weight, but the balance remains. That is what it means to leave power. And still remain in control.

Final note

Sovereignty is not something that can be granted by others, nor inherited as a permanent gift; it is something you design deliberately, piece by piece, until the systems you have built are able to function in silence and remain intact even when you are no longer visibly present. This book has not aimed to offer strategies of escape, because escape is always temporary and fragile. Instead, it has provided a framework for continuity: a way of thinking and building that allows you not only to withstand attacks, but also to emerge from them with greater clarity, deeper control, and less noise.

True power does not depend on spectacle, because power that feeds on noise can be silenced at any moment, and presence that constantly demands explanation is a presence already weakened. If your structures collapse when you step aside, they were never truly yours. Defense, though necessary at the beginning, cannot be the final horizon; reaction must evolve into rhythm, and survival into design. Continuity is not enough if it does not transform itself, because what fails to transform eventually stagnates, and stagnation under scrutiny inevitably leads to decline. To govern your reality is to go further than protection, it is to create the environment in which you exist on terms that belong only to you.

Legacy, in this sense, is not memory or the stories told once you are gone. It is the quiet persistence of the systems you leave behind, still opening doors, still producing outcomes, still holding together without the need for your signature. That is the highest proof of sovereignty: not what is said of you, but what continues to function in your absence.

You do not need to be seen in order to command, nor to raise your voice in order to prevail. You do not need permission to build in silence. What began as the instinct to protect yourself must end as the capacity to govern your world. And that is the true meaning of sovereignty.

Chapter VIII. Jurisdictions

The logic of jurisdictions for HNWIs

Every high-net-worth life is shaped by geography, even when the individual believes they have risen above it. The place where you live, the place where you pay taxes, the place where your companies operate, and the place where your assets rest, each of these locations imposes rules, expectations, and vulnerabilities of its own. You may not feel the weight of these differences day to day, but the systems behind them are always at work, quietly recording, classifying, and interpreting your presence.

Jurisdictions do not simply define legal obligations. They create the *context* in which your entire architecture is understood, by banks, by regulators, by courts, by tax authorities, by counterparties, and even by your own advisors. Two people with identical assets can face entirely different outcomes depending on where they reside, where their companies are incorporated, or where their wealth is held. The map is not decorative; it is operational.

Most individuals learn this only when pressure begins. A sudden audit, an unexpected disclosure request, a bank reviewing your file under updated compliance rules, a cross-border inquiry triggered by automatic exchange of information, these moments reveal what your environment really is. Some jurisdictions absorb pressure calmly and predictably because the legal framework is stable and decisions follow established procedure. Others become unpredictable under stress, especially when the law gives broad discretion to institutions or when enforcement fluctuates with political climate, public opinion, or administrative priorities.

For HNWIs, the difference is not academic. A jurisdiction that treats complexity as normal allows you to design structures that protect continuity. A jurisdiction that mistrusts complexity interprets the same structure as evasion or concealment. Neither interpretation is personal; it is simply a reflection of local legal culture and institutional temperament. The same holds for privacy, disclosure obligations, reporting requirements, property rights, succession rules, and tax exposure. Each system carries its own logic, and that logic governs you whether you acknowledge it or not.

The modern regulatory landscape adds another layer. Automatic exchange of financial information under CRS, FATCA-related obligations for us people, beneficial ownership registers, anti-money laundering directives, and enhanced due diligence for politically exposed or high-value clients, all of these frameworks now operate across borders. The world has become more connected, not less. The jurisdiction you choose influences how your data circulates internationally, how banks classify your risk profile, and how easily you can defend the coherence of your structures when questioned.

This is why jurisdiction strategy is not a matter of secrecy or escape. It is a matter of alignment. You must choose environments whose legal, fiscal, and cultural frameworks fit the life you lead and the level of visibility you naturally generate. A mismatch between your reality and your legal environment does not remain invisible. It eventually appears in the way institutions react to your presence: delays, hesitation, excessive documentation requests, or sudden changes in treatment that seem personal but are simply systemic.

A jurisdiction is not only a place. It is an interpretation of you. It shapes how authorities read your movements, how banks classify your accounts, how courts understand your entities, and how your personal story is contextualized when pressure arises. Choosing the right jurisdiction is not about seeking the most advantageous rule in isolation. It is about placing your life where your intentions make sense, where your structures can operate without friction, and where your presence does not create unnecessary suspicion.

For someone with wealth, mobility, and influence, geography is no longer a backdrop. It is part of the architecture itself. The laws of a country become the laws of your life, and the institutions of that country become the first responders when uncertainty arrives. If the environment is incompatible with your profile, you will feel it not in theory, but in practice, delays, questions, audits, frozen decisions, or narratives shaped without your input.

Understanding this logic is the foundation of jurisdiction strategy. It is not about choosing where to hide, but choosing where your life functions coherently, predictably, and lawfully. The right jurisdiction does not promise invulnerability. It promises clarity, in how you are seen, how you are governed, and how you can operate without becoming the story.

Levels of personal exposure: residency, domicile, citizenship

Three legal concepts shape how a high-net-worth individual is interpreted by the international system: *residency, domicile,* and *citizenship.* They appear simple on paper, yet each carries consequences that reach across borders, influencing how you are taxed, how you are reported, and how your presence triggers institutional scrutiny. Understanding the difference between them is not academic. It determines how exposed you are without realizing it.

Residency is usually the most visible layer. It is the jurisdiction where you live long enough to be treated as tax resident under that country's rules. Some countries apply day-count formulas, some use center-of-life criteria, and some examine economic ties or habitual presence. Whatever the method, residency determines where the state expects you to declare global income, where financial institutions send tax reports under CRS, and which legal system becomes your primary point of interpretation. Residency is not emotional. It is operational. Banks, tax authorities, and counterparties rely on it as the default frame through which they classify you.

Domicile is deeper. In many jurisdictions, especially common-law countries, it defines long-term tax exposure, inheritance rules, and the way courts interpret your permanent ties. Domicile is not the place where you currently live, but the place you are legally anchored to in a more enduring way. It may remain unchanged even after decades abroad unless you take deliberate steps to sever it and establish a new one. For HNWIs, domicile influences succession planning, trust structuring, and the way wealth is treated at the moment of transfer. A person can move to another country, pay tax there, and still be bound by the inheritance rules of a previous domicile. Few realize this until the consequences arrive.

Citizenship is the most permanent of the three, and often the most misunderstood. It is not only a matter of passports or travel convenience. Some countries tax citizens globally regardless of residence. Others extend reporting obligations to citizens living abroad, expecting consistency between their declared structures and their cross-border movements. Citizenship can also determine automatic data sharing between jurisdictions and may influence how banks apply due diligence. Even without any wrongdoing, certain nationalities trigger enhanced scrutiny simply because the global regulatory framework treats them as higher-risk for compliance purposes. Nothing about this is personal; it is structural.

These three layers interact constantly. A person may hold citizenship in one country, be domiciled in another, and be tax resident in a third. If these jurisdictions contain conflicting rules, especially regarding tax, reporting, or succession, the individual becomes visible in ways that are difficult to anticipate. A bank in one country may interpret your profile differently from a court in another. A reporting obligation in your country of residence may not align with expectations in your country of citizenship. The result is friction: delays, questions, forms, and reviews that seem arbitrary but are simply the system trying to reconcile conflicting legal anchors.

For HNWIs, misalignment between residency, domicile, and citizenship is one of the most common sources of unnecessary exposure. It creates confusion in due diligence, complexity in succession, and uncertainty in long-term legal positioning. When institutions cannot immediately classify you, they treat you cautiously, not because of who you are, but because of what the system cannot predict.

The solution is not to minimize complexity, but to make complexity coherent. Each layer must be aligned with the life you actually live, the structures you operate, and the visibility you naturally generate.

Residency must be defensible. Domicile must be intentionally managed. Citizenship decisions, whether maintaining, renouncing, or adding, must be evaluated not as lifestyle choices, but as legal frameworks that determine how the world interprets your presence.

These are not abstract distinctions. They are the coordinates of your legal identity. When they conflict, exposure grows. When they align, the system reads your life clearly and predictably, and predictability is one of the strongest forms of protection you can build.

The three layers of a multi-jurisdictional life (designed legally)

A global life only becomes stable when it has depth. A single residence, a single financial center, or a single strategic environment is never enough for someone whose movements, visibility, and responsibilities extend across borders. The more influence or wealth you carry, the more each country interacts with you according to its own rules, and the greater the need to distribute your presence across several layers rather than one exposed point. The idea is not to fragment your life, but to structure it in a way that matches how the international system actually works today: geographically distributed, data-driven, and highly sensitive to inconsistencies.

The first layer is your *functional base*. It is the place where you physically live most of the year, where your personal rhythm unfolds, and where institutions see your daily presence. This layer anchors your tax residency in a way that must be defensible. It shapes how banks classify you under CRS, how authorities understand your center of life, and how your personal footprint is interpreted. A functional base must not be chosen only for lifestyle. It must be a place where your presence makes legal and economic sense. If your daily life, spending habits, and travel patterns contradict the residency you declare, the system will detect the mismatch long before anyone asks questions directly. A functional base must withstand scrutiny without requiring explanations.

The second layer is your *financial base*. This is the jurisdiction where you hold your core banking relationships, where your companies are governed, and where your assets are protected. It does not need to be the place where you live, but it must be a jurisdiction that recognizes and accepts international complexity as normal. A strong financial base provides stable institutions, predictable courts, and banking systems that understand cross-border clients. It also offers clarity in reporting, which is essential in a world where automatic information exchange is the default. A financial base is not chosen for secrecy but for continuity. When personal life becomes unstable, a divorce, a lawsuit, a political event, or a sudden relocation, the financial base remains steady. It keeps liquidity accessible, protects assets from misinterpretation, and ensures that governance structures remain operational even when other parts of your life move.

The third layer is your *strategic base*. This is the part of your architecture that does not need to be visible to your daily environment. It includes long-term holding structures, succession planning frameworks, philanthropic entities, and any asset or structure designed to outlive immediate circumstances. A strategic base is not where you spend time or where you conduct daily banking. It is where you place the elements that must remain stable regardless of political changes, public exposure, or personal events. It is the layer that creates distance between your personal life and your long-term architecture. The goal is not opacity but resilience: placing certain structures in jurisdictions that remain predictable, regardless of shifts in the places where you live, invest, or operate.

These three layers must function together. A global life becomes fragile when the layers contradict each other, for example, when a functional base suggests one lifestyle, while the financial base reflects different priorities, or when a strategic base contains structures that lack substance or clear logic from the perspective of the jurisdictions involved. When layers align, institutions see coherence: the residency makes sense, the governance is defensible, the financial flows follow an understandable logic, and the long-term architecture fits the person who built it. When the layers misalign, the system interprets the inconsistencies as potential risk, even without any wrongdoing.

Designing a multi-jurisdictional life legally means accepting that each layer must stand on its own while still forming part of a single, coherent narrative. The functional base must reflect your physical presence and personal reality. The financial base must reflect your economic activity and governance. The strategic base must reflect your long-term intentions. When these layers support each other, your global architecture becomes stable, predictable, and capable of withstanding pressure without sudden disruptions.

The purpose of this model is simple: to ensure that your life is not dependent on a single jurisdiction that may one day become incompatible with your reality. A well-designed global structure does not promise invisibility. It promises continuity. And continuity, in a world defined by cross-border reporting and institutional interpretation, is the most valuable form of protection a high-net-worth individual can build.

How to structure a multi-jurisdictional life the legal way

A multi-jurisdictional life is only sustainable when every element can be defended in the jurisdiction that reviews it. This is the foundation of a lawful global architecture. It is not built on secrecy, speed, or improvisation, but on coherence: your movements match your declarations, your structures match your economic reality, and your documentation matches your intentions. The system does not require perfection. It requires a logic that holds under pressure.

The first principle is understanding that any change of residence is not just a lifestyle decision but a legal event. When you relocate, the system examines more than your physical presence. It looks at your spending patterns, your travel rhythm, your center of economic and personal interests, and the consistency of your documentation. The goal is not to avoid scrutiny but to ensure that, if questioned, everything aligns without requiring explanations that seem reactive. A change of residence must be documented with clarity, supported by evidence, and consistent with your real life. When it is, no jurisdiction sees it as suspicious.

When you open entities in different countries, the logic must be equally clear. A company incorporated abroad is not a risk when it has genuine purpose, real governance, and activity that reflects the jurisdiction chosen. Problems arise when the structure exists only on paper or when the location of the entity contradicts your economic footprint. Authorities have become increasingly skilled at detecting entities that lack substance. If an entity contributes to your economic life, its purpose must be defensible, and its presence must make sense to anyone reviewing it. A legitimate international structure is never defined by where taxes are lowest, but by where the value is created and where management and decision-making actually occur.

Diversifying jurisdictions is also a legal exercise. You cannot simply accumulate residencies, companies, and banking relationships in places that seem advantageous on paper. Each additional jurisdiction creates another point of interpretation. When those points align, your life appears well-structured. When they contradict each other, the system interprets complexity as opacity even if the underlying choices are lawful. A diversified global life must therefore be built slowly, intentionally, and with full awareness of how each jurisdiction reads the others.

Compliance is not the enemy of discretion. In fact, it is the foundation of it. The more predictable your filings, the less attention you attract. When your reporting is accurate and consistent, institutions process your information without hesitation. Compliance is not about surrendering privacy. It is about maintaining control of your narrative. A high-net-worth individual who understands their obligations and fulfills them on time is treated with far more trust than one who appears disorganized, reactive, or inconsistent.

Documentation is the final layer of legal design. A coherent global life can be read without confusion because every element is supported by evidence: residence, income, asset flows, governance, and decision-making. You do not need to explain your life; your documents do that for you. When your paperwork reflects the same structure that your jurisdictions expect to see, you eliminate the risk of misunderstanding. You also reduce the likelihood of institutional hesitation, because clarity prevents escalation.

Structuring a multi-jurisdictional life legally does not require complexity. It requires intentionality. You choose where you live because it fits your personal and professional reality. You choose where you operate companies because it matches the location of real value creation. You choose where you hold assets because the jurisdiction offers stability, predictability, and a consistent legal framework. You choose your strategic base not for secrecy, but for continuity.

A global life constructed this way does not trigger red flags. It does not rely on last-minute explanations. It does not depend on fragile interpretations or ambiguous positions. It stands on a clear, defensible foundation. And when pressure arrives, as it inevitably does, the system understands you, processes you, and allows you to continue.

This is what it means to build a lawful international architecture: coherent presence, defensible intention, and structural clarity that holds everywhere you exist.

Analysis framework for jurisdictions (no opinions, only criteria)

A high-net-worth individual cannot choose jurisdictions based on reputation, fashion, or generic rankings. What matters is not how a country is perceived publicly, but how it behaves legally, institutionally, and operationally when your life intersects with its system. A jurisdiction is neither "good" nor "bad" in abstract terms. It is either compatible with your profile or incompatible with it. That compatibility can be assessed only through criteria, not opinions.

The following analytical framework allows you to evaluate any jurisdiction in a way that is neutral, professional, and legally grounded. It does not rely on stereotypes or assumptions. It focuses on measurable characteristics: stability, predictability, disclosure exposure, and institutional temperament. The goal is not to label jurisdictions, but to understand how each one interprets you and how it will respond under pressure.

The first dimension is the legal infrastructure. This includes the quality of the judicial system, the predictability of rulings, the independence of courts, the clarity of procedural standards, and the degree to which enforcement follows written law rather than political priorities. Some countries maintain consistent, structured legal processes even during periods of stress. Others allow discretion or administrative interpretation to dominate decision-making. For HNWIs, predictability is not a luxury; it is a risk-management tool. When rules are stable, you can plan. When rules shift with the political environment, planning becomes speculation.

The second dimension is the fiscal logic. Every jurisdiction has a tax philosophy that reveals how it views wealth, mobility, and international activity. This includes marginal tax rates, treatment of foreign income, exit taxes, withholding rules, participation exemptions, and special regimes for new residents or investors. More important than the rate itself is the stability of the system: whether rules change abruptly, whether reforms are retroactive, and whether administrations apply the law uniformly. A jurisdiction does not need to be low-tax to be favorable; it needs to be coherent, rational, and respectful of long-term commitments.

The third dimension is the banking climate. Financial institutions act as the first interface between your global life and the jurisdictional system. Their comfort level with international clients, their internal compliance culture, and their interpretation of risk determine whether your accounts remain stable or constantly reviewed. You must assess how banks treat cross-border income, corporate structures, trusts, politically exposed persons, and high-value accounts. Stability is determined not only by local banking laws but by the institutional personality of the financial sector: whether it acts conservatively, aggressively, or administratively. A calm banking environment reduces friction in every aspect of your affairs.

The fourth dimension is privacy and data exposure. Modern risk does not come only from courts or agencies, much of it arises from public registries, open data policies, beneficial ownership disclosure requirements, press culture, and the degree to which third parties can access or republish information. Some jurisdictions publish extensive records, including company shareholders, property ownership, or litigation data. Others restrict access, limiting exposure. Neither model is inherently better; what matters is how the data environment interacts with your profile. A person with high public visibility requires a more discreet registry environment. A person with large corporate holdings requires clarity in what is disclosed and what remains private. Exposure is not only about visibility; it is about cumulative traceability.

The fifth dimension is the reputation of the jurisdiction itself. International institutions, banks, and regulators classify countries implicitly through their perceived risk level. This affects how they interpret the people who come from, reside in, or operate through those countries. A neutral jurisdiction will not add friction to your profile. A jurisdiction perceived as unstable, opaque, or politically unpredictable may cause institutions to review you more closely, not because of who you are, but because of the narrative associated with that environment. This is not about geopolitics; it is about operational consequences. Country risk affects personal risk, even when your activities are entirely lawful.

These five dimensions, legal infrastructure, fiscal logic, banking climate, privacy environment, and jurisdictional reputation, form a complete analytical system. When assessed together, they reveal how a jurisdiction will fit into your architecture and how it will behave when you need predictability most. The purpose of this framework is not to help you choose "the best" country, but to help you choose the jurisdiction that aligns with your real life, your operating needs, and your long-term resilience.

A jurisdiction is a partner in your stability. When chosen intentionally, it becomes part of your defensive architecture. When chosen casually, it becomes a source of exposure that follows you everywhere.

Red flags, yellow flags, green flags

Institutions do not judge you based on personality, intentions, or past behavior. They judge you based on patterns, visible, measurable signals that either confirm coherence or reveal contradiction. These signals determine whether a bank processes your file without hesitation, whether a tax authority views your residency as credible, or whether a regulator decides that your structures require enhanced review. The interpretation is never personal. It is systemic. For high-net-worth individuals, these signals form the difference between a smooth cross-border life and a life constantly interrupted by questions, delays, or suspicion.

Red flags appear when your profile disrupts the institutional logic of a jurisdiction. They emerge in situations where your declared residency conflicts with your economic footprint, where your spending patterns contradict your recorded presence, where assets sit in jurisdictions that hold no relationship to your actual activity, or where companies exist without substance, governance, or geographic relevance. A structure may be perfectly legal and still trigger institutional doubt if it resembles patterns typically associated with evasion, concealment, or unexplained mobility. Red flags do not imply wrongdoing; they indicate ambiguity. And ambiguity is the one thing most systems are designed to investigate.

Yellow flags occupy the middle ground between concern and comfort. They signal complexity that is legitimate but requires clarification. Many wealthy individuals naturally generate yellow-flag patterns: multiple homes, multiple residencies over short periods, international investments, companies registered in several countries, assets spread across legal systems, or lifestyles that blend private travel with cross-border business activity. None of these elements are inherently risky, but each prompts institutions to look for consistency. A yellow flag is essentially an unspoken request for documentation: an invitation to present a coherent explanation for why your life is structured the way it is.

Green flags emerge when your personal and economic footprint aligns cleanly with the narrative presented in your documents. These signals show that your residency matches your presence, that your companies operate where value is created, that your financial flows reflect your stated activity, and that your reporting is consistent across jurisdictions. Institutions reward this clarity with trust. Files move quickly, accounts remain stable, and authorities limit their inquiries because they see no contradiction between what you declare and what your data reveals. Coherence is the quiet foundation of every global life that functions without friction.

These signals, red, yellow, and green, do not operate in isolation. They accumulate and interact. A single red flag may not matter, but several of them create a profile that institutions must analyze more carefully. A collection of yellow flags can either phase out with proper documentation or escalate if the narrative remains unclear. Green flags, when consistent, act as an invisible shield, reducing the likelihood of scrutiny even in jurisdictions known for strict compliance. Institutions are not looking for perfection; they are looking for alignment.

The purpose of understanding these signals is not to shape your life around external expectations but to avoid accidental exposure created by inconsistencies. Most high-net-worth individuals who face institutional problems are not facing them because they broke the law. They face them because their life, assets, and movements tell different stories in different jurisdictions. When your presence in one country contradicts your filings in another, or when your structures operate without a clear connection to your declared center of life, the system reacts. This reaction is procedural, not emotional.

A coherent architecture solves the problem before it arises. When your residency, spending, corporate activity, asset location, and reporting form a unified story, red flags disappear on their own. Yellow flags resolve with a single explanation. Green flags accumulate naturally because your life makes sense in institutional terms. The system reads your presence the way you intend it to be read.

This is the core principle: complexity is not a risk when it is coherent. Incoherence is the true source of exposure. Understanding how jurisdictions read you allows you to design a life that withstands scrutiny without requiring justification, performance, or excessive visibility. The international system does not punish wealth or mobility. It punishes contradiction. When the signals you project align with the structures you have built, you move through borders calmly, predictably, and without friction, because the system sees what you want it to see: a life that makes sense.

Banking across borders: continuity, not secrecy

For a high-net-worth individual, banking is never just a practical necessity. It is an extension of your legal identity, your jurisdictional footprint, and your perceived risk level. Banks do not evaluate you only as a client; they evaluate you as a regulatory event. Every account you open, every transfer you initiate, and every jurisdiction in which you operate becomes part of a broader interpretation of who you are and how predictable your activities appear. This makes cross-border banking one of the most sensitive components of a global life, not because secrecy is the objective, but because continuity must be protected.

Modern banking no longer revolves around privacy. It revolves around compliance, reporting, and risk classification. Banks today are not simply custodians of wealth; they are gatekeepers for the global financial system, required to interpret your movements through increasingly strict frameworks. This creates a paradox: the more international your life becomes, the more you rely on institutions that may not fully understand it. If your banking footprint appears inconsistent with your residency, your economic activity, or your documentation, the institution does not see flexibility; it sees risk.

Continuity depends on coherence. A bank is far less concerned with how many jurisdictions you interact with than with whether those interactions make sense. When your residence, income sources, and corporate activity form a clear narrative, international banking becomes smooth. If, however, your accounts are scattered across jurisdictions without a logical pattern, or if your financial flows travel through countries unrelated to your declared life, the bank begins to interpret your presence through a stricter lens. This is not suspicion, it is procedure.

The most common threat is not account closure but interruption. A bank may freeze an account while it seeks clarification. It may delay a large transfer without explanation. It may request several rounds of documentation because the compliance team cannot reconcile your file. These moments feel personal, but they are not. They reflect the institution's obligation to justify your profile under its internal risk models and under the rules of the jurisdictions to which it reports. If your profile cannot be justified quickly, the institution protects itself first.

A cross-border banking perimeter must therefore be designed for predictability, not opacity. You need accounts in jurisdictions that understand your economic footprint, institutions that can process your activity without constant escalation, and governance that ensures your financial behavior matches the narrative presented in your filings. This does not mean limiting your banking relationships to one country. It means ensuring that each banking presence has a clear purpose, one that can be defended through documentation at any time.

The strongest banking perimeters share the same foundation: each account is tied to a meaningful part of your life. A residency account receives income and supports daily living. A business account operates in the jurisdiction where the company actually functions. An investment account exists where regulation is stable and asset protection is reliable. When each account is connected to a real economic or operational anchor, institutions interpret your profile as legitimate, even when it spans multiple countries. Coherence removes the appearance of risk long before risk departments begin asking questions.

Continuity also relies on understanding how banks classify clients. Some jurisdictions enforce aggressive compliance requirements that treat HNWIs as high-yield risk profiles, even when everything is lawful. Other jurisdictions maintain stable, predictable banking cultures that consider multi-jurisdictional clients normal. Choosing a banking home is not about secrecy or tax arbitrage. It is about placing your financial life inside systems that can process your mobility without panic.

A resilient banking structure does not break when a single institution changes policy, freezes an account, or requests additional documentation. It survives because it is built with redundancy and clarity. You are not dependent on one jurisdiction, one financial institution, or one compliance officer's interpretation. Your accounts, movements, and reporting form a narrative strong enough to withstand scrutiny anywhere.

In a globalized world, wealth is not protected by silence or evasion. It is protected by structure. When your banking footprint is intentional, coherent, and defensible, institutions do not react to your wealth with suspicion. They respond with stability. That stability is the real luxury: the ability to operate across borders without fear of interruption, misinterpretation, or institutional hesitation.

Continuity is the objective. Secrecy is not. Secrecy collapses under pressure. Continuity survives it.

Travel, mobility and the non-physical footprint

In a global life, movement is rarely just movement. Every border you cross, every ticket you book, every residence you enter or leave, and every pattern you repeat becomes part of a quiet dataset that institutions use to interpret your presence. For most people, travel is private. For a high-net-worth individual, travel is an institutional event. It creates signals that influence tax classification, banking decisions, immigration assumptions, due diligence reviews, and even reputation assessments. Mobility is freedom, but it also produces a trail, and that trail must be understood before it becomes a source of exposure.

The first layer of risk comes from predictability. When your movements follow a consistent rhythm, institutions use that rhythm to infer residency, center of life, or economic presence, even if you have never formally declared any of these. Days spent in a country, the frequency of your returns, hotel bookings, cards used abroad, airline loyalty programs, and even the metadata in your travel apps all contribute to a picture of where you appear to live. If this picture contradicts your declared residency, the discrepancy is treated as a potential irregularity. The system is not accusing you, it is attempting to reconcile what you say with what your movements suggest.

The second layer is inconsistency. When your travel patterns appear fragmented, erratic, or disconnected from the locations where you claim to operate, banks and authorities may interpret your mobility as an attempt to avoid anchoring. Even perfectly legitimate movement can appear suspicious if it has no visible structure. A professional who spends long periods in countries unrelated to their declared economic activity, or who alternates between multiple jurisdictions without maintaining a stable narrative of why those movements matter, risks being categorized as an undefined profile. Undefined profiles trigger additional scrutiny, not because of wrongdoing, but because institutions cannot predict them.

The non-physical footprint is often more revealing than physical travel. A device that connects regularly from multiple jurisdictions, an ip address that shifts across regions, a pattern of online activity that indicates presence in countries where you rarely appear physically, or metadata from emails sent while in transit can all become indicators of your global rhythm. Even when you try to keep a low profile, the tools you use to move, phones, laptops, wearables, apps, cloud systems, continue broadcasting fragments of your journey. These fragments travel farther than you do, often entering systems that you will never see, handled by institutions you will never meet.

Managing mobility does not mean restricting travel. It means ensuring that the pattern your travel creates is compatible with the jurisdictions that classify you. If you maintain tax residency in one country but spend most of your time elsewhere, the narrative must be clear. If you operate businesses across borders, your travel must reflect genuine engagement with those activities. If you relocate or shift your center of life, the movement must be documented in a way that prevents institutions from interpreting it as concealment. Mobility becomes dangerous only when it contradicts your declared identity.

The goal is not to erase your footprint, but to align it. A coherent mobility pattern demonstrates legitimacy. It shows that your presence in each jurisdiction corresponds to personal life, business operations, or legal obligations. When your footprint matches your documentation, institutions treat your travel as ordinary, even when it spans several continents. When your footprint contradicts your declared anchors, institutions begin asking questions you may not be prepared to answer.

The art lies in avoiding predictability without activating suspicion. Predictability can lock you into an implied residency. Excessive unpredictability can resemble attempts to evade it. The solution is intentional movement: travel with purpose, align your patterns with your declared jurisdictions, and ensure that your non-physical footprint supports rather than contradicts the narrative of your life.

A global life is not defined by the number of places you visit. It is defined by the coherence with which you move between them. When your mobility is structured, when your presence across borders makes sense, and when your digital trail mirrors your reality, travel becomes an asset rather than a liability. You retain the freedom to move without allowing your movements to interpret you incorrectly. That balance is what protects you.

Life events that trigger jurisdictional risk

Certain life events carry an administrative and legal gravity that goes far beyond the immediate personal or financial impact. For most people, these transitions unfold quietly. For a high-net-worth individual, they recalibrate how multiple jurisdictions interpret your presence, your assets, your intentions, and your long-term anchors. A divorce, a succession, a change of residence, the creation or dissolution of a company, or the acquisition of a visible asset all have consequences that travel farther than expected. They signal shifts in structure, geography, power, and economic logic, and institutions react to these signals even before you realize what they imply.

The greatest risk in these moments is not the event itself, but the institutional interpretation that follows. When your circumstances change, the system expects your legal and financial footprint to adapt. If the adaptation is unclear or incomplete, ambiguity emerges, and ambiguity is always treated as potential exposure. A divorce, for example, alters not only personal life but also residency patterns, asset distribution, and financial flows. A succession can trigger cross-border reporting, reassessment of domicile, and questions about the origin and destination of wealth. A relocation can reshape the center-of-life analysis that determines where you are truly resident. These events do not happen in isolation; they create ripples across jurisdictions that must be managed intentionally.

Unplanned relocations carry their own complexity. Moving suddenly, because of personal reasons, professional shifts, or external pressure, often leaves behind a trail of inconsistent filings, unresolved obligations, and unexplained changes in economic behavior. Institutions see these inconsistencies long before you have time to correct them. A country may consider you to have never left. Another may assume you have arrived permanently. Banks may detect shifts in transaction patterns that contradict your declared residency. When movement is not documented properly, multiple jurisdictions may claim authority over the same aspects of your life, creating friction that becomes difficult to unwind.

Corporate events behave the same way. Opening or closing a company, transferring shares, changing directors, or altering management structures are all actions that create institutional signals. Even if the business is small or inactive, the jurisdiction where it is registered may expect tax filings, governance records, and compliance updates. When these expectations are not synchronized with your personal life or with other countries' requirements, institutions perceive inconsistencies that require clarification. The problem is rarely the company itself, it is the narrative around it.

Acquiring visible assets adds another layer. Real estate, yachts, aircraft, and high-value art pieces each trigger reporting obligations, metadata generation, registration processes, and interactions with compliance systems across borders. A property purchase reveals presence. A yacht reveals crew, logistics, and movement. A piece of art reveals provenance and financial flows. If these assets do not align with your residency, your economic activity, or your declared footprint, institutions interpret the disconnect as a signal worth examining.

The key is preparation. Before any major life event unfolds, the jurisdictional consequences must be understood and integrated into your overall architecture. A divorce requires a map of how both jurisdictions will read the separation: residency decisions, asset division, future reporting. A succession requires planning that respects the inheritance laws of each country involved, not only your own preferences. A change of residence must be accompanied by clear documentation, updated economic ties, and careful synchronization with your former jurisdiction's exit rules. Even apparently simple events, such as closing an old company or purchasing a home, must be integrated into a coherent narrative that institutions can interpret without suspicion.

When handled proactively, these transitions strengthen your structure. They allow you to redefine your legal anchors intentionally, update your economic footprint, and reinforce the coherence of your global life. When handled reactively, they create a trail of inconsistencies that follow you for years, resurfacing during audits, immigration reviews, banking updates, or cross-border inquiries.

The purpose of managing life events from a jurisdictional perspective is not to complicate private matters. It is to ensure that personal transitions do not become institutional disruptions. When each event is understood, documented, and aligned with the logic of your overall architecture, the system reads your life with clarity. And in a world where ambiguity generates risk, clarity is one of the most powerful forms of protection you can create.

How to build stability across borders

A global life only becomes stable when it stops looking like a puzzle to the institutions that observe it. Stability is never the result of having many structures, many residencies or many bank accounts. It comes from coherence: the degree to which your physical presence, your financial footprint, your legal obligations and the narrative that holds everything together can be understood without contradiction.

Most high-net-worth individuals experience instability not because they have violated a rule, but because their lives appear inconsistent from the outside. A person can be fully compliant and still face questions, delays or institutional hesitation if the elements of their life do not align in a way that the system can interpret clearly. The goal is not to simplify a global life, but to ensure that its logic is visible and defensible.

The first step is establishing a primary jurisdiction, even if you move frequently. Mobility is perfectly lawful, but institutions need a central reference point to understand who you are. That anchor is not merely the place where you spend time; it is where the story of your life makes sense: your spending patterns, your personal ties, your long-term plans and your governance decisions. A person without a clear anchor does not look free; they look undefined, and undefined profiles attract attention.

Stability also requires that your presence aligns with your obligations. If you declare residency in a jurisdiction but barely appear there, or if you spend most of your time in a country with strict day-count rules while insisting you are resident elsewhere, the system will attempt to reconcile what it sees with what you claim. That reconciliation process often leads to questions, because inconsistency suggests that something is missing. The institutions are not judging you; they are trying to understand you.

Your financial footprint must follow the same logic. Banking activity, income flows, spending patterns and the jurisdictions where assets are held all form part of the institutional picture. A person who is resident in one country but banks entirely in another, or whose lifestyle contradicts their declared fiscal position, will be examined more closely simply because the narrative is unclear. The more your financial signals match the legal story you have built, the more predictable your interactions with banks and regulators become.

Substance plays an even deeper role. A company without real activity, governance or purpose may be perfectly legal, but it rarely survives scrutiny because it looks fragile. A structure supported by genuine decision-making, real oversight and a clear economic or strategic role needs no performance to prove itself. Institutions trust what they can see; hollow structures only survive until someone asks what they actually do.

Documenting your logic is equally important. You do not need a manifesto or an autobiography, but you must be able to explain your life in a way that another professional can follow. A short, clear internal note describing why you live where you live, why your structures exist where they exist, how your income is generated and how your day-to-day movements match your obligations can prevent countless misunderstandings. In cross-border environments, being able to articulate your own structure often matters as much as the structure itself.

Stability also requires anticipation. Regulations change, sometimes abruptly, and frameworks like CRS, FATCA, beneficial ownership rules and AML directives evolve every year. A structure that was coherent five years ago may now be outdated. Reviewing your cross-border architecture regularly, at least once a year, is not a luxury. It is part of maintaining continuity in a world where compliance systems operate faster than individuals expect.

Ultimately, building stability across borders has nothing to do with secrecy. It has everything to do with fitting the logic of the system. The international environment does not attack complexity when complexity is coherent. It does not punish mobility when mobility is documented. What destabilizes individuals is contradiction: presence that does not match obligations, structures that do not match activity, and narratives that do not match reality.

A stable global life is one where the elements speak the same language. Your residency matches your rhythm. Your financial signals match your narrative. Your structures match your intentions. And your documentation matches everything. When that happens, institutions handle you quickly, quietly and without suspicion. The absence of friction becomes your real advantage.

Stability is not created by defending yourself. It is created by designing your life so clearly that there is nothing to defend. And in a world governed by information rather than borders, that clarity is the closest form of sovereignty you can build.

Life events that trigger jurisdictional risk

Even the most carefully designed global architecture is vulnerable to certain life events, moments that seem personal or administrative, but that activate legal and institutional mechanisms across borders. These events are predictable, yet many individuals treat them as incidental until they create friction with banks, tax authorities, or regulators. In a multi-jurisdictional life, every major change sends a signal. If the signal is not anticipated and managed, it becomes exposure.

One of the most disruptive events is divorce. For HNWIs, divorce is not merely the dissolution of a relationship; it is a legal process with jurisdictional consequences. Different countries claim authority over marriage, assets, maintenance, and property division based on residence, domicile, nationality, or even the place where the couple last lived together. A divorce that begins in one jurisdiction can rapidly spill into others, sometimes unpredictably, triggering disclosure obligations, asset freezes, or demands for documentation. Even when both parties act in good faith, the legal systems involved may interpret the situation differently. If your assets, companies, or trusts are spread across several countries, each jurisdiction may attempt to assert competence, and each institution involved will look for signs of inconsistency between your declared positions. Managing divorce discreetly requires preparation: choosing the forum before someone else chooses it for you, aligning documentation across jurisdictions, and ensuring that any movement of assets is defensible and properly recorded.

Succession carries equal complexity. Whether anticipated or sudden, a death triggers a cascade of legal consequences governed by domicile, not residency. Many individuals believe their estate will follow the rules of the country where they live, only to discover that the law of their original domicile still governs inheritance, wealth transfers, and even the validity of certain structures. Banks freeze accounts, trustees pause distributions, and notaries or courts demand information from all relevant jurisdictions. If heirs are located in different countries, each system may claim authority. Without preparation, succession becomes a cross-border negotiation in which the institutions, not the family, set the pace. Preparing for succession is not only an estate-planning exercise; it is a jurisdictional one that determines whether your architecture can survive transition without disruption or institutional suspicion.

Relocation is another event that authorities monitor closely. A change of residence, even when fully legal, can trigger reviews from the country you are leaving, the country you are entering, and the financial institutions that bridge the two. Day-count rules, exit taxes, center-of-life criteria, and automatic exchange of information mean that a move is visible long before you formally register it. If your spending patterns, travel history, or asset flows contradict the residency you declare, institutions will notice the inconsistency. A move made without documentation or coherence can create a multi-year trail of questions, audits, or delayed approvals. Relocation must be structured, not improvised. Authorities want to see logic, why you moved, how your economic footprint matches your new residence, and why the timing is consistent with your broader architecture.

The creation or dissolution of companies is equally significant. When you open a new entity in one jurisdiction while residing in another, banks and regulators expect to see substance: clear reasons for the company's existence, proper governance, and activity that matches your professional reality. If you dissolve a company shortly after a life event, such as a divorce, an inheritance, or a sudden change of residence, institutions may interpret the timing as an attempt to shield assets. Even when the decision is legitimate, the perception can create unnecessary questions. Documents must therefore explain the business logic of each step. A company that closes because its purpose is complete is unproblematic; a company that disappears without narrative coherence invites scrutiny.

Unplanned moves also create risk. Events such as political instability, health emergencies, or family disputes may force you to change countries abruptly. Authorities understand that life is unpredictable, but institutions still expect alignment between your physical presence, your declared residence, and your financial footprint. When an unplanned move creates discrepancy, the goal is not to hide it but to document it. A clear explanation, supported by travel records, contracts, or medical evidence, prevents institutions from assuming deception or inconsistency.

Visible asset acquisitions, especially yachts, aircraft, significant properties, or high-value art, can inadvertently connect your life to a jurisdiction you never intended to be associated with. A property purchased in a country where you are not resident may trigger assumptions about lifestyle or economic presence. A yacht registered in one jurisdiction but used primarily in another may raise questions about vat, importation, or beneficial ownership. Art purchased across borders can trigger customs declarations and tax inquiries. None of these problems arise from the asset itself; they arise from the absence of narrative. Institutions want to understand why the asset exists, how it is used, and how it fits into your broader footprint.

The common element across all these life events is visibility. Each event leaves a trail, legal, financial, or administrative. That trail becomes part of your profile in the eyes of institutions. When the story is coherent, nothing happens. When the story contradicts itself, the system reacts. The solution is not to avoid these events, they are part of life, but to manage them as jurisdictional transitions. Each must be prepared, documented, and aligned with your broader architecture so that banks, authorities, and courts see continuity rather than contradiction.

When these events are handled with consistency, they do not create risk. They reinforce stability. The system reads you clearly, understands your movements, and treats your architecture as legitimate rather than unpredictable. The key is anticipation: understanding which life events trigger scrutiny, and designing the narrative in advance so that the institutions interpreting you see coherence rather than confusion.

How to build stability across borders

A global life only works when it is stable. Not stable in the emotional sense, but in the institutional one. Banks, tax authorities, regulators, courts, immigration systems, and even counterparties expect your life to follow a logic they can understand. When that logic is missing, the friction begins. When the friction accumulates, the system reacts. And when it reacts, the burden of explanation falls entirely on you.

Stability across borders is not a matter of living quietly or reducing your footprint. It is the result of designing a life that makes sense in every jurisdiction that touches it. Many individuals fail at this because they try to live in one system while benefiting from another. They keep the lifestyle of country a while claiming the residence of country b. They open companies in one place but generate income in another without showing substance. They hold assets in jurisdictions that do not match their declared ties. This disconnect may work during calm periods, but the moment pressure appears, an audit, a bank review, a family dispute, or a regulatory inquiry, the inconsistency becomes visible.

The first step toward stability is alignment. Your residency must match the geography of your life. If you declare tax residence in a country with strict physical-presence rules, your spending patterns, travel records, and day-to-day reality must reflect that truth. If your life is split between several locations, you need documentation showing why the center of life is where you claim it to be. Authorities are not trying to trap you; they are trying to understand you. When the facts are consistent, they leave you alone. When they conflict, they escalate.

Your assets must follow the same principle. If they are held in a jurisdiction for tax reasons, there must be a practical justification as well: governance, investment access, management infrastructure, or long-term planning. When the logic is clear, institutions see legitimacy. When the logic is absent, they see concealment. The difference is narrative, not law.

Your companies also require coherence. A company incorporated abroad must show substance when substance is legally required. Even when the law does not demand it, banks still look for evidence that the structure fits your professional reality. If your operational life is in Europe but your companies are elsewhere, you must be able to explain why. In the modern regulatory environment, "because it is efficient" is not enough. Efficiency is accepted when it sits on top of a real operational purpose; it becomes suspicious when it appears to be the only reason for the structure.

Stability also requires clarity in financial flows. Money that moves across borders must follow a pattern consistent with your declared economic footprint. Income earned in one jurisdiction but reported in another creates unnecessary questions. Payments originating from jurisdictions with no clear connection to your activity raise flags. Even legitimate movements may be misinterpreted when the pattern is not obvious. Stability means that your flows mirror your structures, and your structures mirror your life.

Documentation is the quiet foundation of all this. A coherent global architecture is not built on secrecy; it is built on evidence. You do not need to disclose everything to every institution, but you must be able to provide documentation whenever required. Banks look for contracts, invoices, board minutes, lease agreements, residency certificates, tax filings, and proof of presence. Authorities look for patterns that match what you declare. When the documents tell a consistent story, the system does not escalate.

The emotional obstacle for many individuals is the belief that structure limits freedom. In reality, it does the opposite. Structure is what allows freedom to exist without consequence. Without structure, freedom becomes suspicion, and suspicion becomes friction. A stable multi-jurisdiction life frees you from constant explanation, because the architecture speaks for you when institutions ask questions.

Stability across borders is therefore not about minimizing movement. It is about designing movement that leaves a coherent trail. It is not about avoiding scrutiny. It is about giving scrutiny nothing contradictory to hold on to. When your life, your assets, your companies, and your financial flows align naturally, every jurisdiction that observes you sees the same story.

Stability is the moment when your global life stops looking like an improvisation and becomes a system. A system that withstands pressure not because it is hidden, but because it is coherent. And coherence, more than wealth or complexity, is what allows a high-net-worth individual to operate across borders without becoming a target.

Creating jurisdictional redundancy (a–b–c layers)

A global life becomes fragile when it relies on a single country, a single bank, a single advisor or a single regulatory environment. Most high-net-worth individuals do not realize this until something breaks: a bank freezes an account, a government changes policy overnight, an advisor disappears, or a jurisdiction becomes unpredictable for reasons far beyond personal control. Redundancy is not paranoia. It is structure. It is the architecture that ensures continuity when one element fails.

Jurisdictional redundancy operates on three levels. The first level is the place where you live most of the year, where your presence is visible and where your daily interactions occur. This is your a-layer: the environment that absorbs your physical routines, your administrative obligations and the unavoidable visibility that comes with being present. If something goes wrong here, a political shift, a legal dispute, a sudden increase in scrutiny, you must know that your life does not collapse with it.

The second level is the jurisdiction that protects your assets, the institutional environment that holds your banking, investment structures and corporate governance. This b-layer does not need to be your home, but it must be stable, predictable and compatible with the a-layer. Many individuals choose asset jurisdictions based on tax or convenience without considering the broader institutional climate. Yet the safety of your assets does not depend on low tax; it depends on consistency, legal protection, regulatory integrity and the ability to operate without being treated as a foreign irregularity. If your a-layer becomes unstable, the b-layer ensures nothing essential is lost.

The third level is the jurisdiction that holds what must remain immune to local crises: long-term structures, legacy vehicles, intellectual property, trusts, foundations, backups of critical documents and, in some cases, secondary residencies or alternative citizenships. This c-layer is rarely used in daily life. Its role is silent continuity. It exists so that even if the a-layer becomes uninhabitable or the b-layer becomes restrictive, the core of your architecture remains untouched. This is not an escape plan. It is the final perimeter that ensures sovereignty under pressure.

These three layers must be compatible. A residence in one jurisdiction, assets in another and long-term structures in a third can work beautifully when the logic behind the combination is coherent. When the logic is unclear, when presence, capital and governance contradict each other, institutions begin to interpret the structure as a risk. Redundancy becomes exposure if it is not designed with intention.

To build true redundancy, each layer must be independent enough to survive failure in another, yet aligned enough to appear consistent to institutions. You must be able to live temporarily without access to the a-layer, operate without full access to the b-layer, and preserve your long-term structures without depending on either. The goal is not to abandon one jurisdiction for another when life becomes uncomfortable. The goal is to ensure that no single point of institutional failure can destabilize your entire system.

This requires discipline. If your residency depends entirely on a country that is politically volatile, you must build a secondary path long before volatility becomes a crisis. If your banking depends on a single institution or a single regulatory system, you must diversify while you are still in a position of strength. If your long-term structures exist in a jurisdiction that is evolving rapidly in terms of compliance or transparency, you must evaluate whether your architecture will still make sense five or ten years from now.

Redundancy is not built during crisis. It is built during calm. The worst time to seek a second residency, move a structure or open an additional banking perimeter is when institutions already perceive you as high-risk. Continuity must be designed before it is needed. When redundancy is done correctly, you do not feel its presence. You simply live with the quiet certainty that your life can pivot smoothly if circumstances require it, without frantic decisions or defensive explanations.

The real power of redundancy is psychological. When you know that your life does not depend on a single government, a single institution or a single environment, your decisions become calm, deliberate and strategic. You are not trapped by fear of change, because you have already built the pathways you would need if change arrived. What others perceive as resilience is, in reality, preparation.

Jurisdictional redundancy is not a luxury. It is the architecture of freedom. It allows you to exist across borders without being controlled by any of them. It ensures that pressure in one place never becomes vulnerability everywhere. And ultimately, it transforms your global life from something that must constantly be defended into something that simply continues, no matter what happens around you.

The quiet art of coherence: how to avoid looking like a global puzzle

A global life becomes risky only when it stops making sense from the outside. Institutions do not need to know your story; they only need to understand your structure. When your documents, movements, expenses, assets, and legal anchors all point in the same direction, your life can be processed without hesitation. When they contradict one another, even slightly, the system begins to view you as an anomaly. And anomalies are rarely ignored.

Coherence is not about simplifying your life. It is about giving your life a readable shape. Your residence, your spending patterns, your banking activity, and your corporate footprint must all reflect the same narrative. If you declare one country as your primary residence but most decisions, expenses, and interactions occur somewhere else, institutions assume they are missing a piece of the picture. Missing pieces generate questions, and questions generate exposure.

The first source of incoherence usually appears in the difference between declared residence and lived reality. If your tax filings claim presence in one jurisdiction while your financial activity suggests another, the system interprets the gap as potential misalignment. This is not an accusation; it is a response to patterns. Banks, for example, rely heavily on behavioral signals. When they see that your credit card spending, travel schedule, and economic footprint contradict the country where you claim to reside, they escalate your file automatically because they cannot explain the inconsistency.

Another source of incoherence arises from assets and entities scattered across jurisdictions without a clear purpose. Owning property in one place, banking in another, incorporating companies in a third, and spending most of your time in a fourth is perfectly lawful. But it must have a logic that institutions can understand. When these elements exist by habit rather than by design, you appear fragmented. Fragmentation is treated as a form of opacity, even if nothing improper is happening.

Your personal footprint also matters. If your lifestyle suggests one jurisdiction, through schools, health contracts, recurring subscriptions, or domestic staff, while your filings suggest another, authorities interpret the mismatch as a sign that they need to verify your actual center of life. This does not require any wrongdoing to trigger administrative curiosity. The mere absence of coherence is enough to attract attention.

Digital traces complicate the picture further. Travel patterns, device metadata, login locations, and the geographical rhythm of your communications all create a silent map of your life. When this map conflicts with your declared legal position, the inconsistency becomes measurable. Institutions now rely heavily on metadata to corroborate residency, economic ties, and lifestyle indicators. The more the digital evidence contradicts the paperwork, the more the system concludes that the architecture behind your life may be incomplete or artificially constructed.

Coherence does not require absolute consistency. It requires alignment. If you spend significant time in multiple jurisdictions, your documentation should reflect that reality. If your economic activity spans continents, your structures should explain the distribution. If you rely on several countries to manage your affairs, your governance and reporting must show the logic behind these choices. Institutions do not expect simplicity from people with complex cross-border lives. They expect intention.

The advantage of coherence is that it neutralizes suspicion before it arises. When your documents, movements, and governance reflect the same story, institutions classify you as predictable. Predictability lowers your risk category without you having to do anything extraordinary. A global life that makes sense is treated as legitimate. A global life that appears improvised is treated as something to examine more closely.

Coherence allows you to move freely, restructure discreetly, and operate internationally without triggering unnecessary verification. It does not restrict your options; it protects them. When the visible signals of your life align with the legal foundations beneath them, you no longer resemble a puzzle. You resemble someone who knows exactly what they are doing.

Final note

Sovereignty is not isolation. It is the ability to continue your life on your own terms, regardless of what happens around you. Geography shapes that ability more than most people realize. The jurisdictions where you live, earn, invest, and hold assets determine how easily you can move forward when the world changes, when institutions shift their priorities, or when personal events disrupt your equilibrium.

Choosing a jurisdiction is not an act of escape, privilege, or strategy for advantage. It is an act of self-definition. You decide which legal system interprets your intentions, which institutions hold your information, which authorities protect your rights, and which environment becomes responsible for your continuity. A country is not only a place. It is a framework that decides how your life is understood.

A coherent, well-designed jurisdictional structure grants you something rare in the modern world: the ability to withstand pressure without losing access, control, or clarity. When your anchors are stable, when your legal position is defensible, and when your narrative matches the facts, you are not exposed even when someone tries to expose you. Institutions react calmly because your architecture is built to make sense.

Sovereignty through geography does not mean disappearing. It means choosing where you exist with intention, placing each part of your life where it can function without friction. You do not need perfect privacy. You need a structure that remains intact when attention arrives. You do not need to be invisible. You need to be unreadable to those who should not interpret you, and entirely clear to those who must.

The world is no longer divided by borders, but by systems. Some systems reward coherence. Some punish inconsistency. Some protect you. Others expose you without meaning to. Sovereignty comes from understanding these differences and designing your life accordingly.

You do not control the global environment. You control the way you move through it. And when your geography reflects your intentions instead of your circumstances, you no longer navigate the world. You shape it around you.

Chapter IX. The architecture of control

Every structure you create, whether it is a trust, a foundation, a holding company, or a special-purpose vehicle, is ultimately an instrument of control. Not control over others, but control over your own life, your assets, your decision-making, and the way your presence is interpreted across jurisdictions. The purpose of private structuring is not secrecy. It is continuity. A structure exists so that your financial, personal, or strategic life does not collapse simply because circumstances around you change.

Wealth is fragile when it depends entirely on personal presence. When every signature must be yours, every instruction comes from you, and every asset responds to your direct command, your life becomes the weakest point in the system. A sudden illness, a travel disruption, a political misunderstanding, a bank officer misreading your profile, an investigation, even if unjustified, can interrupt your ability to act. Without structure, interruption quickly becomes vulnerability.

A well-designed structure creates a layer between you and the pressure. It absorbs friction so that you do not have to. It provides legal continuity when you are unavailable, strategic continuity when the environment becomes unpredictable, and operational continuity when your name should not appear directly in the day-to-day mechanics of an asset or entity. Control is not lost when you use structures; it is transformed. You shift from direct management to directional governance, still in command, but not exposed.

This is why the quality of the architecture matters more than the sophistication of the tools. A simple structure built on stable legal ground is stronger than a complex structure built on contradictions. A trust created with a clear purpose and coherent documentation is safer than a multi-layered arrangement assembled without substance. A holding company that reflects real economic activity withstands scrutiny more effectively than a complicated offshore chain with no discernible logic.

The most effective structures share three traits: they are legally sound, narratively coherent, and operationally defensible. Legally sound means they respect the laws of every jurisdiction involved, not only the favorable ones. Narratively coherent means that the structure makes sense to an outsider who sees only its surface: a regulator, a bank, a judge, or an auditor. Operationally defensible means that the structure produces actions, governance, documentation, and economic substance that match its declared purpose.

The architecture of control also requires understanding the difference between ownership and power. Owning something directly exposes you. Controlling it through governance, voting rights, or decision frameworks gives you influence without unnecessary visibility. Structures are not about avoiding responsibility; they are about distributing responsibility correctly so that you are not the only point of failure. The wealthiest families and institutions in the world operate this way not because it is fashionable, but because it works.

Finally, a structure is only as strong as the intentions behind it. If you create entities merely to manipulate appearances or to obscure obligations, the system will eventually reveal the contradiction. But when a structure reflects a real need, protection of heirs, management of international assets, philanthropic purpose, business continuity, it stands firm under analysis. Intentionality is the one aspect that cannot be retroactively added. It must exist from the beginning.

A private structure is not a hiding place. It is a legal instrument that allows your life to function even when the world around you does not. It is the quiet architecture behind every person who carries significant responsibility, visibility, or vulnerability. And when built correctly, it becomes the backbone of sovereignty, not in the political sense, but in the personal one: the ability to remain stable, effective, and protected under pressure.

Substance and reality: the line between protection and exposure

Every structure you create—whether it is a company, a trust, a holding, or a foundation—lives in two parallel worlds. One is the world you see: documents, signatures, bank accounts, directors, and contracts. The other is the world that institutions see when they analyze your life. In that second world, the key question is always the same: does this structure reflect reality, or is it an artificial layer that collapses as soon as someone touches it?

Substance is the element that bridges these two worlds. In simple terms, substance means that a structure behaves the way it claims to behave. It has real activity, real decision-making, real governance, real documentation, and a real economic purpose. It is not an ornament. It is not a nameplate on a lawyer's door. It is not a company that exists only because a form was filed years ago. It is a functioning part of your architecture, with a life that can be demonstrated through actions rather than intention.

Substance becomes visible in many ways. A company with genuine substance has directors who actually meet, sign decisions, and understand their responsibilities. It has contracts that reflect real activity, not templates copied between jurisdictions. It has accounting that makes sense, operations that match its purpose, and a rhythm of activity that aligns with your financial footprint. By contrast, a company with a nominal director, no meetings, no agreements, no invoices, and no internal documentation may still exist legally, but it will not survive scrutiny. When a bank, regulator, or tax authority examines it, they will see a disconnect between the structure and the life around it.

The same principle applies to trusts. A trust with substance is one where the trustee acts independently, makes decisions according to the trust deed, and keeps records that demonstrate real governance. It follows its logic. It behaves like the legal organism it is meant to be. But a trust where the settlor continues to give instructions through text messages, where assets are used personally without formal approval, or where the trustee simply signs whatever is placed in front of them sends a different message. Even if the documents are perfect, the behavior shows that the trust is not truly separate from its founder. Institutions have learned to recognize this contradiction immediately.

Holdings follow the same rule. A holding company that controls assets, receives dividends, manages investments, and serves as a genuine financial center has substance. A holding that holds nothing, does nothing, and exists only because someone once said it was "good for structuring" does not. When a holding has no activity, banks interpret it as a cosmetic layer. When it has real flows, governance, and purpose, it becomes the backbone of your architecture.

Substance also determines how your structures are treated in different jurisdictions. Many countries, including Switzerland, the United Kingdom, and the United States, now rely on substance tests to distinguish between legitimate arrangements and artificial ones. These tests examine where decisions are made, where board members live, where the activity takes place, and whether the structure reflects economic reality. If the structure's footprint contradicts your real life, institutions will ignore the structure and treat you as the true center of control. This is how tax reclassifications, asset seizures, or reporting disputes often begin—not through illegality, but through inconsistency.

Regulators and banks do not expect grandeur. They do not need you to employ dozens of people or rent a large office. They expect coherence. A company should look like a company. A trust should look like a trust. A holding should look like a holding. These expectations are simple, but they must be met with discipline.

Substance is not expensive, but the absence of substance is. The moment a system questions the credibility of one structure, it begins questioning all of them. When your architecture is built on real governance and real purpose, the burden shifts: institutions trust the logic of your design because the structure can defend itself.

Substance is not a technical requirement. It is the difference between a structure that protects you and a structure that exposes you. It is the quiet element that allows your architecture to survive pressure, because it demonstrates that what you built is not an illusion—it is part of the real world, and it can stand on its own when someone asks it to.

Companies and Legal Entities: The Basic Building Blocks

Before you enter the world of trusts, foundations, holding companies, and more advanced structures, you need to understand the simplest unit of any architecture: the company. A company—regardless of jurisdiction—exists to perform one essential function. It separates the individual from the activity. It creates a legal person that can own assets, sign contracts, hire employees, incur liabilities, and operate independently of your private life. That separation is what allows risk to be contained, continuity to be preserved, and decisions to be made without exposing you personally every time something happens.

At its core, a company has a personality of its own. It has owners or shareholders, a management body, an internal governance system, and responsibilities defined by the law of its jurisdiction. When a company functions properly, it gives structure to your intentions. When it is poorly maintained or chosen without regard for jurisdiction, it becomes a point of vulnerability. Many high-net-worth individuals underestimate how different corporate forms truly are from country to country. A company is never "just a company." It is a legal identity shaped entirely by the environment in which it exists.

The United Kingdom, for example, offers several types of corporate vehicles that appear similar from the outside but operate under different principles. A private limited company (Ltd) is the standard business form, while a public limited company (plc) has stricter reporting obligations and may offer shares to the public. An LLP looks like a company but functions more like a partnership, with flexible internal rules and a different tax treatment. All of these are governed by the Companies Act 2006, which imposes clear duties on directors, filing obligations, and accountability standards. Yet these forms cannot be compared directly with their equivalents in continental Europe or the United States, because the legal culture behind them is different.

In the United States, the contrast between a corporation and an LLC is even more pronounced. A corporation (Inc.) has a rigid governance structure, with directors, officers, and formalities that resemble the European company model. An LLC, by contrast, is far more flexible; it can be member-managed, manager-managed, or governed by a bespoke operating agreement. But this flexibility comes with a trade-off: outside the US, an LLC is often misunderstood or treated cautiously by banks and regulators. A Delaware LLC, for instance, is not viewed the same way as a Swiss SA or a Spanish SL because it may lack the formal substance that foreign institutions expect from a corporate vehicle. On paper, they all have limited liability. In practice, they do not carry the same weight.

Switzerland offers a different model. The SA (or AG) is a classic corporation with strict capital requirements, clear duties for directors, audited accounts in many cases, and strong expectations around governance and transparency. The Sàrl (or GmbH) is more accessible, used frequently for private business or smaller structures, but still subject to meaningful regulation. Recent reforms introduced stronger transparency rules, including mandatory identification of beneficial owners. Swiss companies are respected globally because they tend to reflect the country's culture: disciplined, well-documented, and predictable.

Spain, like many EU countries, relies on the SL and SA as its primary corporate forms. The SL is widely used for private business and asset holding, while the SA is more formal and often used for larger enterprises. Both require annual accounts, board meetings, and filings with the Registry. Directors carry fiduciary duties, not symbolic ones, and can face liability for mismanagement. Again, the form looks familiar, but the obligations and expectations differ significantly from those of the UK or the US.

These examples illustrate a fundamental point: there are no universal equivalents. A Swiss SA is not the same as a US corporation, even if both are "companies." An LLC is not a substitute for a European limited company. A Panamanian foundation bears no resemblance to a Swiss Stiftung, even though both use the word "foundation." The law behind each form is unique, and institutions–including banks, regulators, and foreign courts–evaluate them according to their own standards, not according to your intention.

Ownership rights also shift depending on the jurisdiction. Dividends may be distributed freely in one country but restricted by capital-maintenance rules in another. Shareholder rights in an LLC depend entirely on the operating agreement, while rights in a plc are imposed by statute. In some countries, dissolving a company is a simple administrative step; in others, it triggers tax consequences, audits, or scrutiny. Even the duties of directors change dramatically from one place to another. In the UK, directors must act in the best interest of the company. In Switzerland, they must also consider creditors and maintain solvency standards. In the US, obligations depend on state law and the company's own governance documents.

For a high-net-worth individual, the practical lesson is simple: a company is not merely a tool, it is a legal organism with a personality shaped by its jurisdiction. You cannot treat companies from different countries as interchangeable, and you cannot assume that what works in one system will automatically work in another. When you build a structure that spans multiple jurisdictions, these differences become amplified. A decision made casually in one country may carry consequences in another where the rules are stricter or interpreted differently.

Everything that follows in this chapter—trusts, foundations, holdings, SPVs, donations, and long-term governance—rests on this foundation. Companies are the building blocks of your architecture. If the building blocks are chosen without understanding, or maintained without discipline, the entire structure becomes vulnerable. When they are selected intentionally, governed coherently, and aligned with the rest of your footprint, they form the basis of an architecture that can withstand scrutiny, adapt to change, and operate quietly in the background of your life.

Trusts: revocable, irrevocable, hybrid, how they really work

A trust is not magic, and it is not a loophole. It is a legal relationship built on three elements: a person who contributes assets, a person who manages them, and a purpose that explains why the assets must exist under that arrangement. When done correctly, a trust is one of the most powerful instruments for continuity, succession, and protection. When done poorly, it becomes a source of exposure, contradiction, and sometimes disaster.

For high-net-worth individuals, the importance of a trust does not lie in secrecy. The modern world has eliminated secrecy from the equation. What remains is structure. A trust allows you to redefine ownership in a way that reduces your personal surface of attack without placing assets in a legal vacuum. You transfer assets into a framework governed by clear rules, supervised by a trustee, and protected by the courts of the jurisdiction where the trust is created. That protection becomes most visible at moments of stress: litigation, divorce, political pressure, or disputes between heirs. The trust becomes the stabilizing element that tempers volatility.

Understanding the different types of trusts is essential, because the degree of protection depends almost entirely on how much control you retain. A revocable trust gives you the freedom to change, amend, or terminate the structure at any time. That flexibility makes it attractive for lifetime planning, but it weakens the protective effect because you remain the ultimate authority. If you can reverse the trust, so can the law. In many jurisdictions, revocable trusts are treated as transparent. They may offer no shield against creditors, no separation in litigation, and no real insulation from tax or reporting obligations. Their value lies in organization, not defense.

Irrevocable trusts function differently. Once assets enter the structure, the trust, not you, becomes the legal owner. You can still influence governance through carefully drafted documents, but you can no longer treat the assets as an extension of your personal estate. That loss of ownership, while uncomfortable for some, is what creates the protective strength. Creditors, litigants, or adversarial parties cannot access what you no longer control. Courts cannot treat the assets as yours if the trust was created properly, long before any conflict arose, and with clear economic and legal intent. Irrevocability is not a punishment; it is the price of real protection.

Hybrid trusts sit between these two worlds. They allow you to retain certain powers while still creating a degree of insulation. Perhaps you keep the right to appoint or remove trustees, or to direct certain investments, or to influence distributions within limits. Properly drafted, a hybrid trust balances control and protection, but it requires precision. Too much retained power and the structure collapses under legal scrutiny. Too little, and the trust feels disconnected from your actual needs. Hybrid models are useful when you want flexibility without sacrificing the integrity of the structure, especially in families with complex dynamics or assets spread across multiple jurisdictions.

Whatever form you choose, the critical element is always the same: purpose. If the purpose is weak, artificial, or inconsistent with your life, the trust will not withstand institutional pressure. A trust created "to protect assets" is not a purpose. The law requires clarity. Succession planning, family governance, philanthropic intent, preservation of a business, consolidation of holdings, intergenerational continuity, these are purposes that courts understand and respect. A trust built on genuine purpose looks legitimate because it is legitimate.

Modern compliance adds another layer. Banks no longer accept trusts without full documentation. Trustees must demonstrate independence. Beneficiaries must be identified. Economic substance must be visible. None of this weakens the value of the trust. On the contrary, it reinforces it. The era of shadow structures is over; the era of resilient structures has begun. A trust survives not because nobody sees it, but because it makes sense when someone does.

The greatest mistake wealthy individuals make is treating a trust as an ornament, something created for perceived benefits but never integrated into their actual governance. A trust must be alive. It must be administered, reviewed, and adjusted as life changes. Family circumstances evolve, businesses expand or dissolve, jurisdictions alter their laws, and beneficiaries mature. A trust that is never updated slowly becomes a liability. A trust that grows with you becomes a fortress.

In the end, a trust is not about escaping responsibility. It is about defining your responsibilities with clarity so that your wealth, and the people who depend on it, remain protected regardless of what happens around you. When designed intentionally, administered professionally, and aligned with the rest of your architecture, it becomes one of the few structures that can withstand time, pressure, and the unpredictability of life.

Foundations & philanthropy: protection vs. exposure

A foundation is often perceived as a symbol of maturity in wealth: a structure that stands above personal interests, directing resources toward long-term goals, public benefit, or intergenerational purpose. But for a high-net-worth individual, a foundation is not merely a philanthropic gesture. It is a legal organism, shaped by the jurisdiction that hosts it, and it can either strengthen your architecture or expose it, depending on how it is designed.

The first truth about foundations is simple: they are public by nature, even when their operations are private. A foundation is created to serve a purpose outside the founder, which means regulators demand transparency, governance, and accountability. You cannot treat a foundation like a private vault. You cannot mix personal interest with institutional purpose. Even when the law allows discretion, the boundary between "founder influence" and "founder control" must remain clean and visible. This is why the foundation can either be a shield or a spotlight.

When built correctly, a foundation provides continuity that no personal structure can match. Unlike a trust, which may be governed by flexible common-law principles, a foundation is rigid and institutional. It has a board, statutes, supervision, and a purpose that cannot be easily altered. That rigidity is what creates resilience. It protects assets from personal litigation. It enables long-term governance across generations. It transforms wealth into something that survives personal crises, political shifts, or family disputes. Courts understand and respect foundations because they operate within defined, supervised frameworks.

But this same rigidity creates vulnerabilities if misused. A foundation that acts like a personal vehicle attracts immediate suspicion. Excessive founder control, discretionary benefits without proper governance, opaque transactions, or personal expenses disguised as philanthropy are all red flags in modern compliance. Today's regulatory environment expects foundations to reflect genuine intent, not performative generosity. When intent is unclear, authorities assume the structure is cosmetic. And when they assume it is cosmetic, they treat it as a tool for concealment, even if no wrongdoing exists.

Philanthropy itself requires caution. Large donations, sponsorships, or public commitments create visibility that may be beneficial in one context and dangerous in another. A well-designed philanthropic footprint can build reputation, support social or diplomatic leverage, and create legitimacy. But a poorly timed or poorly structured donation can trigger scrutiny from tax authorities, regulators, or political observers. Visibility is a currency here: it must be used carefully, with clarity of purpose and precision of timing.

The foundation becomes most powerful when it serves multiple functions at once: social value, reputational stability, succession planning, and asset protection. But none of these functions can exist in contradiction. A foundation that tries to provide benefits without governance collapses under pressure. A foundation that is purely symbolic lacks legal credibility. A foundation that exists only for tax advantage is treated as such, and institutions respond accordingly.

A well-designed foundation is independent but aligned, opaque in what it must protect but transparent in what it must show, close enough to reflect your values but far enough to withstand your absence. Its governance must work with or without you. Its board must be competent. Its statutes must reflect real purpose, not convenience. And its activities must be defensible when viewed through the lens of international compliance.

For families with complex dynamics, foundations provide structure where emotion often creates instability. They define inheritance rules when no consensus exists. They prevent disputes between siblings or heirs. They ensure continuity for businesses, art collections, properties, or philanthropic missions without relying on personal agreements. The foundation becomes the stabilizer that keeps the family, and its wealth, from fragmenting.

But none of this works without coherence. A foundation must sit comfortably within your jurisdictional architecture, your tax position, your domicile rules, and your long-term strategy. Misalignment between these elements does not go unnoticed. Authorities are quick to examine whether a foundation serves genuine purpose or merely an attempt to distance assets without economic substance.

The goal is not to hide. The goal is to create a structure that stands even when you do not, that protects without attracting suspicion, and that outlives personal volatility. When a foundation is built with clarity, governance, and purpose, it becomes a pillar of sovereignty. When built without discipline, it becomes exposure in institutional form.

In the end, a foundation is not about generosity or image. It is about design, design that transforms wealth into continuity, responsibility into stability, and personal intent into long-term structure.

Holding companies & multi-layer ownership

A holding company is one of the most misunderstood tools in private wealth. Many view it as a simple container for assets or as a way to “separate things,” but a holding company is far more than that. It is a governance instrument, a visibility filter, a tax-organizing layer, and a strategic firewall between your wealth and the environments in which you operate. When designed correctly, it simplifies a complex life. When designed poorly, it multiplies risk across every layer of your architecture.

The first function of a holding company is concentration of ownership. Instead of owning assets directly, real estate, operating companies, intellectual property, art, aircraft, or investments, you own participation in a single entity that consolidates these interests. This consolidation creates clarity for banks, regulators, and courts. Instead of analyzing each asset individually, institutions evaluate the holding structure itself, which becomes the interpretive center of your financial universe. Clarity protects you because institutions hesitate when faced with fragmented ownership, inconsistent records, or assets scattered across unrelated jurisdictions. A well-structured holding eliminates that hesitation.

The second function is separation. A holding company creates a legal and operational gap between personal life and professional exposure. Litigation, commercial disputes, or regulatory inquiries aimed at an operating business do not automatically reach the holding. The structure distributes risk instead of letting it fall directly on you. This separation only works, however, when the holding has proper governance. Nominal companies with no meetings, no decision-making records, and no substance rarely withstand scrutiny. Institutions have learned to distinguish between a true holding and an empty shell.

The third function is narrative coherence. When all personal and business assets flow through a structure with consistent governance, financial logic, and jurisdictional stability, your profile becomes easier for the system to process. Banks see predictable flows. Tax authorities see predictable reporting. Regulators see predictable governance. Predictability creates trust, and trust is what keeps your file from moving into enhanced due diligence. The opposite is equally true: ownership that looks improvised or scattered invites questions, even if fully legal.

Multi-layer ownership adds another dimension. Sometimes one holding is not enough. You may require multiple layers for reasons such as shielding a sensitive asset, isolating liability from a volatile business, or separating reputational risk from financial logic. Multi-layer does not mean unnecessary complexity. It means vertical coherence. Each company exists for a reason, documented internally and defensible externally. When the purpose is clear, additional layers do not appear suspicious; they appear deliberate.

Jurisdiction selection is the foundation of a strong holding. The company must exist in a legal environment that respects governance, allows clear ownership rules, and aligns with your personal residency and long-term intentions. A holding in a jurisdiction that interprets complexity as suspicion creates friction. A holding in a jurisdiction that understands international profiles creates stability. The system evaluates not only the structure but also the country that hosts it. A mismatch between the sophistication of your life and the simplicity of the jurisdiction creates unnecessary exposure.

Substance remains essential. Even when the law does not require full physical presence, the company must be able to demonstrate real decision-making. This can include board meetings, professional directors, accounting records, and clear internal logic behind asset acquisitions or transfers. A holding that exists only on paper is fragile. A holding built as a functioning entity is resilient. Substance is not a luxury; it is your insurance policy when institutions examine your structure.

The tax dimension must be handled with the same discipline. A holding is not a tax trick; it is a tax organizer. Its purpose is to centralize income, dividends, and asset transfers in a way that remains compliant in every jurisdiction involved. When designed correctly, it reduces friction without relying on artificial arrangements. When designed irresponsibly, it exposes the entire architecture to reclassification. Modern tax authorities no longer react to the existence of a holding, they react to whether the holding makes sense.

Visibility is the final variable. A holding company should not draw attention to itself. It should sit quietly behind the scenes, visible where necessary, invisible where appropriate. Its filings must be clean. Its ownership records must be consistent. Its narrative must match your residency, your financial footprint, and your movement across borders. When these elements align, a holding becomes the backbone of sovereignty. When they do not, it becomes the first point of failure under pressure.

A holding company is not designed to impress. It is designed to protect, organize, and stabilize. When the logic is clear, the governance is real, the jurisdiction is aligned, and the substance is credible, the holding does not merely own assets, it sustains the architecture that allows you to operate without noise, without contradiction, and without unnecessary exposure. It becomes the quiet center from which the rest of your world remains coherent.

SPVs & operational shields

Special-purpose vehicles, SPVs, are among the most misunderstood instruments in the world of wealth. To some, they appear mysterious or overly complex. To others, they seem like tools reserved only for corporations or institutional investors. In reality, SPVs are nothing more than containers: self-contained legal units designed to isolate risk, organize ownership, and keep specific activities separate from the rest of your financial architecture. When used correctly, they become one of the most effective shields a high-net-worth individual can deploy.

An SPV works by narrowing the scope of exposure. Instead of conducting an activity under your personal name or through a central holding company, you place that activity inside a dedicated entity with its own governance, its own accounting, and its own liabilities. If something goes wrong, litigation, contractual disputes, regulatory issues, operational accidents, the consequences remain inside the vehicle. They do not spill over into unrelated assets or structures. Asset segregation is the essence of the shield. It is not secrecy, and it is not avoidance. It is discipline.

This separation becomes essential in complex lives. When you invest in a business, acquire a property, operate a yacht or aircraft, launch an international venture, or hold an asset that carries operational or reputational risk, placing it inside an SPV keeps the risk where it belongs. Without this separation, you create a single point of fragility. One dispute could threaten unrelated holdings; one operational failure could jeopardize your entire architecture. SPVs exist to prevent these scenarios.

The strength of an SPV lies not in the entity itself but in the clarity of its purpose. A vehicle created without a defined function attracts institutional suspicion. A vehicle created with a coherent logic, acquisition of a specific asset, operation of a project, participation in a joint venture, or management of a limited activity, reads as normal. Banks, regulators, and courts understand SPVs because they are built into the global financial system. When they are aligned with commercial reality, they require little explanation.

However, SPVs must be governed with precision. Even the most sophisticated structure collapses if the lines between personal and corporate activity are blurred. Commingling, mixing personal expenses with corporate accounts, undermines the shield instantly. Decisions must be documented. Directors must have real responsibilities. Accounting must be separate. Agreements must be signed by the SPV itself, not by you personally. These practices are not formality, they are the evidence that the SPV is a genuine operational unit rather than a façade.

Jurisdiction matters as well. An SPV must be placed where its activity makes sense. An aircraft SPV belongs where the aircraft is registered. A property SPV belongs where the property sits. A venture SPV belongs in a jurisdiction that recognizes the commercial purpose of the venture. When the jurisdiction matches the asset or project, the structure stands on firm legal ground. When the jurisdiction is disconnected from activity, institutions begin asking questions. A mismatch does not make the structure illegal, but it forces you to constantly justify decisions that should be self-explanatory.

SPV also serve as communication shields. They allow you to engage with counterparties, banks, employees, contractors, or regulators without exposing your personal identity unnecessarily. When a contract is signed by an SPV, your name becomes one step removed from operational risk and reputational noise. This is not concealment; it is proportionality. It ensures that only the actors who need to know your involvement actually know it. In a world where personal data, signatures, and public filings circulate with increasing ease, this layer of separation becomes part of your privacy architecture.

Another benefit is strategic flexibility. When an asset becomes obsolete, risky, or incompatible with your long-term direction, dismantling an SPV is far cleaner than unwinding activity that sits inside a core holding. You close the vehicle, transfer out what must be preserved, and walk away without destabilizing unrelated systems. This modularity is essential for individuals whose lives evolve across sectors and borders. You are never trapped inside an old decision. The SPV lets you close a chapter without rewriting the entire book.

But SPVs are not magic. They do not protect against criminal liability, fiscal obligations, or personal guarantees. They cannot be used to hide assets, disguise ownership, or avoid legitimate reporting. Their power comes from legality, not opacity. The moment an SPV is used with the wrong intention, it stops being a shield and becomes a risk factor. The safest structures are always the ones that could withstand scrutiny from any jurisdiction because everything inside them follows clear, honest, and documented logic.

What makes SPVs invaluable is not their complexity. It is their simplicity. They allow you to place each aspect of your life inside the container where it belongs. They isolate risk, clarify purpose, and reduce the burden of explaining a global life to institutions that rely on coherence. They are tools of order, not tools of escape.

When you design your architecture around well-structured SPVs, your life becomes cleaner, your exposure becomes narrower, and your operational world becomes far easier to manage. You gain the ability to move, expand, retreat, or redesign without destabilizing the entire system. And in a world where pressure can appear at any moment, freedom is worth more than any single asset you may place inside the vehicle.

Donations, endowments & political visibility

Donations and endowments are often presented as purely philanthropic instruments, but in the life of a high-net-worth individual they also function as structural components of visibility. They shape how institutions read your intentions, how your name appears in public records, and how regulators or media interpret your proximity to influence. Nothing about this means philanthropy is dangerous; it simply means that every act of generosity has legal and reputational consequences far beyond the gift itself. Understanding these consequences is essential if you want your contributions to strengthen your architecture rather than destabilize it.

The first element is purpose. A donation that is anchored in a clear, documented rationale is easy for institutions to understand. A donation that appears sudden, disproportionate, or disconnected from your declared interests can trigger unwanted attention. Banks evaluate the flow of funds. Tax authorities evaluate the deductibility and structure. Media evaluates the symbolism. A donation made without context may look like an attempt to shift assets, conceal intention, or buy influence. A donation made with context reads as part of your established philanthropic identity. The difference lies not in the act but in the surrounding narrative.

Endowments carry even greater structural weight. An endowment is not merely a donation; it is the creation of an ongoing financial organism that continues to operate in your name or under your influence. This introduces long-term obligations relating to governance, oversight, reporting, and compliance. An endowment without proper structure can become a point of vulnerability, especially if it spans multiple jurisdictions or interacts with politically sensitive sectors. When designed correctly, however, an endowment becomes a stabilizing instrument, one that signals continuity, purpose, and discipline.

The interaction between philanthropy and political visibility must be handled with care. Donations tied to public figures, political projects, or entities with regulatory influence can shift the way your entire profile is interpreted. Even legal contributions may be seen through the lens of influence-seeking, and institutions are increasingly cautious about anything that resembles proximity to political power. Not every political connection is dangerous, but every politically exposed linkage triggers enhanced scrutiny. The more visible your donation, the more carefully the structure must be documented. Clarity protects you; ambiguity exposes you.

This is why subtlety often matters more than magnitude. Quiet philanthropy, executed through well-governed foundations, donor-advised funds, or long-term endowments, tends to generate trust within institutions. It demonstrates consistency rather than opportunism. Conversely, sudden high-visibility donations can create a narrative that is difficult to control, even when your intentions are sincere. In the world of cross-border regulation, perception becomes part of the architecture. A philanthropic act that appears benign in one jurisdiction may raise questions in another with stricter political-exposure rules.

The legal dimension is equally important. Donations must be structured in a way that respects the tax, reporting, and anti-money-laundering rules of every jurisdiction involved. A donation made from the wrong entity, at the wrong time, or without proper documentation can be reclassified as an undeclared transfer of wealth. Timing matters. Source of funds matters. The identity of the recipient matters. The structure through which the gift is delivered matters. A philanthropic strategy that is legally sound in your country of residence may not be recognized the same way in your country of citizenship or domicile. A donation intended to help can become a point of friction simply because the framework was not aligned.

Philanthropy intersects with reputation as well. Some individuals use donations as a way to signal legitimacy or influence. This approach often fails because institutions are trained to detect when philanthropy is being used as a shield. The safest posture is the most honest one: act where you truly care, contribute where your involvement makes sense, and structure the contribution in a way that withstands scrutiny from any jurisdiction. When philanthropy is consistent with your real interests and is executed through robust governance, it strengthens your reputation rather than exposing it.

The long-term question is governance. A donation is an event. An endowment is a system. If your philanthropic footprint is meant to endure, it must be designed with the same rigor as any asset structure. That includes succession planning, oversight mechanisms, geographic alignment, and independence from your personal circumstances. An endowment that collapses after your involvement ends weakens your architecture. An endowment that continues without disruption becomes part of your legacy, not as ornament, but as a functioning structure built on legal and ethical coherence.

But the most important principle is this: philanthropy must never outpace your clarity. Give for the right reasons, through the right structures, at the right time, documented with the right discipline. When your intention is sincere and the architecture is coherent, donations and endowments become stabilizing forces in a global life. When the intention is rushed or the structure is improvised, they become pressure points that institutions treat with suspicion.

A donation is never just a donation. It is a signal, a structure, and in some cases a long-term commitment that shapes how the world reads you. When handled with precision, it reinforces sovereignty. When handled without discipline, it becomes a vulnerability disguised as generosity.

Why structures fail: global vulnerability patterns

Many people believe that a structure fails because it was built incorrectly. In practice, most structures fail for a much simpler reason: nobody maintains them. A trust, a foundation, a holding company, or an SPV can be legally perfect on the day it is created, drafted with precision and good intentions, and still fall apart years later. Failure rarely arrives suddenly. It develops slowly, through habits, omissions, and contradictions that accumulate quietly until one day an institution examines the structure and sees what has been neglected.

The first point of vulnerability is the absence of substance. A structure that exists only on paper may appear acceptable as long as nobody looks closely. But the moment a bank, regulator, or court reviews it, the lack of real activity becomes obvious. Substance is not about size. It is not about having employees or renting large offices. It is about coherence: clear governance, documented decisions, real oversight, and a direct link between the structure and the purpose it is meant to serve. When those elements are missing, even an entirely legal entity can be reinterpreted as something artificial or incomplete.

A second weakness appears when the way a structure operates does not match the life surrounding it. A trust intended for succession cannot work properly if the settlor continues to give instructions casually or uses trust assets as if nothing had changed. A holding company cannot be presented as the center of governance when decisions are made informally in another country. A foundation cannot claim charitable purpose if its activity shows none. When the declared purpose and the real behavior do not align, institutions interpret the inconsistency as risk.

Narrative confusion is another common cause of failure. A structure may be technically sound but still raise questions if its purpose is not documented clearly or has not been updated as circumstances evolved. Banks and regulators need to understand why a vehicle exists. When the purpose is vague, outdated, or impossible to reconstruct from the records, the structure becomes uncertain in their eyes. Uncertainty alone is enough to trigger concern.

Structures also weaken because the people responsible for them change. Trustees retire. Directors stop being active. Advisors leave or shift roles. When a structure depends on individuals rather than processes, the departure of a single person can disrupt everything. Continuity requires systems that work even when the people involved change. A structure without stable procedures is always one unexpected resignation away from instability.

Legal and regulatory environments also evolve. Rules change. Reporting obligations expand. Standards for transparency increase. A structure that was fully compliant ten or fifteen years ago may no longer meet today's expectations. Many failures occur simply because no one reviewed the structure after it was created. It remains anchored in a legal context that no longer exists, and the gap between past rules and present requirements becomes a source of exposure.

Emotional decisions create their own form of fragility. Wealthy individuals often remain attached to structures that once served them well: an old company, a familiar advisor, a bank account that feels comfortable. Yet sentiment is not a strategic foundation. When a structure remains in place because of habit rather than purpose, it becomes a liability. What once offered stability can become the weakest point when circumstances change.

Finally, structures fail when they are built with the intention of avoiding visibility rather than withstanding scrutiny. Anything designed to "hide" is vulnerable, not because it is illegal, but because the logic behind it does not hold up when examined. A robust structure does not depend on secrecy. It depends on coherence. When the intention, the documents, and the behavior align, the structure stands firm. When they do not, the structure collapses as soon as someone begins asking questions.

Across all these scenarios, one pattern remains constant: fragility accumulates quietly over time. A structure rarely collapses because of a single event. It collapses because many small issues—ignored obligations, outdated documents, inconsistent behavior—combine at the wrong moment. The structure becomes vulnerable not because it was built poorly, but because it was left untouched.

A structure that is reviewed regularly, updated when your life changes, and kept coherent with your current reality does not fail. It evolves. It adapts. It absorbs pressure because it reflects who you are today, not who you were when it was created. In the end, the difference between a liability and a shield is not the jurisdiction, the form, or the drafting. It is the discipline applied after the structure exists.

Building structures without signaling suspicion

One of the most persistent misunderstandings among wealthy individuals is the idea that a structure becomes suspicious because of its legal form. In reality, banks and regulators do not react to the existence of a trust, a foundation, a holding company, or an SPV. These instruments are common around the world and fully accepted when they make sense. What draws attention is not the vehicle itself, but the way it looks when an institution tries to understand it. A structure becomes problematic when its purpose is unclear, when the documentation does not match its behavior, or when it seems disconnected from your real life. Suspicion is born from uncertainty, not from the structure.

The safest way to avoid unwanted attention is clarity. A structure should be able to stand on its own and "explain itself" without you having to justify it. If a banker or regulator reviews it, they should immediately see why it exists, what function it performs, and why it was created in that particular jurisdiction. This does not require revealing personal strategy. It simply requires internal coherence. A structure that is logical, proportionate, and aligned with your life feels normal to institutions. A structure that looks ornamental or oversized in comparison to your footprint does not.

Substance strengthens this clarity. When a structure has real governance, documented decisions, proper oversight, and an internal rhythm that shows it is alive, institutions interpret it as credible. They do not expect large offices or complex activity, but they do expect a minimum level of reality. Minutes, correspondence, agreements, and simple operational signals show that the structure is functioning as intended. When these elements are present, even a modest structure passes quietly through compliance review. When they are absent, the structure is viewed as unstable or improvised.

Proportionality matters as much as substance. A trust holding a multigenerational estate matches the expectations placed on families with significant assets. A trust created suddenly with disproportionate funding or ambiguous beneficiaries does not. Likewise, a holding company used to centralize investments is predictable. A holding that sits in an unrelated jurisdiction without real ties to your life will raise questions. Institutions look for harmony between the scale of the structure and the scale of your wealth, mobility, and activities. When that harmony exists, the structure appears natural.

Timing also plays an important interpretive role. A structure created just before a change of residency, a divorce, or a major tax event may be technically legal but still read as defensive rather than strategic. Timing creates narrative, and narrative shapes perception. Structures that are built well before sensitive events appear thoughtful and planned. Structures built during or after those events appear reactionary. Institutions trust planning. They distrust improvisation.

Documentation is part of the same logic. A structure does not need complexity, but it needs a traceable history. Agreements should exist. Decisions should be recorded. Changes should be explained. Documentation is not bureaucracy; it is the foundation that allows a structure to withstand examination without relying on your memory or personal explanations. When documents are missing, the institution does not assume wrongdoing – it assumes uncertainty. And institutions dislike uncertainty more than they dislike complexity.

Narrative alignment is another silent filter. A structure should not contradict your residency, your business activity, your mobility pattern, or the public information surrounding your life. If you live in one country, operate in another, and hold entities in a third, the links should be visible through the structure's behavior. When your jurisdictions support each other, institutions accept them. When they clash, even lawful arrangements require explanation—and explanations always carry risk.

For this reason, restraint is often more effective than sophistication. Many people believe that more layers equal more protection. In reality, unnecessary layering creates noise and confusion. Complexity helps only when it reflects genuine needs. When it becomes decorative, it creates suspicion. A structure should make sense without a long explanation. If it does, it survives examination even from someone who knows nothing about you.

In the end, a structure becomes suspicious only when it sits outside the logic of your life. When it aligns with your footprint, your obligations, and your objectives, it becomes part of the background—visible when required, unremarkable when reviewed. The goal is not invisibility. The goal is normality. When your structures look normal for someone with your level of mobility and wealth, they pass through institutional systems without friction.

A structure that explains itself will never force you to explain it. And in a world where explanations can create more risk than transparency, that is one of the strongest forms of protection you can build.

Restructuring vs. Dissolving a structure

At some point in every long-term architecture, a structure simply stops doing what it was meant to do. Your life changes, your assets move, regulations evolve, or the world around you no longer resembles the moment in which the structure was created. The difficulty is not recognizing that something feels outdated—the difficulty is knowing whether the structure should be repaired, redesigned, or allowed to disappear. Many individuals postpone the decision until pressure forces their hand. Others act too quickly, dissolving a structure without understanding the consequences. In practice, the choice between restructuring and dissolving is rarely straightforward, and the wrong move can create far more visibility than the structure ever did on its own.

Restructuring begins with understanding the gap between intention and reality. A trust created for succession may still serve that purpose even if it has fallen dormant; it may only need updated governance, clearer distribution guidelines, or better documentation. A holding company that once controlled a diverse group of assets might remain valuable if its role is redefined to match your current investment pattern. Structures age organically. They collect inconsistencies, outdated contracts, irrelevant clauses, beneficiaries who should no longer be in the picture, and assets whose trajectory separated from the paperwork years ago. Restructuring realigns these elements without breaking continuity.

Continuity is one of the strongest arguments in favor of restructuring. To banks, regulators, and tax authorities, a structure that adapts over time is a sign of planning and discipline. A structure that disappears suddenly, especially one holding significant assets, tends to raise questions even when the dissolution is entirely lawful. Ending a structure often triggers reporting obligations, taxable events, information exchanges, and visibility across multiple jurisdictions. In some systems, dissolution itself is a moment of heightened scrutiny. When you dissolve, you start again from zero—and zero is the point of maximum exposure.

Still, dissolution becomes necessary when the structure is fundamentally flawed. If the vehicle was built on outdated assumptions, weak legal logic, or an economic rationale that no longer survives in the current transparency environment, repairing it may only prolong the problem. A structure that lacks substance, coherence, or a defensible purpose cannot be reinvented into something credible. In those cases, preservation becomes a risk. The right decision is to close it, but only after preparing the terrain so that the closure does not create additional noise.

The real skill lies in determining which option reduces friction. Dissolving a structure that still holds assets may require revealing their value, movements, and beneficiaries at a moment that is not ideal. Restructuring may allow you to transfer the structure—or its purpose—into a more stable legal environment without triggering unnecessary tax consequences or compliance flags. The question is never just legal. It is institutional. How will the bank interpret the change? How will the tax authority read the sequence? How will automated reporting systems connect the dots? These interpretations matter as much as the underlying law.

Timing can amplify or neutralize these interpretations. Dissolving a structure just before a change of residency, or immediately following the sale of a company or the receipt of liquidity, creates patterns that look defensive. Compliance teams do not know your motives—they only see the sequence. When dissolution is necessary, it should occur at a moment when your life pattern is stable and predictable. A structure that disappears far from any pressure point looks routine. A structure that disappears during a major life change looks strategic, and strategic actions attract attention.

Restructuring also demands a clear internal narrative. You cannot simply change a structure because it “feels outdated.” The file must explain the evolution: why the structure was created, how circumstances shifted, and why its design needed to adapt. This narrative is not for courts or newspapers; it is for institutions. Banks and authorities rely on internal files to understand intention. A structure that evolves with documented logic becomes stronger over time. A structure that changes without explanation invites questions when questions are least helpful.

Dissolution should be a quiet endpoint, not a visible beginning. Before a structure is closed, assets must be positioned correctly, beneficiaries aligned, tax exposure measured, and reporting obligations mapped. Dissolving prematurely creates fragmentation, and fragmentation produces contradictions. Contradictions are interpreted as risk.

In the end, the difference between restructuring and dissolving is the difference between evolution and rupture. Evolution preserves continuity. Rupture invites interpretation. Not every structure deserves to survive, but every structure deserves to end cleanly. A well-managed dissolution closes a chapter without creating echoes. A poorly managed one follows you across borders for years.

There is no universal rule–only one guiding question: which option creates the least friction, preserves coherence, and allows institutions to understand your intention without needing to investigate it?

When the answer is clear, the decision becomes simple. When the answer is not clear, the safest choice is the one that maintains coherence. In the world of private structures, coherence is the closest thing to invisibility you will ever achieve.

Operational discipline

Even the strongest structure can collapse if the way it is operated does not match the logic on which it was built. A trust, a foundation, a holding company, or an SPV is only as solid as the discipline that governs its daily functions. Most structures do not fail because of drafting errors; they fail because people forget that legal vehicles are living systems. They require attention, consistency, and a rhythm of maintenance that reflects the reality of the life they protect.

Operational discipline begins with something simple: acting in accordance with the structure you created. If a trust is meant to be independent, the settlor cannot give instructions casually through informal channels. If a company has a board, the board must actually meet. Decisions cannot be implied; they must be recorded. If a foundation represents a philanthropic purpose, the activities must match that purpose in a recognizable way. Institutions evaluate behavior as much as they evaluate documents, and behavior that contradicts the structure tells them that the structure is only formal, not functional.

Documentation plays a major role in this discipline. Minutes, resolutions, correspondence, contracts and reports do not exist to create bureaucracy; they exist to create continuity. When decisions leave no trace, they are easy to reinterpret. When a structure has no internal memory, it appears improvised, and improvisation is the opposite of credibility. Documentation does not need to be complex – it only needs to show intention, sequence, and responsibility. A regulator or bank should be able to understand the evolution of a structure without needing you to explain it verbally.

Another key element is governance. A structure must have people who understand their roles and are able to perform them. Directors, trustees, protectors, council members, or managers cannot simply lend their names to the file. They must be reachable, prepared, and capable of making decisions in a timely and coherent manner. Many structures fail because the individuals appointed years ago have disappeared, retired, or lost contact. A structure without an active decision-maker becomes inert, and an inert structure becomes vulnerable the moment a question arises.

Consistency across jurisdictions is equally important. If a company is registered in one country but all real activity happens elsewhere, there must be a clear and defensible reason. If a director lives in one jurisdiction but decisions are made in another, the file must reflect this structure in a way that makes sense. Modern compliance systems compare patterns: travel, spending, contracts, emails, filings, bank behavior. When jurisdictions do not match, or when economic logic appears weak, institutions investigate. Operational discipline is the art of ensuring that every element points in the same direction.

Financial flows also require discipline. Payments must follow a recognizable pattern. Assets should not move in ways that contradict the stated purpose of the structure. A holding company that distributes irregular amounts without clear rationale appears unstable. A trust that pays personal expenses directly for the settlor can create the impression of control, even if the trust is legally independent. Financial coherence is one of the first things institutions examine because numbers reveal what words often try to conceal.

Digital discipline has become equally central. Communications related to a structure should occur through secure, organized channels. Informal instructions sent through personal messaging apps, shared documents stored in unsecured clouds, or sensitive files exchanged through unprotected devices create invisible weaknesses. Digital environments have jurisdictional implications, evidentiary consequences, and, in some cases, regulatory expectations. Operational discipline today includes digital hygiene.

Finally, operational discipline requires periodic review. A structure created five or ten years ago may no longer reflect your life, the laws of the jurisdictions involved, or the expectations of global compliance systems. Annual or biannual reviews are not a formality—they are a survival mechanism. During review, you examine governance, documents, beneficiaries, asset movements, tax positions, regulatory changes, and any inconsistency that may have accumulated quietly. A structure that is updated regularly becomes stronger over time. A structure that is never reviewed eventually becomes a trap.

The purpose of operational discipline is simple: to ensure that your structures behave exactly as they appear on paper. When the way you operate aligns with the way the structure is designed, institutions interpret it as legitimate. When there is alignment, questions disappear.

When alignment is missing, even a perfectly legal structure becomes difficult to defend.

In the world of private architecture, discipline does not restrict freedom. It preserves it. It is the discipline in the background that allows the rest of your life to move freely in the foreground, without unnecessary friction, and without creating vulnerabilities that could have been avoided with a bit of structure and attention.

Final note

When you operate across borders and your life interacts with multiple legal, financial, and regulatory systems at once, only one foundation remains stable under every form of pressure: *the law.* Not shortcuts, not secrecy, not the hope that institutions will overlook contradictions, but the quiet certainty that your structures can withstand examination because they were built to function, not to hide.

Resilient architectures do not survive because nobody sees them. *They survive because they make sense.* Every element described in this chapter—companies, trusts, foundations, holdings, SPVs, philanthropic vehicles—can protect you or expose you depending on how well it aligns with your real life, your jurisdictions, and your long-term intentions. The decisive factor is not ingenuity. It is legality supported by substance, coherence, and disciplined operation.

The most effective protection a global individual can build is a system that does not rely on explanations. A structure that reflects real activity. Governance that exists in practice, not only on paper. Documentation that shows evolution instead of improvisation. Timing that fits naturally within your life rather than reacting to pressure. When a structure can speak for itself, you are no longer required to defend it.

The world has shifted. Automatic exchange of information has eliminated the shadows in which outdated planning once lived. Compliance departments now operate with tools more sophisticated than many legal systems. Risk algorithms classify people long before a human reviews their file. In this environment, coherence is not an aesthetic preference; it is survival. Only structures built on defensible logic can function without friction. Only those that reflect reality can scale with wealth, mobility, and visibility.

Legality is not the limit of what you can do. It is what gives you the freedom to act without fear. When your architecture respects the rules of every jurisdiction you touch, you move without hesitation. When your governance is consistent, you are not dependent on advisors or intermediaries whose errors could compromise you. When your structure is aligned with your presence, institutions process your file smoothly instead of interpreting it.

Power built outside the law collapses the moment it is tested. Power built within the law becomes stable, not because it is hidden but because it is structurally sound. In a world where visibility is unavoidable, the only sustainable form of protection is one that can endure visibility.

If this chapter leaves you with one idea, it is this: *a structure is only as strong as the legal, economic, and operational reality beneath it.*

For someone who lives globally, the law is not a constraint. It is the shield that allows you to maintain continuity, independence, and sovereignty in a world that never stops examining the decisions you make.

Chapter X. Surveillance, private intelligence & counter-surveillance

Institutional & regulatory surveillance

How authorities monitor individuals of interest

Most high-net-worth individuals imagine surveillance as something only existing in movies with spies, something exceptional, triggered only when a government has a specific reason to investigate them. The reality is far more mundane and far more systematic. Modern institutional surveillance is not aimed at discovering wrongdoing; it is designed to verify coherence. Authorities monitor not because they are suspicious, but because the international regulatory landscape requires them to understand who you are, where you exist legally, and how your structures interact with the financial system. This form of surveillance is predictable, rule-based, and largely automated. It is also unavoidable for anyone whose life spans multiple jurisdictions.

The first layer of this monitoring comes from tax authorities through automatic information exchange. Under CRS and FATCA, financial institutions across the world report account balances, income, and identifying information to the jurisdictions that claim you as tax resident or taxpayer. This exchange does not require suspicion and does not wait for a legal trigger. It happens every year by default. The goal is to ensure that your declared residency aligns with the financial activity visible in the global data network. When the pattern is coherent, the system moves on. When the pattern contradicts itself, authorities examine it more closely.

A parallel layer operates through domestic audits and compliance reviews. These processes vary by country, but the logic is consistent. Authorities verify day-count rules, economic ties, center-of-life criteria, and the presence or absence of declarations that should accompany your level of wealth or activity. For most individuals, these checks are administrative. For HNWIs, they can be comprehensive. Jurisdictions with aggressive enforcement scrutinize lifestyles, spending patterns, ownership structures, and cross-border movements to ensure that claims of residency or non-residency are consistent with observable behavior. The scrutiny is not personal; it is structural.

Banking institutions add another dimension. Banks are legally obligated to classify every client under risk-based frameworks, and the classification is dynamic. It changes when your residency changes, when your income sources shift, when your corporate structures evolve, or when global regulatory rules tighten. Banks monitor inflows, outflows, concentration of funds, beneficial ownership, and transaction patterns. They compare your profile with the expectations that arise from your declared economic life. Any inconsistency, however benign, triggers enhanced due diligence. This does not mean the bank believes you are doing something wrong. It means that the internal system cannot yet reconcile the information it has.

Regulators also monitor through licensing bodies, corporate registries, and financial-market compliance networks. These systems do not target individuals; they monitor the ecosystem. If a company you control becomes subject to review, if a manager you rely on faces sanctions, or if a jurisdiction where you hold assets undergoes regulatory tightening, you appear on the institutional radar without ever being directly involved. Modern compliance frameworks are interconnected. An inquiry in one country automatically notifies another. A clarification requested by one institution may be mirrored by others weeks later.

Even border agencies participate in this landscape, though not through deliberate targeting. Travel patterns, entry stamps, immigration filings, and visa applications all contribute to how your residency is understood. When the recorded movement aligns with your narrative, the system interprets your presence as stable and legitimate. When it does not, inconsistencies accumulate silently until an authority decides to clarify the situation. Most HNWIs only discover the importance of travel records when a dispute arises over tax residency or center-of-life tests.

None of this resembles the cinematic version of surveillance. It does not involve agents, covert operations, or targeted monitoring. It is a network of automated systems, compliance obligations, and legal frameworks that intersect whenever your profile crosses borders. The more jurisdictions you touch, the more frequently these systems interact. And the more public your economic footprint becomes, the more important it is that the information flowing through these networks presents a coherent picture.

Institutional surveillance is not your enemy. It is the structure within which your global life must operate. When you understand how it works, its rhythm, its logic, its triggers, you stop fearing it and begin designing your life so that institutions interpret you accurately. Clarity protects you better than invisibility, and coherence shields you more effectively than silence. The goal is not to avoid being seen. It is to ensure that what is seen makes sense.

How individuals of interest are monitored by third-party ecosystems

Beyond governments and financial institutions, a second layer of surveillance operates quietly through the private sector. This ecosystem is not coordinated, ideological, or conspiratorial. It is simply large, fragmented, and commercially motivated. Yet its combined effect creates a form of indirect monitoring that shapes how you are perceived long before any authority takes interest. For high-net-worth individuals, this is often the most underestimated dimension of exposure.

The first component is the private-sector compliance industry. Banks, law firms, accounting firms, fiduciaries, corporate service providers, insurance companies, and luxury-asset intermediaries all maintain internal risk models. These models evaluate you not because they are suspicious, but because they are required to protect themselves. When you interact with them, by opening an account, forming an entity, buying real estate, acquiring a yacht, participating in a fund, or even making a large purchase, they classify your profile, assign you a risk level, and sometimes share this classification with external systems or counterparties. These evaluations accumulate silently across institutions. None of them are malicious, but together they create a shadow profile of who you appear to be.

Another component is commercial data aggregation. Marketing companies, analytics platforms, travel services, telecommunications providers, loyalty systems, and digital ecosystems routinely store information about your movements, spending patterns, habits, devices, and preferences. They are not tracking you personally; they are tracking everyone. But because wealth increases activity across multiple platforms, your data footprint becomes unusually dense. When aggregated, this density produces patterns that reveal more than you expect: where you typically are, where you rarely are, what you spend on, what you avoid, what your lifestyle communicates, and how your digital identity evolves over time. In isolation, each dataset is harmless. Combined, they form a detailed portrait.

A third component emerges from OSINT practitioners and commercial intelligence services. These actors operate legally, using public records, corporate filings, leaked registries, court databases, media archives, social networks, aviation and maritime trackers, property registries, and even public procurement documents. Their objective is not surveillance; it is research. Yet the information they assemble can become part of due-diligence reports, journalistic investigations, litigation strategies, or competitive intelligence assessments. HNWIs often underestimate how much of their life is traceable not through secrecy breaches, but through publicly accessible sources that no one ever intended to be private.

Service providers with access to your logistical life also play a role. Travel agents, private jet brokers, yacht crews, real estate managers, art advisors, and high-end suppliers all see fragments of your life. None of them function as surveillance actors, yet their operational knowledge can become valuable to third parties when leaked, disclosed, hacked, or casually mentioned in the wrong environment. High-trust professions such as personal assistants, chauffeurs, and estate managers hold even more sensitive knowledge. Their exposure is rarely intentional, but mistakes, gossip, and external pressure all contribute to vulnerabilities that sophisticated actors can exploit.

The final layer of this ecosystem consists of digital platforms whose algorithms monitor everything by design. Search engines log your queries. Cloud services store your documents. Messaging platforms retain metadata even when content is encrypted. Social networks record interactions, proximity patterns, and behavioral signatures. These systems do not target HNWIs specifically, but wealth often amplifies the amount of digital territory a person occupies, and with it, the amount of metadata that becomes available to entities with access, whether commercial, institutional, or adversarial.

None of these third-party actors intend to monitor you. They are simply doing their jobs, running their systems, and protecting their own liabilities. But because each sees a small piece of your life, and because many of these pieces are stored, processed, and sometimes cross-referenced, the combined effect is a form of continuous observation. It is diffuse rather than targeted, structural rather than personal, and unavoidable for anyone living a global, high-mobility, high-value life.

Understanding this ecosystem is not about paranoia. It is about realism. When you recognize that surveillance today is the sum of ordinary processes functioning exactly as designed, you stop fearing hidden enemies and begin focusing on what you can control: reducing unnecessary visibility, preventing accidental contradictions, managing who sees which fragment of your life, and building an architecture that remains coherent even when interpreted through systems you do not directly influence.

When you master this, third-party ecosystems stop being a threat and become an environment you can navigate with precision.

Detecting profiling, mapping, or pre-attack curiosity

Targeted attacks almost never begin with an attack. They begin with curiosity. Someone, somewhere, starts looking, discreetly at first, then more persistently, until the pattern becomes visible to those who know how to read it. For most high-net-worth individuals, the real danger is not that someone is watching, but that they notice it only after the observation has already escalated.

Profiling usually starts with information gathering that seems harmless. A journalist reviews corporate filings. A competitor searches public registries. A lawyer representing an adversarial party requests historical documents. A family member in conflict starts collecting emails, messages, or financial statements. A regulator quietly updates your file after receiving an automated cross-border report. None of these signals are hostile in isolation. What makes them meaningful is repetition.

Mapping goes a step further. It appears when someone begins to trace connections: between your entities, your advisors, your assets, your relationships, or your movements. You may notice this through unusual questions from institutions that previously required nothing, or through third parties who suddenly show interest in your governance, your holdings, or your residency status. Sometimes it appears through indirect channels, people asking about staff members, attempting to verify your presence in a location, or contacting service providers to confirm innocuous details. Mapping is systematic by nature. It seeks not information, but structure.

Pre-attack curiosity is the most dangerous phase because it usually feels benign. Someone submits a request "just to confirm a detail."

Someone asks about a transaction "as part of routine review." A regulatory authority requests documents that should already be on file. A business partner asks questions that seem slightly outside the scope of your relationship. A bank reevaluates your profile, citing internal policy updates. These events are easy to dismiss individually, but together they form a line of inquiry aimed at understanding how you are positioned, what can be exploited, and where pressure would be most effective.

In some cases, the first visible sign is institutional hesitation. A bank delays a transfer that should take hours. A notary asks for additional proof of substance. An immigration authority extends a review period without explanation. These are early indicators that someone, somewhere, is examining pieces of your life more closely than before. Institutions rarely reveal the origin of this scrutiny, but their behavior reflects it.

A more subtle sign appears when people around you, staff, advisors, intermediaries, begin receiving questions instead of you directly. Attackers, journalists, and litigants know that high-net-worth individuals are often shielded. They approach those with easier access: assistants, accountants, managers, brokers, or even friends. The moment someone begins asking about your schedule, your activities, or your structures, the inquiry has already expanded beyond casual curiosity.

Digital signals also reveal pre-attack behavior. Sudden spikes in searches of your name, unusual patterns of social media activity around your profile, new accounts monitoring your online presence, or unexpected attempts to access old email addresses or forgotten accounts, all of these indicate that someone is trying to piece together a narrative or locate a vulnerability. This often coincides with automated systems flagging you due to new visibility, a legal event, or a change in jurisdiction.

The key is not to panic but to interpret. Curiosity becomes profiling when it repeats. Profiling becomes mapping when it becomes structured. Mapping becomes pre-attack behavior when it focuses on your weak points: inconsistencies, unprotected assets, dormant entities, exposed relationships, or recent life transitions. By the time an attack becomes public, it has already passed through each of these phases quietly.

For this reason, the most effective form of protection is awareness. You must know when attention around you shifts, even when the shift seems minor. Most crises can be mitigated, or prevented entirely, when detected at this stage. What appears as a distant echo is often the first signal that someone intends to step closer. And once you learn to detect curiosity before it matures into threat, you regain control over the timeline, the narrative, and the outcome.

Due diligence triggers & false flags

Most high-net-worth individuals believe that due diligence is something that happens only when they request a service: opening an account, forming a structure, applying for residency, completing a transaction. In reality, due diligence operates constantly and often silently. Institutions reassess you not only when you initiate contact, but whenever your profile changes, whenever regulations shift, or whenever external signals cause your name to enter a different risk category.

Triggers appear for many reasons, and most of them have nothing to do with wrongdoing. An unusual inflow, a transfer from a new jurisdiction, a change of residency, a company restructuring, or even a newspaper mention can activate internal reviews. These reviews are often automated. A bank's algorithm may flag a transaction because it resembles a pattern associated with risk, even if your situation is entirely lawful. A compliance officer may request additional documents simply because your file has not been updated in several years. A tax authority may cross-check your declared residency after receiving foreign data automatically under CRS.

The mistake many individuals make is assuming that due diligence is a punishment. It is not. It is a mechanism institutions use to protect themselves. If they request more documents, it is because they need to reconcile information, not because they suspect you personally. Understanding this saves you from unnecessary stress and helps you respond in a way that restores institutional confidence.

False flags are situations where the system interprets a signal as risk when it is actually the result of ordinary life. A sudden movement of funds may be flagged even if the transfer represents a simple restructuring. A company registered in a jurisdiction known for tax incentives may appear suspicious even when the structure meets every legal and substance requirement. A rapid change of address may resemble relocation for tax avoidance even when it is driven by family or business necessity.

False flags also arise when your life shifts faster than your documentation. If your travel patterns change, if you spend extended time in a jurisdiction without updating your formal records, or if you maintain accounts in places that no longer match your economic activity, institutions struggle to understand your profile. The system does not interpret context; it interprets patterns. And patterns without explanation become risk signals.

Some false flags are generated by external actors rather than institutions. A partner in conflict may hint at irregularities. A disgruntled employee may exaggerate facts. A journalist may frame a narrative in a way that makes your structures appear aggressive or opaque. Even a minor lawsuit can create echoes in financial and regulatory systems, triggering reviews long before the case reaches any meaningful stage. These situations are not caused by your behavior but by how your behavior looks from a distance.

The safest response is clarity, not overexposure. Institutions do not need your entire story, they need enough coherence to close the review. When your documentation is consistent, when your structures are lawful and aligned with your presence, and when your narrative matches the facts, due diligence becomes a formality.

The danger lies not in the trigger but in the reaction. If you respond defensively, inconsistently, or with unnecessary detail, institutions may interpret the noise as an attempt to conceal something. If you ignore the request, the review escalates. If you panic and restructure too quickly, you create new anomalies. Most damage arises not from the trigger itself but from the mismanagement of the moment.

The goal is not to avoid due diligence, you cannot. The goal is to ensure that when the system looks at your life, the picture is so consistent and legally grounded that the review ends as quickly as it began. A well-designed architecture transforms due diligence from a threat into an administrative routine. And in the modern environment, that transformation is one of the most powerful forms of protection you can build.

Building a private intelligence perimeter

A high-net-worth individual is never protected by isolation. They are protected by awareness. Protection does not come from locking yourself away from the world, but from understanding how information flows around you, how people interpret your movements, and how institutions form conclusions before you ever speak to them. That awareness is the essence of a private intelligence perimeter: a discreet, continuous system that allows you to anticipate risks long before they crystallize, and to detect curiosity before it becomes action.

A private intelligence perimeter is not surveillance. It is the disciplined habit of knowing what the world can see, what others can infer, and how your decisions create ripples that travel across borders, institutions, and relationships. It begins with the basics, understanding how your name appears in public registries, how your companies are reported across jurisdictions, how your digital footprint behaves over time, and how your associations shape the narrative surrounding you. Most HNWIs are surprised to discover that the system remembers far more than they do, and that fragments of information they forgot years ago continue to circulate quietly in the background.

This perimeter also includes awareness of the actors who map you. Banks monitor your activity to remain compliant. Immigration systems cross-check your movements. Journalists, researchers, and adversaries collect fragments that may seem insignificant individually but revealing when assembled. Even well-intentioned individuals around you, partners, employees, advisors, family, may unintentionally publish details that expose patterns you never meant to reveal. A private intelligence perimeter exists to notice these ripples before they become currents.

The perimeter extends inward as well: understanding who has access to what, where information travels without your explicit consent, and how your own routines create predictability. Assistants who handle travel arrangements, advisors who communicate across platforms, service providers who maintain your properties, staff members with partial access to your schedule, all of them generate signals that can be observed from the outside. This is not a matter of distrust; it is a matter of structure. Access must exist, but it must exist with control, and control requires visibility.

A well-designed private intelligence perimeter is quiet. It does not provoke or escalate. It does not try to monitor the entire world. Instead, it observes the areas where your profile, your structures, or your movements intersect with systems that classify, record, or analyze you. Those intersections are where risk begins. The perimeter helps you see shifts in tone from institutions, patterns in information requests, changes in how a bank communicates, or signs that someone has begun assembling a picture of your life without your knowledge. These signals are subtle, and you notice them only when you are trained to look for them.

The perimeter also requires regular audits, not only of structures but of narrative. What do search engines associate with your name today? Which public records have been updated? What corporate filings reveal more than they should? Which jurisdictions now publish information that used to remain obscured? What documents appear in online archives after a legal proceeding or a routine administrative task? What stories circulate in environments that rarely reach you directly? Without periodic review, the perimeter becomes porous, and you become discoverable in ways that you never intended.

None of this implies paranoia; it implies preparedness. A private intelligence perimeter does not turn you into an investigator. It turns you into someone who cannot be surprised. It transforms exposure from a sudden event into something you can detect early, manage calmly, and neutralize with precision. It ensures that curiosity, whether from institutions, journalists, partners, or opportunistic actors, never reaches you directly, because you see it before it crosses the threshold.

The goal is simple: to know what others can see, to understand how they interpret it, and to shape your life so that no misunderstanding, no fragment, and no isolated detail can be used against you. When your perimeter works, you do not need to fight threats. You simply prevent them from forming.

Operational security for travel, staff & advisors

High-net-worth individuals do not move alone. Even when they travel quietly, speak cautiously, or maintain a limited digital presence, their life generates signals through the people who surround them. Travel patterns, staff routines, advisor communications, and service interactions all form part of a broader ecosystem that reveals more about a person than any direct disclosure. Operational security is not about restricting this ecosystem, but about designing it so that it cannot be weaponized through oversight, carelessness, or simple misalignment.

Travel is one of the most revealing aspects of a global life. Flight bookings generate data trails long before you board a plane. Hotels collect identification, preferences, and payment information. Immigration systems record entry and exit logs with precision. Ride-hailing services track routes, habits, and companions. Even the rhythm of your movements becomes a pattern: the cities you frequent, the seasons you prefer, the intervals between each trip. None of this is secret; it exists as part of the normal functioning of international life. The risk appears when these patterns contradict your declared residency, tax position, or professional footprint. Institutions scrutinize contradictions, not travel itself. Operational security begins by ensuring that your movements reflect the life you claim to lead, and that every trip, short or long, fits a larger logic that institutions can quickly understand.

Staff amplify your footprint even more. Assistants handle reservations, communicate with intermediaries, and store copies of your documents. Household employees manage access to your properties. Drivers, security personnel, and service providers see your routines with a level of detail that no institution could access directly. None of this is problematic when managed correctly; the problem arises when access exists without structure. Staff must know what belongs within their role and what does not. They must understand which communications require formality, which details should never be shared, and which aspects of your life must remain unconnected to daily operations. The goal is not secrecy; it is clarity. When staff know what they can handle and what must be escalated, they stop generating accidental exposure.

Advisors pose a different type of risk. Lawyers, accountants, bankers, and consultants operate under confidentiality obligations, but they also communicate across jurisdictions, using emails, messaging platforms, and cloud systems that store data far beyond their control. Advisors often work with fragments of information and may attempt to solve problems without full visibility, inadvertently generating inconsistencies that institutions later detect. The challenge is not competence but coordination. Your advisors must operate from the same narrative, supported by documents that are consistent across borders. When one advisor acts without understanding the implications for another jurisdiction, they create openings that the system interprets as red flags. Operational security demands that information moves through a single, coherent architecture, not through parallel channels that contradict one another.

You cannot eliminate data trails created through travel or professional networks; they are part of a functional global life. What you can eliminate is noise. Noise is created by unstructured communication, by informal decisions made in a hurry, by staff acting on assumptions, or by advisors working in isolation. Noise attracts attention because it creates irregularities, and irregularities provoke questions. Operational security removes noise by ensuring that every movement, every booking, every communication, and every delegation can withstand the scrutiny of someone who does not know you personally, but who must interpret your actions through rules.

The heart of operational security is rhythm. Your life must follow a rhythm that reflects your true priorities, not a rhythm shaped by improvisation. If you move frequently, the pattern must match your declared profile. If you maintain multiple homes, the time spent in each must be documented with accuracy. If your staff handle sensitive tasks, their access must be proportional to their role and their tools must be appropriate for the level of exposure you carry. If your advisors collaborate across borders, their communications must preserve coherence rather than fragment it.

A well-designed operational system allows you to remain mobile, visible where necessary, and understated where appropriate. It lets you travel with confidence because your movements follow logic. It allows your staff to support you without creating vulnerability. It guides your advisors so that every action reinforces your architecture instead of undermining it. The goal is not to hide or to restrict your life. The goal is to ensure that everything around you functions with precision, so that no mistake, no assumption, and no fragment of routine becomes the doorway through which exposure begins.

Information leakage & structural weak points

Information rarely escapes through dramatic breaches. It escapes through routine. The greatest leaks in a high-net-worth life do not come from hackers, investigators, or adversaries. They come from the small, predictable openings built into everyday systems: poorly handled documents, unmonitored intermediaries, unstructured communication, repeated habits, or mismatched disclosures across jurisdictions. Exposure begins slowly, and almost always from within.

Every life produces information automatically. Hotels store your preferences. Airlines record your travel patterns. Banks log your transfers with precision. Digital platforms collect metadata that says more about your movements than the content of your messages. Advisors keep drafts, notes, and correspondence that live on servers in different countries.

Even your calendar, stored on a cloud system, becomes a source of insights into your priorities, relationships, and timing. None of this is dangerous on its own. It becomes dangerous when multiple fragments align to reveal a picture you did not intend to share.

Weak points appear whenever information is handled without structure. A document forwarded "just this once" to a personal email account. A copy of a passport stored on a device that syncs across uncontrolled platforms. A sensitive conversation held over an unsecured app because it was convenient. Staff using their own phones for work errands. Advisors sending files through channels that create versions you cannot track or retract. Information leakage is rarely malicious; it is procedural. And procedural weakness is predictable.

Another form of leakage emerges through what institutions observe indirectly. When your lifestyle contradicts your declared profile, the data generated by your own habits becomes a signal. If your official residence suggests a modest footprint but your travel patterns show constant presence elsewhere, the system notices. If your declared income does not align with the assets you acquire or the properties you maintain, institutions begin reconciling the gap. If your communication history shows commitments or timelines that diverge from your documented decisions, inconsistencies accumulate. These are not accusations. They are interpretations produced by automated systems trained to detect anomalies.

A more subtle weak point comes from the people around you. Staff who are loyal but unaware of the importance of discretion. Advisors who share information casually with third parties because they believe it accelerates a task. Service providers who treat your profile as a case study.

None of this is malicious, yet each interaction leaves traces that someone else may access or aggregate. Information moves quickly through hands, devices, jurisdictions, and platforms. Without clear protocols, even the most trusted environment becomes porous.

The most dangerous leaks occur when fragments connect. A single detail rarely exposes you. But a pattern of small details, travel dates, property registrations, corporate filings, media mentions, bank movements, or personal routines, can be stitched together by institutions or third parties to form a storyline you did not authorize. Modern compliance systems are built to detect these connections automatically. What feels like a private life is, in reality, a network of small, publicly and semi-publicly accessible signals that gain meaning only when combined.

The solution is not to erase information. Erasure is neither realistic nor legal. The solution is to control the flow: who sees what, when, and why. You must treat every piece of information as something that will eventually exist on a server, in a database, or within an institutional file. If the piece is harmless on its own but dangerous when combined with others, limit its spread. If the information belongs to one jurisdiction but not to another, keep it geographically contained. If a document can be replaced by a summary, do so. If a communication can be formalized instead of improvised, formalize it.

Operational cleanliness is the antidote to leakage. Not secrecy, not silence, cleanliness. Clean information flows are consistent with your legal profile. Clean documentation matches your declared positions across jurisdictions. Clean communication reduces ambiguity. Clean patterns leave no contradictions for institutions to reconcile. When your systems are clean, leakage loses its power. The fragments may still circulate, but they no longer form a story that can be misinterpreted.

Information leakage is not a failure of privacy. It is a failure of design. Once your architecture is clear and intentional, the risk diminishes without needing to hide. What you protect is not the existence of information, but the coherence of the narrative it forms. When the narrative is consistent, even leaks have nothing damaging to reveal.

Pattern erasure: reducing predictability without raising flags

There is a common misconception among high-net-worth individuals that the only way to protect their privacy is to disappear from view. In reality, disappearing creates more suspicion than presence ever did. Institutions, algorithms, and even private-sector actors react more aggressively to absence than to movement. What protects you is not opacity, but unpredictability, carefully designed, legally coherent unpredictability that prevents others from mapping your life without making you look evasive.

Pattern erasure begins with recognizing how predictable most global lives actually are. People tend to travel at the same times of year, stay in the same properties, use the same advisors, follow the same professional rhythms, and maintain routines that barely change over time. These patterns become visible not only to institutions, but to commercial systems, digital platforms, and anyone who chooses to observe closely. Predictability is exposure. When your movements can be anticipated, your vulnerabilities can be planned around.

Reducing predictability does not mean introducing chaos. It means removing the kind of repetition that allows third parties to build a narrative around your life. If you always travel on the same weeks every year, change the timing. If you stay in the same city for the same duration every quarter, vary it slightly. If you always use the same entry point into a country, alternate between airports, routes, or even airlines. These are not acts of concealment; they are signals of normal global mobility. What institutions interpret as risk is not change, it is inconsistency. As long as your movements align with your declared residency, tax position, and professional obligations, variation strengthens your profile instead of weakening it.

The same principle applies to digital habits. If you always log in from the same devices, networks, or locations, the pattern becomes a signature. When that signature changes suddenly, systems react with caution. But when variation is part of your natural behavior, the system reads the change as normal rather than anomalous. This applies to cloud backups, messaging patterns, platform usage, and digital presence. Predictability creates a digital silhouette. A silhouette can be targeted. A flexible pattern cannot.

Financial behavior follows the same logic. Regular, mechanical transfers between the same accounts, at the same times, for the same amounts, create a profile that institutions can chart with precision. When your financial life follows the rhythm of your real economic activity rather than automatic repetition, institutions interpret the pattern as organic and low-risk. Pattern erasure does not require eliminating structure; it requires replacing artificial patterns with real ones.

Social exposure must be understood the same way. If you appear in the same circles, events, or public contexts on a predictable schedule, adversaries can anticipate your presence. When your public visibility emerges only when it serves a purpose, and not as a recurring habit, you regain control over how the outside world maps your influence, your environment, and your alliances. Reducing predictability is not about hiding your life; it is about preventing others from scripting it for you.

The goal of pattern erasure is to ensure that no single observer, whether institutional, commercial, adversarial, or opportunistic, can draw straight lines between your movements, your financial flows, your digital behavior, and your structural decisions. When these lines cannot be drawn, you cease being predictable. When you cease being predictable, you cease being easy to target.

Pattern erasure is not an act of paranoia. It is an act of narrative control. You are not erasing yourself, you are erasing the assumptions that others could make about you. You remain visible where you choose, accessible where necessary, and consistent where the law requires. But you stop being a diagram that others can trace. Your life becomes fluid, coherent, and strategically un-patterned, exactly the kind of presence that protects you without provoking scrutiny.

When unpredictability becomes a natural part of how you live, institutions read you as stable, legitimate, and low-risk. And those who might wish to map your life discover that the lines stop before they form a picture.

Final note

In a world where surveillance is structural, data flows freely across borders, and institutions interpret your life long before they ever meet you, the strongest form of protection is not invisibility. It is legality. Nothing shields a high-net-worth individual more effectively than a life that aligns with the law, speaks the language of compliance, and presents a narrative that institutions can understand without hesitation.

The temptation to hide, obscure, or outmaneuver systems is always strongest when one feels exposed. Yet every attempt to escape visibility creates more of it. Complexity without purpose becomes noise. Silence becomes a signal. Avoidance becomes a pattern that systems are designed to detect. The modern world does not punish wealth. It punishes contradiction. And the only reliable antidote to contradiction is a legal framework that supports every movement, every structure, every decision, and every layer of your international life.

Legality is not the opposite of privacy. It is the foundation that allows privacy to exist without arousing suspicion. When your residency is defensible, when your companies have substance, when your travel aligns with your declared status, when your financial flows match your economic footprint, and when your advisors can articulate your position without improvisation, you become unassailable not because you are hidden, but because you are coherent.

The legality principle is simple: a global life must be designed so that it functions smoothly under examination. Not because you expect to be examined, but because scrutiny today is a normal part of international existence. When authorities request documents, you can provide them. When banks ask questions, the answers already exist. When your structures are reviewed, they pass because they were built to withstand review. There is no performance, no panic, no rush to rewrite the past. Your life is already aligned with the rules.

This is the deep protection that most people misunderstand. Illegality makes you vulnerable. Opacity makes you visible. But coherence, legality, and well-designed substance make you disappear, not by erasing you, but by removing any reason for the system to focus on you. You become the client institutions trust, the resident whose profile makes sense, the investor whose structures are predictable, the individual whose life can be processed without escalation.

When your architecture is clean, you do not fear surveillance. You outgrow it. Institutions see exactly what they expect to see: a person whose decisions follow a rational, lawful, and stable logic. Everything else becomes irrelevant.

In the end, protection is not built through secrecy or sophistication. It is built through the quiet confidence that comes from living inside a structure that does not break under pressure. Legality is not a constraint. It is the infrastructure that allows you to move freely, think clearly, and maintain control over your life in a world that constantly observes.

A coherent life is a protected life. A lawful life is a sovereign one.

Chapter XI. Adjacency risks: lifestyle, assets & symbolic exposure

Why adjacency risks matter more than direct threats

Most high-net-worth individuals assume that the greatest threats to their privacy, security, and continuity come from direct attacks: an investigation, a lawsuit, a leak, a hostile actor. In reality, direct attacks are rare. The true danger comes from everything that surrounds you, your lifestyle, your assets, your habits, your staff, your movements, your preferences, and even the environments in which you spend time. These are the adjacency risks: the signals you do not intend to send, but that the world interprets with precision.

The modern system does not need access to your private documents to understand who you are. It reads your life through patterns. A watch you wear publicly reveals part of your wealth profile. A property you purchase exposes where you spend your time. A yacht or a jet discloses your mobility rhythms. A single social event links you to people whose public risk profile may be higher than yours. Even silence becomes a signal when the rest of your environment is loud enough.

Adjacency risks operate quietly. They do not create noise, they create clarity. Institutions, service providers, journalists, and adversaries often learn more from what surrounds you than from anything you consciously protect. When they cannot access your structures, they observe your behavior. When they cannot read your documents, they study your environment. When they cannot see your finances, they look at what you own, how you move, and who moves with you.

Lifestyle becomes a dataset. Properties become coordinates. Staff become sources of insight. Digital presence becomes a map. Mobility becomes a signature. Social proximity becomes an indirect measure of influence, vulnerability, or conflict. None of these elements are problematic on their own. They become problematic only when they combine to create a picture you did not intend to reveal.

For HNWIs, adjacency risks matter more because they are easier to access. Court filings may be sealed, but real estate registries are not. Corporate structures may be complex, but flight trackers are public. Wealth may be discreet, but a single photograph online, posted by someone else, can reveal locations, assets, companions, or routines. Even your absence from public records can raise questions when your lifestyle suggests otherwise.

The paradox is that the more disciplined and private a person believes themselves to be, the more exposed their environment often becomes. A highly protected individual with inconsistent lifestyle signals attracts far more attention than someone moderately visible but structurally coherent. Institutions do not need a confession to form an opinion; they rely on indicators. And in a global, hyper-connected world, indicators are everywhere.

This chapter examines how these adjacency risks emerge, how they shape institutional interpretation, and how a high-net-worth life can remain stable without retreating into paranoia or austerity. The goal is not to eliminate lifestyle, assets, or mobility, but to understand how they speak on your behalf long before you ever say a word. When you control these signals, you regain the ability to shape how the world sees you, and more importantly, how the world reacts to you.

Social media, digital presence & algorithmic exposure

In the past, privacy was something a person could choose. Today, it is something a system decides. Social platforms, search engines, recommendation algorithms, and behavioral-analysis tools capture more about a high-net-worth individual than any investigator could have collected twenty years ago. This happens even when you never post a single photo, even when you believe you live quietly, and even when you go out of your way to remain discreet. Your digital presence is no longer defined by what you publish, but by what the system infers from the traces you leave behind.

For HNWIs, the exposure does not come from intentional visibility. It comes from the ecosystem around them. Family members share moments that reveal patterns. Friends post group photos that disclose your locations, companions, or movements. Staff capture background details, art, properties, aircraft interiors, that can be cross-referenced with public sources. Even strangers who appear briefly in your orbit generate digital evidence simply by posting their own content. The system does not need your cooperation to assemble the puzzle. It only needs fragments, and fragments are everywhere.

Platforms do far more than store images or messages. They analyze relationships, interpret proximity, and identify behavioral trends. When a person appears repeatedly in the digital circle of another, algorithms assume a connection and begin suggesting content that strengthens that association. If your presence overlaps with certain environments, the system categorizes you accordingly. A single tagged location is enough for travel platforms to adjust their predictions about your mobility patterns. A single image can help facial-recognition models refine their assumptions about your appearance across different contexts. The digital world does not ask permission to interpret you; it simply observes and concludes.

The danger increases when lifestyle intersects with algorithmic logic. A luxury purchase becomes an advertising signal. A travel pattern becomes a consumption profile. A search query creates commercial assumptions that ripple across platforms. Wealth amplifies these echoes because it multiplies interactions: more services, more transactions, more devices, more environments, more intermediaries. Each of them produces data, and each dataset becomes a lens through which the digital system interprets your life, even when you remain entirely silent.

Many individuals attempt to protect themselves by staying offline, but absence is not invisibility. A profile with little activity is still analyzed: who searches for you, who tags you, which networks mention you, which platforms associate your name with certain topics or industries. Silence becomes its own form of exposure when everything around you speaks loudly. Moreover, when a person of means has almost no digital footprint, institutions often interpret the absence as intentional opacity rather than discretion. Algorithms treat it as an anomaly and flag the profile for manual review. In this sense, over-protection can create the very attention one hopes to avoid.

The most overlooked source of exposure is the passive trail generated by everyday tools. Cloud backups store photos with embedded coordinates. Messaging platforms retain metadata even when messages are deleted. Shared calendars reveal meetings and rhythms. Voice assistants capture ambient audio that becomes training data. Apps track location to optimize services, unaware that the information may later be accessed through legal requests, commercial apis, or security breaches. None of this activity seems significant when viewed individually. Together, it forms a detailed, involuntary biography.

Managing digital exposure is not about avoiding technology. It is about understanding how it interprets you and designing your presence so that what exists online remains coherent, limited, and predictable. You cannot control how people behave on social media, but you can control what they can reveal unintentionally. You can define boundaries for staff, clarify expectations for family, and create structures for how travel, events, and assets appear in the digital world. You can also shape your own footprint by ensuring that what exists about you reflects the life you are prepared to defend under institutional scrutiny.

At its core, algorithmic exposure is not malicious. It is mechanical. Systems respond to patterns, not intentions. They do not distinguish between a billionaire, a politician, or a private individual. They categorize based on signals, and signals are everywhere. The challenge is not to silence them entirely. It is to ensure that the signals you emit, voluntarily or involuntarily, do not create stories you never meant to tell.

When you understand this, social media stops being a threat and becomes a landscape you navigate with awareness. And when you navigate it with awareness, you no longer fear what the system can reveal, because you have already shaped what the system can see.

Risks hidden in luxury assets

Luxury assets are never just objects. They are statements, data points, coordinates, and often inadvertent disclosures of wealth architecture. Whether it is a piece of art, a vintage car, a yacht, a jet, or a rare collectible, every high-value asset introduces a new surface of exposure, not because of its price, but because of the ecosystem required to acquire, maintain, insure, move, or display it.

The risk does not come from the asset itself. It comes from the visibility that surrounds it.

A luxury asset creates a trail long before it is in your possession. Auction houses record bidding histories. Galleries maintain detailed client files. Insurers analyze background, liquidity, provenance, and storage. Transportation companies log routes, conditions, and delivery schedules. Ports, customs offices, and registries generate documentation for items that cross borders. Even the private databases of art dealers, jewelers, and brokers become part of a network of signals that reveal far more than the transaction you intended to make.

The moment an asset enters your life, the circle expands. Staff interact with it. Advisors register or insure it. Appraisers document it. Maintenance teams gain access to locations, routines, and security systems. Art handlers know the layout of private residences. Yacht crews understand your habits at sea. Jet operators know your flight schedule and the individuals who travel with you. Every luxury asset, no matter how discreet, becomes a point of contact between your private world and a constellation of people, institutions, and systems that do not belong to your inner circle.

The financial visibility of a luxury asset is often greater than the owner realizes. Banks track large purchases as part of their risk-based review obligations. Insurance records can reveal the scale of your holdings. Customs documentation exposes cross-border movement of valuables. Import declarations, export permits, conservation reports, and restoration histories are stored in systems far outside your control. These datasets do not need to be public to create exposure; they simply need to exist in environments where they can be accessed, analyzed, or shared under regulatory pressure.

For individuals with complex personal or corporate structures, the ownership path of a luxury asset can inadvertently reveal the architecture behind it. A painting purchased through a holding company may appear in a registry under the entity's name. A yacht registered in one jurisdiction but crewed through another may expose substance inconsistencies. A jet owned by an SPV can reveal travel patterns when international aviation logs become part of OSINT analysis. Anything that moves, floats, or flies generates data, and data always lands somewhere.

Even static assets carry their own vulnerabilities. Real estate, even when held discreetly, creates tax footprints, municipal records, renovation permits, and utility usage patterns that show who is present and when. High-value furniture, art, or jewelry stored in freeports, vaults, or specialized facilities may reveal both location and scale of wealth during routine audits or inspections. What appears to be safely hidden behind layers of structure is often visible to those who know where to look.

The greater risk comes from the symbolic meaning of luxury assets. Wealth attracts narratives, and assets provide symbols that journalists, litigants, adversaries, and even family members can use to construct stories. A yacht can be portrayed as excess. A jet can be used to question residency. Art can be framed as a vehicle for concealed value. Real estate can be interpreted as a center of life when evaluating tax claims. These narratives do not need to be accurate to be damaging; they simply need to be plausible enough for institutions to investigate.

The solution is not to avoid owning luxury assets. It is to integrate them into a broader architecture that makes sense. Every asset must have a legal and financial reason to exist. Its ownership path must be clear, its documentation consistent, and its relationship to your life coherent under scrutiny. When an asset is aligned with your residency, your structures, and your economic footprint, it stops being a vulnerability. When it is not, it becomes the first point authorities or adversaries use to question your profile.

Luxury assets reveal two things simultaneously: who you are, and who manages your life. The more carefully they are integrated into your architecture, the less they expose. When acquired with intention, maintained with structure, and positioned within defensible legal logic, they enrich your life without endangering it. When acquired without alignment, they become bright markers in a landscape that others can read more easily than you think.

A luxury asset can elevate your lifestyle, or it can reveal your vulnerabilities. The difference depends entirely on the architecture behind it.

Art, auctions & identity traceability

Few assets expose a high-net-worth individual as subtly, or as deeply, as art. Unlike yachts, jets, or real estate, art does not announce itself through physical presence. It travels quietly, often wrapped, sealed, and stored. Yet the ecosystem that surrounds it is one of the most information-dense environments in the world. Every transaction, every appraisal, every import, every restoration, every insurance update leaves a trace. And those traces rarely remain in a single jurisdiction.

Art exists at the intersection of culture, finance, and regulation. That intersection is where exposure begins.

Acquiring a piece of art creates a chain of visibility long before the work reaches your hands. Auction houses record bidding histories, identify participating buyers, and store detailed profiles that are often shared across departments, affiliates, and external partners. Even when the name of the ultimate buyer does not appear publicly, the institution handling the sale knows exactly who you are, where the piece will be delivered, and how its payment was structured. These records survive for decades and circulate quietly inside a professional ecosystem that treats information as currency.

Private galleries maintain even deeper files. They collect background, preferences, patterns of acquisition, and even internal notes about your behavior, reliability, or long-term value as a client. Curators, brokers, and art consultants often share intelligence informally across networks to position clients within certain markets. Nothing malicious, simply the nature of an industry built on relationships rather than formal reporting. But once documented, your profile becomes part of the internal memory of a global community that does not forget.

Insurance adds another layer of traceability. To insure a piece, you must disclose value, storage location, transportation conditions, provenance, and sometimes even restoration history. Insurance underwriters operate under strict compliance rules, and anything they classify must be justified with documentation that later becomes accessible within the company's risk files. If the piece moves, the policy updates. If it is appraised, the valuation enters multiple systems. If it travels across borders, customs records record its presence. The artwork remains silent, but the systems around it are constantly speaking.

The regulatory environment of the art world has also transformed. Many jurisdictions now treat high-value art transactions as financial operations subject to anti-money-laundering requirements. That means identity verification, source-of-funds documentation, and transaction reporting. This shift was designed to target illicit activity, but its effect is broader: it expands the number of institutions holding detailed profiles of private collectors. Even if you comply fully, as you must, your identity becomes part of a dataset that can be accessed during audits, investigations, or cross-border reviews.

Art also reveals architecture. Ownership structures used for art, foundations, SPVs, trusts, often appear in registries, filings, or internal compliance notes. When the structure is coherent, the piece enhances your architecture. When the structure lacks substance, it becomes a vulnerability. Authorities have learned to use art as a proxy for wealth mapping. A single painting, properly traced, can reveal not only where it is stored, but also which entity holds it, who manages the entity, how it was financed, and whether its path aligns with your declared tax position.

Even more revealing is movement. Art that crosses borders generates export permits, transport records, customs declarations, and storage documentation. Freeports, once considered opaque, now operate under tighter regulation that still provides discretion but leaves procedural footprints. These footprints can show patterns: where your assets truly live, which jurisdictions you rely on, how often pieces circulate, and whether your declared residency aligns with the movements of your collection.

The greatest source of exposure, however, comes not from institutions but from people. Art handlers see your properties. Installers learn the layout of private spaces. Consultants know your taste, your liquidity, and your appetite for acquisition. Even a casual conversation at an opening can reveal your presence in a city where your tax filings suggest you rarely live. The art world is a social ecosystem, and social ecosystems are porous.

Identity traceability is not an art-market flaw; it is a feature of its structure. Art is cultural. Culture is public. And anything public becomes a point of connection between your private life and a wider narrative.

Yet none of this means you should avoid collecting. It means you must understand the disclosures built into the process. When ownership structures match your legal architecture, when movement aligns with your residency and reporting obligations, when documentation is consistent across jurisdictions, art ceases to be a vulnerability. It becomes a refined, coherent part of your personal and financial identity.

When misaligned, it tells a story you never agreed to tell.

A painting cannot speak, but the systems around it can. And they do, quietly, persistently, and with more detail than most collectors ever imagine.

Yachts, jets & crew leaks

Private aviation and yachting are often perceived as symbols of privilege, but in reality they are among the most revealing environments a high-net-worth individual can operate in. Few assets generate such a dense combination of regulatory paperwork, digital traces, human access, logistical movement, and informal observation. A yacht or jet may appear to offer privacy, yet the ecosystem surrounding them produces more information than most owners ever realize. Exposure does not come from the vessel or the aircraft. It comes from the systems and the people that make them function.

Every flight begins creating a data trail long before you reach the aircraft. Bookings are logged with brokers, operators, dispatch teams, and aviation authorities. Passenger information is recorded, transmitted, and stored across multiple jurisdictions, even when travel is private. Airports capture identification, crew lists, and routing details. Air traffic control systems and flight trackers publish routes publicly, and while some information can be minimized, the flight itself is rarely invisible. For someone monitoring your movements, aviation data is one of the easiest ways to reconstruct your presence, routines, and connections.

Yachts leave an equally rich trail. Maritime authorities record registry details, movements, port entries, and flag compliance. Crew lists must be filed, insurance updated, and technical inspections documented. Even when trackers are disabled, ports, suppliers, and support services document arrival and departure times. Modern yachting infrastructure depends on communication, between captain and port, between engineers and service providers, between crew and management companies. Every exchange creates another entry in a system that remembers far more than it reveals.

But the greatest point of exposure aboard yachts and jets is human, not technical. Crew members see everything: schedules, guests, habits, tensions, decisions made under pressure, and patterns of movement that reveal far more about your life than any formal system. Crew turnover, informal conversations, personal phones, and the normal flow of operational chatter create openings that can travel outward quickly. Most crew members are loyal and professional, yet loyalty is fragile when people move between employers, when personal matters intervene, or when they feel pressure from external actors who want information that only they can access.

Advisors often underestimate the magnitude of this vulnerability. A single comment overheard by a crew member about a deal in progress, a dispute, a family issue, or a change in residency can travel through informal channels without malicious intent. Human beings talk. They talk to partners, friends, colleagues, and occasionally journalists or brokers who are trained to listen carefully. These fragments, once spoken, cannot be withdrawn. And when combined with the structural data generated by the vessel or aircraft, they can form a narrative that institutions, adversaries, or media actors find highly valuable.

The operational staff surrounding these assets, brokers, maintenance teams, provisioning suppliers, aviation handlers, customs intermediaries, also receive pieces of your life. Each sees only what is necessary to do their job, but these pieces replicate across borders, companies, and platforms. A note added by a handler in one airport may be visible to staff at another. A repair invoice may reveal geography. A provisioning list may reveal your presence in a particular port during a sensitive moment. Even a routine fuel request can confirm your location at a time when you might prefer not to be traced.

The exposure becomes sharper when the use of jets or yachts does not align with your declared residency, professional commitments, or lifestyle narrative. If you spend substantial time in jurisdictions you do not officially inhabit, the movement of your vessel or aircraft contradicts your documentation. Authorities do not need to prove intent; the pattern itself invites questions. Regulatory systems increasingly cross-check aviation and maritime data with tax filings, corporate structures, and border records. A contradiction that feels harmless to you may be interpreted very differently on the institutional side.

Yet none of this means you must avoid private travel or stop using vessels that genuinely support your life. It means that these assets require the same architectural discipline as your companies, your accounts, or your legal structures. Systems should reflect your declared reality. Crew should be professionally managed, trained, and supported. Communication should be deliberate rather than improvised. Access should be defined rather than assumed. And your movements should follow patterns that can withstand institutional interpretation rather than rely on secrecy that does not exist.

Yachts and jets are tools, powerful ones, capable of adding flexibility, autonomy, and comfort to your global life. But like any powerful tool, they generate signals. When those signals align with your architecture, they reinforce your stability. When they contradict the story you present to institutions, they expose weaknesses before you notice them.

The objective is not to erase every trace. That is neither realistic nor necessary. The objective is to ensure that the traces these assets produce are consistent with your legal, financial, and personal position, so that nothing in their movement can be misinterpreted as contradiction, inconsistency, or intent.

A vessel moves through water. An aircraft moves through air. But both move through systems that leave marks. And it is the marks, not the movement, that determine how the world interprets you.

Real estate as a surveillance vector

Real estate feels immovable, solid, and inherently private. A property does not follow you around the world. It has no engine, no crew, no flight plan. Yet in the modern regulatory landscape, real estate is one of the most revealing, and least understood, surveillance vectors in a high-net-worth life. Unlike jets or yachts, a property is permanently tied to a jurisdiction. It anchors you in the eyes of institutions, even when you intend your life to remain fluid. And every property, no matter how discreet, creates a trail of administrative, digital, financial, and behavioral signals that others can interpret with surprising accuracy.

A property begins generating visibility before you even acquire it. The purchase process itself, due diligence, financing, notary filings, land registry documents, title searches, insurance, and valuation reports, produces a web of records across multiple institutions. These records identify you, your structures, your representatives, and your sources of funds. Even when the transaction is conducted through entities, the information eventually forms part of a chain that institutions can interpret. Property is never invisible. It is formal by nature.

Ownership registration creates a second layer of exposure. Land registries vary by jurisdiction, but many are public or semi-public. Even where details are restricted, the information exists, and institutions, journalists, compliance bodies, and litigants can access it under the right circumstances. Beneficial ownership rules, increasingly strict in many countries, link properties to ultimate owners even when held through complex structures. A property held in the wrong jurisdiction can reveal far more about your economic footprint than any bank account.

Use and occupancy create a different type of visibility. The time you spend in a particular property, measured not through official records but through practical signals, quickly becomes part of your residency profile. Utility usage, security logs, entry systems, wi-fi connections, maintenance schedules, deliveries, service providers, neighborhood observations, and even the rhythm of household activity contribute to how your presence is perceived. Institutions do not need direct evidence; they rely on patterns. And real estate generates patterns that are difficult to dispute.

Staff access further amplifies visibility. Housekeepers, maintenance teams, property managers, and contractors see your routines in ways no institution could. They observe when you are present, who accompanies you, how the household functions, and what rhythm your life follows. None of this requires malice. Routine conversation, casual remark, or misplaced disclosure can reveal sensitive information that spreads outward, through agencies, subcontractors, or local networks. A property is not only a home; it is a point of interaction with dozens of people over time.

Real estate also reveals relationships. Joint ownership structures, shared properties, consecutive visits from the same individuals, and repeated use of certain addresses by different members of your inner circle all create signals about personal and professional ties. Litigation involving properties, even minor disputes, produces public filings that can expose business partnerships, financial arrangements, or family dynamics. For someone trying to map your life, a property provides both geography and context.

Luxury real estate contains additional layers of vulnerability. High-end properties require specialized services, concierge staff, architects, designers, art installers, security integrators, garden specialists, and seasonal contractors. Each interaction generates invoices, communications, and operational details that circulate across platforms and jurisdictions. These documents, stored on servers far beyond your control, can be accessed through institutional requests or unintentionally through data leaks. The more sophisticated the property, the more sophisticated the information it produces.

The jurisdiction itself matters equally. Countries differ dramatically in how much real estate information they publish, how closely they monitor property-related tax obligations, and how aggressively they enforce beneficial ownership rules. In some jurisdictions, property ownership immediately triggers assumptions about your residency, your financial capacity, or your economic ties. In others, owning a property without spending enough time there raises red flags about tax avoidance. Real estate shapes the legal interpretation of your life even when you do not intend it to.

Despite all this, real estate is not a liability. It becomes a liability only when the narrative surrounding the property conflicts with your declared positions in other areas. A property that aligns with your residency profile strengthens your credibility. A property that reflects your economic reality reinforces your stability. A property held through structures that make sense, legally, fiscally, and geographically, supports your overall architecture. The danger arises when ownership, usage, and documentation diverge from the story institutions are expected to believe.

The goal is not to avoid property ownership. It is to treat property as part of your global architecture rather than a separate, passive asset. The purchase must reflect your long-term structure. The ownership must align with your jurisdictional strategy. The usage must be consistent with your declared life. And the administrative footprint must remain coherent across borders.

Real estate does not expose you because it is visible. It exposes you when it contradicts your narrative. When property, presence, and paperwork form a single, consistent logic, a home ceases to be a surveillance vector and becomes what it should be: a stable point in an otherwise mobile life.

How lifestyle reveals geography & weakness

Lifestyle is never neutral. It is a map. It reveals where you are, how you move, what you value, who you trust, and which vulnerabilities you carry without ever saying a word. For most high-net-worth individuals, lifestyle exposure is not the result of excess, visibility, or social media. It comes from patterns, predictable rhythms that allow institutions, adversaries, or opportunistic actors to infer far more than you intend.

Every aspect of daily life creates geographic signals. Your preferred restaurants, the gyms you frequent, the medical specialists you visit, the boutiques that know your size, the clubs that recognize your name, the hotels where you feel comfortable, all of these establish territorial anchors. Even when you believe you live fluidly between multiple countries, your actual life tends to settle into recognizable clusters. These clusters form the basis of how authorities interpret your residence, how banks evaluate your profile, and how third parties construct narratives about where you belong.

Routine is especially revealing. People tend to underestimate how consistent their movements are until someone else maps them. The days you usually travel, the neighborhoods you choose, the time you typically leave home, the seasons when you gravitate toward a certain city, these habits create a timeline that is easy to reconstruct through indirect data. Loyalty programs, private memberships, service subscriptions, and the digital trail of appointments and reservations all indicate where your life truly happens. Institutions rely on this information to assess the authenticity of your declared residency. Adversaries use it to anticipate your next steps.

Consumption patterns reveal even more. Luxury goods are heavily tracked, not because they target HNWIs, but because the industry depends on data to prevent fraud, manage exclusivity, and monitor resale markets. Purchases of art, jewelry, high-end fashion, and collectibles often require identification, registration, or internal profiling. Over time, these records indicate where you shop, what you acquire, and how your tastes evolve. Even when purchased discreetly, luxury items often require services, maintenance, storage, insurance, or authentication, that create additional touchpoints across jurisdictions.

Health, wellness, and personal services generate a different set of identifiers. The clinics you visit, the specialists you rely on, the therapies you schedule, the personal trainers you hire, and the wellness retreats you frequent leave a pattern that reveals your physical presence even when your official documents suggest mobility. Medical systems, especially in countries with centralized records or insurance networks, accumulate data that can later be accessed or cross-referenced for legal, financial, or administrative purposes.

Hospitality and events form another layer of exposure. Invitations, guest lists, memberships, and attendance records reveal your social radius. Even when events are private, their logistics are not. Security teams, catering companies, event managers, pr agencies, and venue staff document attendance for operational reasons. Photos circulate. Mentions appear in private newsletters or member communications. These traces help third parties map your networks long before you realize the information has left the room.

Lifestyle also reveals personal weaknesses, not in the dramatic sense, but in the structural one. A person who always returns to one region, one advisor, one property, or one habit becomes predictable. Predictability is not inherently dangerous, but it becomes a liability when it can be exploited. Institutions use predictable patterns to evaluate residency or tax risk. Journalists use them to locate you physically. Litigants use them to identify pressure points. Opportunistic actors use them to infer when you are away, overwhelmed, or distracted.

Even your silence reveals patterns. Not responding to messages during certain hours, disappearing from digital platforms at predictable times, or maintaining communication habits that reflect your time zone, all of these provide clues about where you are and how you operate. In a world where metadata speaks louder than content, these small rhythms carry significant weight.

The solution is not to eliminate comfort or authenticity. A life stripped of routine is not a life, it is a performance. The goal is to ensure that your lifestyle does not contradict your legal or structural position. If your declared residency is in one country but your lifestyle operates in another, institutions will notice. If your official center of life differs from the one reflected through your habits, the inconsistency becomes a risk. Lifestyle must align with narrative, and narrative must align with structure.

The most resilient global lives are not hidden. They are coherent. They allow you to enjoy comfort, freedom, and pleasure without creating signals that misrepresent who you are or where you stand. When your lifestyle reflects your architecture instead of undermining it, exposure loses its power. You live as you wish, but within a framework that cannot be weaponized by those who observe it.

Staff, service providers & social proximity risks

A high-net-worth life is never lived alone. Even the most private individuals depend on a constellation of people who keep their world functional: assistants, drivers, house managers, nannies, pilots, captains, security teams, personal shoppers, it providers, art handlers, real-estate managers, consultants, and friends who orbit close enough to see more than they should. None of them intend to expose you. In fact, most believe they protect you. Yet proximity generates information, and information handled without structure becomes risk.

The exposure begins with routine. An assistant reschedules a meeting and copies the wrong address into an email. A housekeeper mentions a detail about your travel plans to a vendor. A driver posts a photo of your car without realizing the location can be identified. A yacht crew member casually names the port where the vessel will be next week. A family office intern speaks about a project in a co-working space. None of these actions are malicious, and none of them feel significant in the moment. But each one adds a fragment to the external picture of your life, timelines, preferences, locations, habits, vulnerabilities.

People around you also have patterns of their own. Staff use their phones, their apps, their personal cloud storage. Service providers keep messages, pdfs, copies of documents. Advisors forward emails through systems you do not control. Brokers speak to other brokers. Crew members rotate between yachts and bring knowledge with them. Even the most discreet environments produce micro-leaks simply because humans talk, remember, and move across networks. When you live a high-mobility or high-value life, the accumulation of these fragments often reveals more about you than anything you say yourself.

Social proximity adds another dimension. Friends, partners, acquaintances, visitors, and extended circles observe your lifestyle in ways that institutions later interpret. Someone takes a photo at a dinner. Someone tags the location of a private event. Someone comments publicly on a purchase, a relationship, or a trip. In modern life, it takes only one person in your circle to live openly for everyone around them to become partially visible. Your privacy depends not only on what you choose to reveal, but on the judgment of the people who stand close enough to observe your patterns.

The deeper risk comes from misalignment. Staff who do not understand the importance of discretion make operational decisions that contradict your legal narrative. Advisors who are unaware of one another's work generate inconsistencies that banks detect before you do. Service providers, especially in luxury industries, become informal storytellers: they know where you spend, how often you travel, what you buy, and how you behave. They are not malicious, but the market they operate in thrives on stories, and stories circulate faster than you think. Exposure rarely comes from a leak. It comes from a pattern.

The solution is not to withdraw from the world or to distrust the people who support you. It is to bring structure to an environment that naturally produces noise. Staff must understand what belongs inside the professional sphere and what must never leave it. Boundaries must be clear not because secrecy is needed, but because coherence protects every member of the team, including you. Service providers must know which details are operational and which details should remain unspoken. Advisors must align their actions so that your life looks consistent across jurisdictions, institutions, and timelines.

Proximity is inevitable. Exposure is not. When the ecosystem around you understands the role it plays, not only in comfort but in continuity, it stops generating accidental signals that others can read. Your network becomes a shield rather than a mirror. And your life becomes something institutions can interpret without distortion, because the people closest to you are no longer revealing pieces of a story you never intended to tell.

Symbolic exposure: what your choices signal

Wealth communicates long before you speak. A high-net-worth individual does not need to announce anything; their choices announce it for them. The places you appear, the objects you use, the people you stand beside, and the rhythms of your life all form a language that institutions, journalists, adversaries, and even algorithms know how to read. Symbolic exposure is not about what you own, it is about what your ownership means when interpreted through systems designed to classify, predict, and evaluate risk.

Every choice has a symbolic dimension. The neighborhood where you live suggests a level of spending, stability, and social alignment. The restaurants you frequent reveal patterns of association. The schools you choose for your children place you within a specific socioeconomic network. Even your wardrobe, cars, and leisure habits convey information, not because these items are inherently revealing, but because they belong to ecosystems full of people who observe, compare, and interpret.

Luxury goods create an even clearer signal. Watches, art, jewelry, collections, and custom items operate in markets with high transparency and strong recordkeeping. Auction houses publish results. Galleries keep private client notes. Jewelers remember purchases and discuss trends. Dealers track who acquires what. When you participate in this world, you leave a trail, not always public, but always interpretable by the actors who operate within it. A single acquisition can reveal appetite for risk, liquidity levels, and social alliances.

Your presence in certain spaces is read in similar ways. Appearing regularly in a particular country may imply a tie to its tax system or regulatory environment. Visiting exclusive clubs or events places you inside a specific social topology that third parties can map. Being associated with political figures, celebrities, or other high-visibility individuals produces assumptions, accurate or not, about your influence, your connections, and your intentions. Symbolic exposure makes you legible to strangers who understand the code better than you do.

Even silence communicates. If you never appear online, institutions interpret this as a profile requiring deeper verification. If you avoid all visibility, journalists assume there is a story behind the silence. If you withdraw abruptly from social or economic spaces, competitors assume a shift. Absence can be as revealing as presence, depending on the context in which it occurs. Modern systems are trained to detect outliers, and extreme discretion is an outlier when placed in contrast with a high-mobility lifestyle.

Symbolic exposure becomes dangerous when it contradicts your formal positioning. If your declared residency suggests modest daily presence but your lifestyle signals constant activity elsewhere, institutions notice. If your wealth structure appears conservative but your lifestyle communicates excess, banks become cautious. If your public presentation appears understated but your inner circle behaves ostentatiously, OSINT researchers and journalists find the inconsistency too tempting to ignore. Contradiction is not only a legal issue; it is a narrative issue.

The goal is not to erase your lifestyle but to understand what it signals and to manage those signals intentionally. You do not need to live invisibly; you need to live coherently. Your choices should align with the legal, fiscal, and operational architecture that supports your life. When your structures say one thing and your lifestyle says another, the system begins to investigate, not because you are doing anything wrong, but because the pattern no longer makes sense.

Symbolic exposure is a function of interpretation. When you understand the symbols you create, you control the interpretation. When you ignore them, others define the narrative for you.

Social dynamics & relationship-driven exposure

Wealth does not exist in isolation. It moves through relationships, partners, ex-partners, friends, family members, collaborators, and acquaintances who orbit your life at different distances and for different reasons. These relationships are not neutral. Each one carries its own risks, its own signals, and its own capacity to expose parts of your world that were never meant to be visible. For most high-net-worth individuals, the deepest vulnerabilities do not come from institutions or systems, but from the social dynamics that surround them.

Relationships reveal patterns. A romantic partner sees your routines, your spending, your vulnerabilities, and your internal decision-making. A conflict, divorce, or separation can turn that knowledge into leverage. Even when confidentiality agreements exist, emotion has a way of creating pressure points that no contract fully anticipates. Family dynamics, which often combine affection, rivalry, inheritance expectations, and resentment, create their own form of exposure. A family member's financial crisis, legal problem, or emotional instability can bring your name into systems you never intended to interact with.

Friendships expose you in more subtle ways. Friends know your habits and the way you speak when you are relaxed. They hear intentions, frustrations, and ideas you have not formalized. They observe the people you trust and the people you avoid. They see patterns long before institutions do. Most friends would never betray this knowledge, but betrayal is not the only risk. A careless comment, a forwarded message, or a moment of distraction can reveal something that becomes part of someone else's narrative about you.

Your social environment also determines who watches you indirectly. Attending events alongside influential figures, political actors, or controversial personalities places you inside networks that journalists, activists, or opposing parties already monitor. Being photographed next to certain individuals, intentionally or not, can create interpretations that have nothing to do with your actual views or alliances. Even the events you decline to attend send signals, because absence itself becomes a data point in circles where presence is expected.

Service networks add another layer. Managers, brokers, personal assistants, concierge services, handlers, intermediaries, and private staff navigate your life on your behalf. They book flights, handle reservations, communicate with institutions, and maintain relationships with external actors. They see patterns you rarely think about, and they sometimes become the first point of contact for anyone trying to learn about you discreetly. A small question answered innocently can reveal more than you intended.

Conflicts in any of these circles magnify exposure dramatically. A business dispute can push someone to reconstruct your corporate structure. A jealous partner may use your travel records against you. A family argument can create pressure on your advisors. Even a misunderstanding between staff members can lead to information circulating through channels you cannot control. Social dynamics are unpredictable, and their unpredictability is precisely what makes them dangerous for individuals who depend on consistency.

The greatest risk, however, comes from alignment, or the lack of it. When the people around you act in ways that contradict your official position, your narrative becomes vulnerable. If your lifestyle suggests one residency but your partner's domain suggests another, institutions question the coherence of your life. If you maintain discretion but your social circle behaves loudly, the inconsistency becomes part of how outsiders interpret you. If your advisors present different versions of your story, you become a puzzle that institutions feel compelled to solve.

Managing social exposure does not require distancing yourself from the world. It requires clarity. You must understand the role each person plays, the level of access they have, and the risks that accompany their proximity. You must anticipate how conflicts form, how information moves, and how relationships evolve under pressure. You cannot control behavior, but you can control structure, how you delegate, how you communicate, and how you align your legal and personal life so that nothing depends on secrecy.

A high-net-worth life is not destabilized by enemies. It is destabilized by unmanaged relationships. When your social dynamics are understood, intentional, and properly framed, they stop being a source of exposure and become part of your defensive architecture.

How adjacency risks reshape institutional interpretation

Institutions do not see your intentions. They see your patterns. And those patterns are shaped as much by the people and environments around you as by your own actions. This is why adjacency risks have disproportionate influence on how banks, authorities, and compliance systems interpret a high-net-worth individual. You may live a coherent, disciplined, legally impeccable life, but if the signals surrounding you contradict that coherence, institutions will treat the contradiction as coming from you.

For banks, your lifestyle is part of your risk profile. A client with stable income, predictable financial flows, and consistent residency becomes suspicious if their spending shifts dramatically, their entourage expands without explanation, or their social circle suggests exposure to litigation, political pressure, or reputation issues. Banks classify clients according to patterns, not personality. If people around you behave erratically, face legal disputes, or exhibit financial instability, the institution assumes you may be affected, directly or indirectly, because adjacency is statistically correlated with risk.

Regulators interpret adjacency in an even more structural way. If your partner owns companies in high-risk sectors, if your family is involved in complex litigation, if someone close to you appears in a leaked database, or if your name appears repeatedly through someone else's filings, the system automatically reviews your position. These reviews do not accuse you of wrongdoing; they verify coherence. But the moment you are associated with risk, even tangentially, you become visible to systems that were not looking at you before.

The media and OSINT ecosystems amplify these effects. Journalists do not need a direct story about you; they only need proximity to someone controversial. If a person you associate with becomes the subject of investigation, your name may appear simply because it is connected. OSINT tools, property records, aviation trackers, maritime databases, corporate registries, social graphs, interpret your life through your adjacency to others. A single connection, repeated across several databases, forms a narrative even when no relationship exists beyond coincidence.

Public perception reinforces institutional perception. When an individual gains attention, through wealth displays, social media visibility, public conflict, or association with high-profile figures, institutions react preemptively. This is not because they adopt public opinion, but because public attention often precedes regulatory attention. If journalists begin connecting dots, compliance officers become vigilant. If osint analysts discuss your name, banks audit your file. If your social circle enters the spotlight, even briefly, your risk category shifts.

Legal exposure works the same way. A divorce in your extended family may lead authorities to reconstruct financial flows. A lawsuit involving a business partner may require regulators to examine your involvement. A conflict between staff members may create filings that reference your name indirectly. Institutions do not differentiate between primary and secondary exposure. They simply react to what the system records.

In this sense, adjacency risks are not merely personal, they are systemic. Every person, structure, or environment near you becomes part of your institutional identity. Your file contains more than your documents; it contains the signals produced by your entire ecosystem. If those signals contradict your declared profile, institutions investigate. If they align with it, institutions trust you.

The key is understanding that institutions interpret patterns, not explanations. You cannot control how others behave, but you can control how much their behavior intersects with the systems that classify you. You can structure visibility so that your relationships exist in their proper context, without bleeding into domains where they distort your profile. When your environment reflects the stability, coherence, and discretion of your legal reality, institutional interpretation becomes predictable, and predictability is the foundation of continuity.

This is why adjacency risks must be managed with as much care as structures, assets, and legal anchors. Institutions do not build stories from your intentions. They build stories from your signals. And the signals generated around you are often louder than the ones you generate yourself.

Designing a low-signal lifestyle

A low-signal lifestyle is not a minimalist lifestyle, nor does it require hiding, reducing comfort, or living with caution. It is the discipline of ensuring that what the world sees aligns with what the law expects, what institutions can understand, and what your architecture can sustain. High-net-worth individuals are not exposed because they live well; they are exposed because their lifestyle generates signals that contradict their legal and structural reality. A low-signal life removes contradiction, not pleasure.

The *first* pillar of a low-signal lifestyle is narrative coherence. Your habits, spending patterns, properties, travel rhythm, digital presence, and social proximity must all reinforce the same story you would present to a tax authority, a bank, or a court. When the way you live matches the way your structures are designed, institutions process you without hesitation. When your lifestyle expresses something your documentation does not support, the system reacts, not because you have done something wrong, but because it cannot reconcile the two.

This coherence is especially important in the places where your presence becomes visible. Luxury environments, restaurants, hotels, clubs, events, flights, art fairs, and social circles, are not dangerous in themselves. They become dangerous when they position you as living in a location where you are not formally resident, or spending at levels that contradict your declared income. Inconsistencies attract attention. Consistency absorbs it.

The *second* pillar is predictability reduction. Predictability is not inherently dangerous, but repeated routines create patterns that institutions, journalists, competitors, litigants, or even opportunistic actors can exploit. This does not require erasing your habits; it requires designing them. Traveling through different routes, varying your timing, avoiding public check-ins, separating personal and professional movements, and preventing repeatable digital trails all reduce the amount of structural information external parties can infer about you. You are not hiding. You are simply removing unnecessary repetition.

The *third* pillar is segmentation. A low-signal lifestyle is compartmentalized. Personal life, professional structures, investment activity, staff operations, digital tools, and leisure environments each exist in their own coherent frame. Problems arise when these domains collapse into one another: a personal trip paid through a corporate card, a staff member handling tasks beyond their role, a property used inconsistently with its ownership structure, or communication channels that merge private and institutional matters. Segmentation ensures that signals remain clean, understandable, and appropriate for their domain.

The *fourth* pillar is silence, not the silence of secrecy, but the silence of non-broadcasting. In the modern world, most exposure is self-generated through social media, public check-ins, shared photos, location tags, and the posting of lifestyle moments that reveal information inadvertently. A low-signal lifestyle is defined by intentional absence. You are discoverable when necessary, but you do not volunteer details that can be aggregated, analyzed, or misinterpreted. Your life exists in reality, not in feeds.

The *fifth* pillar is relational discipline. The people around you, partners, friends, acquaintances, staff, advisors, shape how you are interpreted. A low-signal lifestyle chooses relationships with intention. You do not need people who are invisible; you need people whose own behavior does not create excessive noise around yours. When your proximity circle behaves predictably, ethically, and discreetly, your own lifestyle becomes easier for institutions to understand and accept. When people close to you generate conflict, spectacle, or contradictions, their signals attach themselves to yours.

Finally, a low-signal lifestyle is not about shrinking your life. It is about elevating it to a higher level of design. A well-structured life does not draw unnecessary attention because every part of it stands in harmony with your legal obligations, your institutional footprint, and the way you wish to be understood. You live well, but you live coherently. You enjoy comfort, but you do not generate confusion. You participate in the world, but you do not leave patterns that misrepresent you.

A low-signal lifestyle is the quiet intelligence that makes everything else, your structures, your mobility, your assets, your privacy, your stability, function smoothly. It is the architecture beneath the architecture. And once it is in place, you no longer need to manage exposure crisis by crisis. You simply live in a way that cannot be misread.

Final note

Your lifestyle is data

A high-net-worth life does not need to be loud to be visible. In the modern world, visibility is no longer something you choose; it is something you generate. Every movement, every purchase, every relationship, every digital interaction, every routine, each one produces a trace. None of these traces is dangerous by itself, and none of them says anything meaningful about who you are. But when they accumulate, they begin to form a pattern. And that pattern becomes data.

Institutions interpret you through that data long before you ever speak to them. Banks do not judge your intentions; they judge the coherence of your footprint. Tax authorities do not read your personality; they read the alignment between your residency, your spending, and your economic activity. Journalists, litigants, adversaries, or opportunistic actors do not need private investigators. They need only to collect the signals you unknowingly release through habits that feel harmless.

Your lifestyle becomes a language, one that institutions are trained to read with precision. The restaurants you frequent, the frequency of your travel, the rhythm of your spending, the jurisdictions where you appear, the people who surround you, the assets you maintain, the properties you visit, the public moments you create or participate in. These elements speak louder about you than any official document. They are not inherently compromising, but they are interpretative. And interpretation is what determines how much scrutiny you attract when your life is viewed through a regulatory, legal, or reputational lens.

The goal is not to erase these signals, but to manage them. A coherent lifestyle protects you because the data you produce aligns with the story your structures tell, with the obligations you fulfill, and with the jurisdictions you inhabit. When your lifestyle contradicts your legal reality, the discrepancy becomes a source of risk, not because you have done something wrong, but because the system cannot understand you. And what the system cannot understand, it escalates.

A well-designed life does not hide. It aligns. It allows you to exist openly without creating unnecessary noise. It allows you to move globally without generating contradictions. It allows institutions to read you clearly without misinterpretation. It protects you not by reducing who you are, but by ensuring that the signals you produce cannot be misused, misread, or combined into a narrative that does not reflect the truth.

In the end, your lifestyle is not an accessory to your architecture, it is part of the architecture. The discipline of aligning your habits, relationships, mobility, digital footprint, and asset behavior with your legal and strategic design is what transforms vulnerability into durability. When your lifestyle is intentional, your risks diminish naturally. When your lifestyle is structured, your protection becomes effortless.

You do not need invisibility to be safe. You need coherence. And once coherence becomes the baseline of your life, the world may still see you, but it will not misinterpret you.

Chapter XII. Crisis playbooks: structured responses to high-risk scenarios

Crisis as a structural test

A crisis is never an isolated event. It is a moment when the world briefly stops accepting your narrative and demands evidence instead. For high-net-worth individuals, this shift feels sudden, but it is almost always the final expression of forces that have been converging quietly for some time. A media story, a regulatory inquiry, a digital leak, a bank freeze, a lawsuit, an unexpected border complication, each appears different on the surface, yet they all test the same thing: the coherence of your architecture.

Crisis does not appear because a system "turns against you." It appears because the system cannot immediately reconcile what it sees with what is documented. When there is alignment, the world moves past you without friction. When there is ambiguity, institutions pause, and in that pause you feel the pressure. Crisis, therefore, is not a judgment of your character or your intentions. It is a structural audit imposed by time, visibility, and circumstance.

The purpose of this chapter is not to teach you how to avoid crisis. No one living a global life, operating across jurisdictions, or holding influence can avoid turbulence entirely. The purpose is to teach you how to navigate that turbulence without losing control of your timeline, your assets, or your narrative. A crisis handled early is a disruption. A crisis handled late becomes a story. And once it becomes a story, you are no longer the author.

Every crisis has a predictable shape. There is an early signal, often subtle, that something has shifted, an unexpected question, a delay in an administrative process, a request for clarification, a change in tone from a bank, a new interest from someone who should be indifferent. Then comes escalation, when the issue gains institutional, legal, or public momentum. The final phase is consolidation, when the consequences stabilize and define your position going forward. At each stage, your leverage, options, and narrative shrink or expand depending on your preparedness and your reaction.

What makes a crisis truly dangerous is not the event itself but the speed at which you must respond. Institutions have procedures; you have minutes. Systems escalate by default; you must impose discipline. Adversaries prepare their actions quietly; your reaction will be measured publicly. This asymmetry is where most damage occurs. It is also where most protection is possible, if your architecture was built intentionally and if your response follows structure rather than fear.

This chapter offers playbooks not to dramatize crisis but to restore your advantage. They are practical, grounded in law, and designed to operate within the boundaries of legitimacy. You will see how to recognize the signals that precede escalation, how to avoid the actions that transform a manageable issue into a public disaster, and how to take the few decisive steps that protect continuity while reducing exposure. Each scenario is different, yet the underlying principles remain the same: control the time, control the information, control the narrative, and protect the stability of your life.

Crisis is not chaos. It is pressure applied to weak points. If your architecture is coherent, the pressure dissipates. If it is fragmented, the pressure concentrates until something gives way. Your goal is not to eliminate every potential threat but to ensure that nothing in your life is fragile enough to collapse when the system looks at you closely.

A crisis is not the end of stability. It is the moment when your stability proves whether it was real.

Media attack scenario, when the story moves faster than you

A media crisis is not born when a journalist publishes a story. It begins much earlier, in the moment someone realizes that your name, your life, or your assets can be used to illustrate a narrative that already exists. Modern media does not search for truth; it searches for clicks. If a detail from your life fits the emotional architecture of a story, wealth, power, controversy, influence, privilege, your profile becomes a convenient frame. And once your name enters that frame, the velocity of the situation changes instantly.

The danger of a media attack is not the content itself but the timeline. Journalists move fast; institutions move slowly; audiences move instinctively. By the time you are informed of the situation, the narrative may already have momentum. A rumor becomes an angle. An angle becomes a headline. A headline becomes a chain reaction across platforms you do not control. Correction is possible later, but containment must happen immediately. Most reputational damage comes not from inaccuracies but from the uncontrolled hours between awareness and response.

The first sign of a media threat is curiosity that feels innocently framed. A journalist reaches out "for clarification." A researcher asks about details that should have no public relevance. A pr agency receives questions about your business or past transactions. Someone requests confirmation of something that has never been public. These moments are not neutral. They signal that a narrative is being drafted, and you are a potential character. The mistake most people make is responding too much, too quickly, or too casually, offering fragments that later appear in the story, out of context and without structure.

When a media attack escalates, your reaction must be guided by two principles: control of information and control of timing. You do not correct everything. You do not engage emotionally. You do not play defense. You define the minimum facts required to neutralize the attack, protect ongoing legal or financial processes, and prevent institutions from misinterpreting the noise. A rushed denial or aggressive statement often becomes the anchor that journalists use to intensify the narrative. Silence, when structured, is stronger than improvisation. Every word must serve a purpose, not a sentiment.

The second danger in a media crisis is institutional echo. Banks, regulators, partners, or counter-parties who see your name in an emerging story may freeze decisions until the situation stabilizes. They do this not because they believe the story, but because they cannot afford uncertainty (or stocks fluctuations). This is why clarity is essential: your legal and financial architecture must remain understandable even in moments when noise surrounds your name. When institutions can reconcile the story with the documented reality of your life, the crisis remains contained. When they cannot, hesitation becomes risk.

Inside the crisis, your goal is not to win the narrative. It is to prevent escalation. This means identifying what the story is truly about. Media attacks rarely focus on the detail they publish. They use a detail to symbolize something larger: privilege, secrecy, excess, conflict, or contradiction. If you respond only to the detail, you miss the target. If you understand the symbolic dimension, you can dismantle the narrative without engaging on emotional or moral terms. The most effective response is one that reduces the symbolic value of your involvement. When you stop being the story's metaphor, you stop being the story.

A media attack becomes destructive only when it forces you to act prematurely in other areas of your architecture, relocating assets, modifying structures, changing governance, or accelerating decisions without proper legal and fiscal preparation. The pressure is psychological but the consequences are structural. Panic is the most expensive reaction available to a wealthy individual. Calm timing is the most protective.

A well-handled media attack ends quietly. Not with victory, not with public triumph, but with institutional stability. Banks continue operating normally. Regulators maintain their distance. Advisors coordinate without friction. Partners observe that the situation is under control. The headline loses momentum not because the truth prevails, but because the story no longer finds energy. In the media world, stories die when they become boring, and coherence is the fastest way to become boring.

The objective of this playbook is not to teach you how to fight journalists. It is to teach you how to prevent a moment of visibility from becoming a structural risk. When you understand how media dynamics interact with legal, financial, and personal architecture, you begin to see a media attack for what it truly is: a temporary distortion, not a permanent threat. When managed correctly, the crisis dissolves into noise. When mismanaged, the noise reshapes your life.

The difference is not luck, but preparation.

Legal attack scenario, when pressure arrives through procedure, not conflict

A legal attack rarely begins with confrontation. It begins with paperwork. A letter, a notice, a request for information, a claim filed quietly in a jurisdiction you barely interact with. The danger does not lie in the document itself, but in the fact that the moment you receive it, someone else has already been working on the narrative, the timeline and the terrain on which the conflict will unfold. Legal systems are slow, but legal attacks are fast. They reorganize your priorities before you even understand their full shape.

For high-net-worth individuals, the risk is amplified because legal action often targets not only the individual, but the architecture around them. A lawsuit, investigation or demand can be designed to trigger institutional hesitation, bank reviews, asset freezes, residency questions, governance concerns, delays in transactions, or complications in ongoing restructurings. The real weapon is not the claim; it is the uncertainty it creates across your ecosystem.

The first signs are often subtle. An advisor receives an unusual request from an opposing lawyer. A partner asks for clarifications they never needed before. A bank requests updated documents without explaining why. A regulatory authority initiates a review that seems routine but arrives at a strangely convenient moment. None of these signals look like conflict on their own. Together, they indicate that a legal attack is forming quietly behind the scenes.

When the formal notice finally arrives, the instinctive reaction is to fight the allegation immediately. That impulse is one of the most expensive mistakes a wealthy individual can make. The first hours of a legal attack must be devoted not to argument but to orientation. You must understand the jurisdiction, the motives, the procedural strategy, the true objective of the opposing party, and the areas of your life that may become collateral. A legal attack is rarely about the legal claim. It is about leverage, economic, reputational or relational.

The first rule is simple: you do not respond emotionally. You do not communicate directly with the claimant. You do not send long explanations. You do not explain your intentions or your innocence to anyone outside your legal perimeter. Every word you express becomes a material that can be reframed, interpreted, or introduced into a procedure you do not yet control. Silence is not weakness. It is containment. Your lawyer speaks; you do not.

Your second task is to protect your architecture from procedural shockwaves. You must ensure that banks, partners, counterparties and institutions do not interpret the legal event as instability or inconsistency. A single ambiguous communication from an institution can create more damage than the claim itself. A well-managed legal attack therefore involves parallel communication: firm with the opposing party, calm with institutions, precise with advisors, and invisible to everyone else. You contain the situation by stabilizing your perimeter.

During a legal attack, documentation becomes both shield and weapon. Everything you have built, residency, structures, contracts, compliance, reporting, governance, must now withstand scrutiny without improvisation. If your architecture is coherent, the attack loses traction.

The opposing party cannot create contradictions that do not exist. Institutions do not escalate a situation that appears technically sound. Courts, regulators and banks rely heavily on documentary signals; when yours align, the pressure diffuses.

A legal attack becomes dangerous when it forces you to move without thinking. When you begin restructuring entities prematurely, shifting assets impulsively, making reactive statements, or changing jurisdictions in a way that appears strategic rather than natural, you create the very signals that institutions interpret as risk. The biggest mistake wealthy individuals make is attempting to solve the legal attack by reshaping their system in the middle of the crisis. A crisis is not the moment to redesign your life. It is the moment to defend the structure you already built.

Your lawyer's role is not merely to respond to the claim. It is to manage tempo. Control of time is the most underrated asset in a legal conflict. Opponents try to accelerate you, to force decisions, provoke mistakes, exploit emotion, or generate procedural fatigue. A strong legal strategy slows the conflict down to a pace where clarity returns. Once time is neutralized, the opposing party loses access to surprise, and your capacity to negotiate or litigate increases dramatically.

It is also essential to understand that not every legal attack needs to be fought publicly. Many must be resolved quietly, strategically and without symbolic victory. The smartest outcome is often the one no one learns about. The objective is not to prevail theatrically but to protect continuity, your assets, your standing, your institutions, and your long-term architecture. Reputation survives silence far better than spectacle.

A well-managed legal attack ends not with triumph but with alignment. Institutions remain calm. Structures remain intact. Your life continues without detours. The opposing party expends energy without achieving destabilization. You regain control of the narrative, not through public statements, but through legal coherence, procedural discipline and strategic patience.

The purpose of this playbook is not to teach you to avoid legal conflict. Conflict is inevitable for someone with assets, visibility and influence. The purpose is to teach you how to prevent a legal attack from becoming a legal crisis. When your architecture is coherent, when your advisors are coordinated, and when your emotional distance is intact, you transform a legal attack into a solvable problem. And a solvable problem is not a threat.

A legal attack is not the moment your life breaks. It is the moment you demonstrate that it cannot.

Digital leak scenario, when information escapes faster than you can contain it

Digital leaks rarely begin with a hack. They begin with a mistake. A forwarded document, an unprotected backup, a misplaced phone, a reused password, a staff member syncing files to a personal cloud, an advisor emailing sensitive drafts from an unsecured network. Most high-net-worth individuals imagine digital exposure as the result of sophisticated attacks, but the truth is far more human: what escapes first is never the secret you guarded fiercely, but the detail you considered insignificant.

A digital leak becomes a crisis not because of the information itself, but because of the timing and the interpretation. When private fragments appear suddenly in the wrong environment, media, adversaries, regulators, litigation, or social networks, the narrative solidifies long before facts can be corrected. And once the narrative crystallizes, reputational recovery becomes infinitely harder than technical cleanup.

The earliest signals of a digital leak are always subtle. You notice increased search activity around your name. A journalist asks a strangely informed question. A former partner or business rival displays knowledge of details you never disclosed. An institution requests clarification about a document you haven't touched in years. Sometimes the signal arrives through silence: a bank hesitates, a partner delays, an advisor becomes unusually cautious. Digital leaks create echo patterns before they create consequences.

The first rule in a digital leak scenario is emotional containment. Nothing accelerates damage faster than panic, panic restructures systems prematurely, shuts down communications that should remain open, and triggers defensive statements that expand the attack surface. A digital leak is an information event, not a moral accusation. You must treat it as a technical failure, not a personal one.

Your second priority is classification. Not all leaks are equal, and not all leaks originate where you assume. You must determine whether the leak is:

- Personal (messages, photos, emails, private data)
- Structural (contracts, filings, entity documents, governance records)
- Financial (transactions, statements, tax data)

- Relational (communications involving partners, advisors or family)
- Behavioral (metadata about travel, preferences, habits, locations)

Each category interacts differently with institutions. Some leaks trigger enhanced due diligence, others create regulatory curiosity, and others affect negotiations, perception, or litigation. The danger is not the leak itself, but the chain reaction it activates. Classifying the type of leak determines which chain reactions are likely.

Containment comes next. You do not start by erasing material, you start by stabilizing the environment around it. Institutions, partners, and advisors need clarity, not explanations. You want to prevent escalation, not justify your life. A controlled message is often enough: acknowledging the technical anomaly without over-communicating details. Overreaction is interpreted as guilt; silence is interpreted as contempt. The right tone is factual, limited, and aligned with your legal and digital perimeter.

Technical containment must be led by competent hands. Digital forensics can determine whether the leak originated from a compromised device, an advisor, a cloud misconfiguration, a staff member, or an outdated system. Most HNWIs underestimate how many copies of a single document exist across jurisdictions, law firms, banks, accountants, service providers, and internal archives. You cannot clean what you cannot map. Mapping is the first step toward control.

Once you understand the leak and its path, the narrative must be addressed. Digital leaks gain power when they are ambiguous. Ambiguity allows adversaries, journalists, litigants or regulators to imagine scenarios that exceed the reality. You never provide more information than necessary, but you remove the ambiguity that allows escalation. You close doors quietly, not publicly. You do not litigate through statements. You do not negotiate with emotions. You do not react to speculation. You replace noise with structure.

The greatest danger in a digital leak crisis is fragmentation. Advisors act independently, staff improvise, institutions form assumptions, and the response becomes inconsistent across jurisdictions. Fragmentation creates contradictions. Contradictions create risk. A successful response requires coordination across your entire perimeter: legal, digital, operational and personal. Everyone must communicate from the same narrative, grounded in facts and aligned with compliance.

Digital leaks often expand because people scramble to fix something before understanding what it means. You do not fix first. You understand first. You classify, contain, coordinate, and only then correct. Most of the damage in digital leak crises comes from premature corrections, not from the leak itself.

In the end, a digital leak is an integrity test of your entire architecture. If your systems are coherent, residency, governance, compliance, structures, patterns, documentation, the leak loses its power because it does not expose contradiction. If your systems are fragmented, the leak becomes a catalyst that reveals inconsistencies you never intended to show.

Digital leaks cannot be fully prevented. But they can be rendered harmless by design. When your architecture is clean, stable, legally sound, and narratively coherent, a leak becomes an inconvenience, not a threat. The goal is not to eliminate the possibility of exposure. The goal is to ensure that exposure has nothing destabilizing to reveal.

Bank freeze scenario, when your financial system locks before you do

A bank freeze feels sudden, but it never is. Long before an account is restricted, signals accumulate quietly inside the institution: shifts in your residency, changes in transaction patterns, unanswered requests for documentation, external alerts triggered by CRS or FATCA, media attention, or internal reclassification of your risk profile. A freeze is not a punishment. It is the institution's attempt to protect itself when the information it holds about you stops matching the profile it expects.

For high-net-worth individuals, a bank freeze is one of the most destabilizing events because it strikes at the foundation of continuity. Access to liquidity defines your ability to negotiate, relocate, defend, absorb shocks, and maintain control under pressure. When an account freezes, the crisis is not the lack of funds, it is the interruption of your operating rhythm. Everything becomes slower, heavier, and exposed to interpretation.

The earliest signs of a forthcoming freeze are always small. A bank asks for documents it has already received. A transaction that normally clears instantly is delayed without explanation. Your relationship manager becomes less certain, less available, or more formal. Compliance requests arrive in clusters instead of individually. Even trivial transfers begin to require justification. Many clients misinterpret these signals as institutional disorganization. In reality, they indicate internal escalation.

The first rule in a bank freeze scenario is composure. Panic is the fastest way to convert a procedural review into a full compliance event.

Abrupt withdrawals, defensive emails, restructuring of entities, or sudden movement of assets signal instability, not transparency. Banks monitor behavior as closely as they monitor transactions. A predictable client appears safe; an unpredictable one appears risky. Your behavior is as important as your documents.

The second rule is to identify the category of freeze. There are three:

Administrative freeze: triggered by incomplete KYC, outdated residency information, or routine compliance reviews. This is the easiest to resolve when your documentation is coherent.

Regulatory freeze: caused by external triggers: CRS discrepancies, FATCA issues, cross-border alerts, or inconsistencies in tax reporting. Resolution requires aligning your institutional narrative across jurisdictions.

Risk-based freeze: the most serious category. Triggered when your pattern resembles one associated with litigation, political exposure, sanctions, or complex restructuring.

This requires a controlled legal and strategic response, not administrative fixes.

Most HNWIs assume they can "explain their way out." That is the fastest path to deeper scrutiny. Banks do not judge stories, they judge alignment between documents, behavior, and cross-border data. Your goal is to remove friction, not to justify your life. Friction disappears only when the bank can reconcile what it sees with what you claim.

Your first practical step is to freeze yourself before the bank freezes you further. That means stopping unnecessary transactions, avoiding new applications, and delaying restructurings that create additional signals. You need to stabilize the profile the bank is evaluating. Only then can you begin cleaning it.

You must then gather your records, every residency document, every tax return, every corporate filing, every proof of substance, every advisory note that establishes the logic behind your structure. Banks do not require perfect lives. They require coherent ones. If your structure is lawful, your role is to make it readable. If your structure has inconsistencies, you correct them quietly, never reactively.

Next, you align your advisors. Fragmented responses create contradictions, and contradictions escalate freezes into closures. Your lawyer, tax advisor, and banker must deliver the same narrative. Not more. Not less. Consistency, not volume, resolves institutional hesitation.

If the freeze relates to cross-border discrepancies, you address the mismatch at its source. CRS conflicts are resolved in the jurisdiction that generated the report, not in the bank that received it. FATCA issues are resolved through certified compliance documentation. Residency conflicts are resolved through objective evidence, not statements of intent.

If the freeze is linked to external pressure, a lawsuit, media exposure, a political event, you focus first on stabilizing the institution's perception of your risk level. Banks fear three things above all: regulatory penalties, reputational contagion, and ambiguity. Your job is to neutralize all three by demonstrating legality, transparency proportional to the situation, and calm consistency.

You never threaten litigation against a bank during a freeze. That transforms an administrative event into an adversarial one. You treat the freeze as a technical process, even when it feels personal. The more professional your tone, the faster the institution restores access.

Parallel to resolution, you activate your redundancy. A bank freeze is not the moment to discover you have none. Your liquidity should never depend on a single institution or a single jurisdiction. Your operational life must remain intact even when one system locks temporarily. If it does not, the crisis becomes personal, not because of the freeze, but because of the absence of preparation.

When handled correctly, most freezes lift quietly. No announcement, no explanation, no apology. The door reopens as soon as the institution regains confidence in the structure it sees. Your objective is not to receive justification. Your objective is to restore rhythm.

A bank freeze is not a verdict on your integrity. It is a test of your architecture. If your life is coherent, documented, and legally defensible, the freeze becomes a temporary administrative event. If your life is fragmented, inconsistent, or undocumented, the freeze becomes a mirror reflecting vulnerabilities you ignored.

The goal is not to eliminate the possibility of a freeze. The goal is to ensure that, when it happens, it cannot destabilize your life.

Family litigation scenario, when private conflict becomes public risk

Family litigation is one of the most underestimated threats for high-net-worth individuals. It arrives quietly, grows in the shadows, and escalates faster than almost any institutional process. What begins as a disagreement, over money, property, custody, succession, or the emotional residue of a relationship, can rapidly evolve into a situation where your private life becomes evidence, your structures become targets, and your reputation becomes collateral.

The danger is not the dispute itself. The true danger is that family litigation is the only arena where emotions, legal pressure, and financial exposure collide without filters. In a commercial dispute, parties behave strategically. In regulatory matters, institutions act methodically. But in family cases, logic often loses ground to resentment, fear, desire for control, or vindication. This emotional environment produces actions that no business adversary would ever attempt, and that no institution would normally pursue, unless someone close to you pushes them forward.

The first signal rarely looks like a threat. It may be a request for documents, a sudden interest in past transfers, questions about a trust or company structure, or subtle comments that reveal someone is gathering information. Family members, partners, or former spouses often begin collecting fragments long before announcing litigation. They monitor your movements, review old messages, retrieve financial statements, or speak to advisors "just to understand." They are not preparing an argument. They are preparing leverage.

In this phase, the most valuable asset you have is awareness. A person who begins documenting you is signaling intent, even if they have not yet spoken to a lawyer. Small shifts in tone, a cooling relationship, a rise in tension, unusual curiosity about finances, often precede legal escalation. Many HNWIs miss these signs because they focus on reconciliation, not risk. And by the time the first letter arrives, the other side has already built the narrative they intend to deploy.

Once litigation is initiated, the structure of your life becomes a battlefield. Residency is questioned. Substance is challenged. Asset transfers are reinterpreted. Communication patterns are weaponized. Even your travel and spending habits become part of the story. Family courts often grant broad powers to examine your finances, review your companies, and request documents that commercial courts would never access without cause. The emotional nature of the conflict legitimizes scrutiny that would be disproportionate in any other context.

The biggest mistake in this scenario is reacting from emotion. Responding defensively, escalating verbally, or making impulsive decisions amplifies the perception that you have something to hide. In family litigation, narrative matters as much as evidence. A calm, consistent, legally grounded posture diffuses suspicion and prevents the other side from framing you as evasive.

Your first task is containment. Do not restructure assets, move funds, or modify entities once litigation becomes foreseeable. Any change, however legitimate, will be interpreted as concealment. Courts and adversarial lawyers treat timing as intention. What you do after conflict begins carries a weight far greater than what you did years before.

Your second task is documentation. Family litigation punishes ambiguity. You must gather every relevant document before the process accelerates: financial records, company governance minutes, proof of substance, tax filings, residency evidence, and communication logs that demonstrate stability and transparency. If your structures are coherent, they will withstand scrutiny. If they have weaknesses, you address them through explanation, not through retroactive changes that could undermine your position.

Your third task is emotional distancing. You cannot negotiate effectively while reacting to personal triggers. Separating the personal from the procedural is not coldness, it is strategy. Emotional reactions become evidence in this arena. They influence mediators, lawyers, judges, and even the narrative that institutions perceive from the outside. Calmness is not only dignity; it is tactical advantage.

You must also control your environment. Staff, advisors, and intermediaries often become inadvertent witnesses. A disgruntled employee, a careless assistant, or a poorly briefed advisor can reveal information that alters the balance of the case. Brief your team carefully. Give them instructions in writing. Define what they may disclose and what must be referred to legal counsel. In family litigation, your network becomes part of the risk map.

If children or shared assets are involved, the sensitivity multiplies. Courts prioritize stability, not wealth. Any behavior that appears inconsistent, unpredictable, or reactive damages your credibility. Consistency in daily routines, communication, travel, and financial behavior reinforces the image of a stable, responsible party. You must embody the continuity you want the court to recognize.

Settlement is often the most intelligent path. Not because you are wrong, but because family litigation rarely rewards victory. It destroys privacy, drains resources, and leaves lasting damage that extends far beyond the legal dispute. A strategic settlement preserves sovereignty: it limits disclosure, avoids prolonged examination of your structures, and restores control over the timeline.

When settlement is not possible, preparation becomes your shield. Assemble a legal team with expertise in cross-border family disputes, asset protection, and complex financial analysis. Ensure that every jurisdiction involved understands the others. Family litigation often spans borders without warning: assets in one country, residency in another, structures in a third. A misaligned legal team creates openings the other side will exploit immediately.

A family dispute becomes dangerous only when you are caught unprepared. If your architecture is coherent, your documentation clear, and your emotional posture stable, the conflict loses its power to destabilize your life. The process may be unpleasant, but it will not break you.

In the end, family litigation is not about law. It is about interpretation, of who you are, how you behave under pressure, and how your life fits into the expectations of the system. Your role is to present a picture so clear, consistent, and legally grounded that no adversary can distort it, no matter how personal their motives may be.

Partner betrayal scenario, when someone inside your circle turns into a risk

Partner betrayal is one of the scenarios that destabilizes even the most disciplined individuals. Unlike a corporate adversary or a regulatory actor, a partner operates from proximity, emotional, financial, logistical, or structural. They know not only who you are in public, but who you are in private: your routines, your vulnerabilities, your blind spots, and the architecture of your life. When that proximity shifts into conflict, the impact can be immediate and destructive.

Betrayal rarely arrives without warning. It begins with subtle changes: distance, uncharacteristic secrecy, inconsistencies in communication, or unexplained delays in decisions that previously flowed smoothly. Partners, whether business partners, romantic partners, or long-standing associates, often begin gathering information before expressing dissatisfaction. They review old emails, revisit agreements, examine accounts, or quietly consult third parties. This stage is not hostile on its face, but it signals a shift from collaboration to calculation.

The risk is amplified because partners carry a form of credibility that outsiders never possess. Banks, advisors, authorities, and intermediaries treat their statements as informed, and therefore potentially reliable. A simple allegation, even one without evidence, can trigger reviews or inquiries simply because it comes from someone presumed to have internal knowledge. Betrayal weaponizes proximity. It turns trust into infrastructure for risk.

The first danger in this scenario is emotional reaction. Betrayal feels personal, but your response cannot be. Anger, confrontation, or impulsive decisions, closing accounts, restructuring assets, cutting access, create visible anomalies that institutions interpret as instability. The correct response begins with calm containment. You must immediately secure access points without creating movement that could be misinterpreted by outsiders. Access is removed quietly, not dramatically. Documentation is reviewed systematically, not defensively.

The second danger is narrative vulnerability. Partners often know the weak points in your story: a structure created years ago without substance, a residency change poorly documented, a family asset held informally, an inconsistency in how your lifestyle aligns with official records. Even when nothing is illegal, inconsistencies can be framed to suggest impropriety. Betrayal becomes dangerous when the other person is willing to reinterpret past facts through the lens of conflict.

This is why you must stabilize the documentation of your life before addressing the conflict itself. Contracts, governance records, residency proof, asset registers, and communication logs must be gathered and reviewed. The goal is not to prepare for attack; it is to eliminate ambiguity. The partner's version of events should not be the only version that appears coherent. The more consistent your narrative, the weaker their leverage.

The next step is to evaluate the scope of access the partner still possesses. In many cases, betrayal happens long after the relationship has begun to fracture. People in emotional or financial conflict make inconsistent decisions: they may continue granting access out of habit or sentiment. But once betrayal becomes visible, access must be assessed objectively. Does the partner still have signing rights? Does their email still receive sensitive documents? Do they know current passwords? Do they have access to shared accounts, joint advisors, or family offices? Every point of access becomes a potential opening, not only for action, but for information leakage that may influence banks, institutions, or other members of your network.

If the partner is part of your corporate structure, the risks expand. They may have authority to approve or delay transactions, initiate filings, contact regulators, or influence staff. In such cases, the response must be legal, not emotional. You cannot remove them unilaterally unless governance documents allow it. Acting improperly at this stage creates more exposure than the betrayal itself. Instead, you must identify the legal mechanisms that allow separation: buyouts, resignation procedures, trustee or director replacement provisions, or governance clauses that protect the company from internal conflict.

In personal relationships, betrayal often intersects with financial entanglement. Joint assets, shared accounts, co-owned property, or informal pooling of resources become sources of conflict. Here, transparency is not a vulnerability but a shield. When records are clear, when transfers have legitimate purpose, when ownership is documented, the partner cannot rewrite history to create suspicion. Courts and institutions respond to clarity, not rhetoric.

Communication during this stage must be deliberate. You speak through legal channels when necessary, avoid ambiguous statements, and never attempt to justify or explain decisions casually. Betrayal thrives on emotional noise. Silence, when strategic, stabilizes the situation. And when you must speak, you speak briefly, factually, and with the understanding that every word may later be interpreted by a lawyer, a judge, or an institution.

Your advisors must also be aligned. Betrayal scenarios often create fragmented advice when lawyers, accountants, or bankers react independently. You cannot afford that fragmentation. All advisors must operate from a unified narrative, guided by a single strategic objective: protect your legal position, contain the narrative, and maintain stability. Coordination is not optional; it is the backbone of resilience when a partner turns into an adversary.

The final stage of betrayal is resolution. Not all betrayals require warfare, and not all conflicts require destruction. In many cases, the most effective path is structured disengagement. Settlements, buyouts, negotiated exits, or carefully drafted separation agreements allow you to restore control without prolonged exposure. The goal is not victory; it is continuity.

When betrayal is unavoidable, preparation becomes your anchor. If your structures are coherent, if your documentation is strong, and if your posture is calm, even someone with intimate knowledge cannot destabilize your life. Betrayal hurts, but it only damages your architecture if you built it on sentiment rather than structure.

In this scenario, sovereignty consists of one thing: refusing to let someone else's emotions become the framework through which institutions interpret you.

Political pressure scenario, when power structures try to shape your decisions

Political pressure is one of the most underestimated risks for high-net-worth individuals, family offices, and international entrepreneurs. It rarely arrives as a threat. It arrives as a request, an expectation, an "invitation," or a subtle reminder that your interests intersect with the interests of a political ecosystem. Unlike media or legal attacks, political pressure does not seek truth or correctness. It seeks alignment.

Pressure can originate from governments, regulators, political parties, regional authorities, or even foreign actors who believe you are strategically positioned. Sometimes it comes indirectly, through a bank influenced by political actors, through a regulator under external instructions, or through social circles where influence is traded informally. The danger is that political pressure is not framed as conflict. It is framed as inevitability.

The earliest signs are subtle. A politician wants to meet "informally." A regulator requests a clarification that could have been handled administratively. A local authority suddenly expresses interest in a permit, a license, or an approval related to your activities. A seemingly friendly intermediary suggests that "supporting" someone, attending an event, or facilitating an introduction would be "in your best interest." None of these actions are overtly hostile, but all of them test your boundaries.

Political pressure follows the logic of momentum. If you accept the first small request, larger requests follow. If you accommodate expectations once, those expectations escalate. If you appear compliant, institutions begin to interpret your cooperation as part of your profile. And if someone perceives you as indebted, financially, socially, or strategically, you lose leverage before you notice it.

The first imperative in this scenario is to preserve your legal and narrative independence. Political actors interpret silence as neutrality, neutrality as strength, and strength as negotiation potential. What you must never do is provide ambiguous support. Ambiguity is the language of political ecosystems, and they will rewrite your silence in whatever way benefits them.

The safest way to handle early signs is procedural, not personal. You direct the request through formal channels. You ask for written clarification. You request the legal basis for any action. You respond politely but with structure. Political actors rarely insist when they realize you operate inside a legal framework they cannot manipulate casually. When interactions become formal, their influence diminishes.

If the pressure comes through institutions, regulators, banks, immigration systems, you must treat the situation as structural risk, not personal targeting. Institutions exposed to political influence often behave inconsistently: sudden delays, unexpected reviews, uncharacteristic requests for information. Do not confront the institution; stabilize the record. Make sure your documentation, your filings, your compliance, and your structure cannot be misinterpreted. Political pressure often fails when your file is impossible to weaponize.

In more severe cases, pressure escalates into attempts to force decisions: withdrawing support from a project, participating in a transaction, helping a third party, or providing information you are not obliged to give. Here, your response must be guided by law. You do what is legally required, nothing more. You avoid informal commitments, avoid private meetings without counsel, and ensure that every step can withstand the scrutiny of an external authority or court. Political actors lose interest when they realize you cannot be maneuvered quietly.

A particularly dangerous form of pressure appears when foreign governments or powerful individuals attempt to use your global presence to influence your decisions. This may include leveraging your assets in their jurisdiction, hinting at regulatory exposure, or exploiting connections in your professional network. The instinct may be to negotiate, but negotiation creates vulnerability. The correct response is jurisdictional repositioning: shifting exposure away from the environment applying pressure. Assets, companies, and accounts move to jurisdictions where political risk is procedural, not personal. You do not oppose pressure; you remove the leverage that enables it.

Political pressure also exploits social proximity. High-net-worth individuals are often invited to high-level events, forums, dinners, galas, or private gatherings where political actors expect alignment disguised as social courtesy. These environments create the illusion of inclusion, but inclusion always comes with cost. You must attend these events with the expectation that every conversation is observed, interpreted, and potentially recorded by someone. The safest posture is polite distance: present, but unaligned; cordial, but unreadable; visible, but uncommitted.

When pressure becomes explicit, threats of delays, retaliatory audits, blocked approvals, or political narratives, your approach must become both strategic and legal. You involve counsel, you create a documented timeline, and you build a defensive narrative that demonstrates consistency. Political pressure thrives in darkness; documentation brings light. When your actions are traceable, justified, and coherent, political actors cannot distort them without exposing themselves.

The most important rule is this: *never allow political pressure to become part of your identity in institutional files.* Once a bank, a regulator, or an international agency believes that political actors influence your decisions, they classify you as high-risk. That classification follows you across borders. This is why your response must always protect your institutional profile. You are a client, a taxpayer, an investor, not an instrument of political agendas.

Political pressure is not defeated through defiance. It is defeated through structure. When your governance is strong, when your documentation is precise, when your advisors are coordinated, and when your exposure is distributed across jurisdictions that do not respond to the same political incentives, pressure loses its force. You become immune not because you resist, but because there is nothing in your architecture that can be used as leverage.

In this scenario, sovereignty is the ability to remain calm while the environment attempts to recruit you, intimidate you, or bend your trajectory. Stability comes from the fact that your decisions are grounded in law, not influence, and political actors have no sustainable strategy against someone who cannot be cornered legally or persuaded emotionally.

Mobility crisis (jets, yachts, borders)

A mobility crisis always arrives with an element of surprise—not because the event is truly unexpected, but because it tends to interrupt a moment when the individual assumes everything is under control. A jet denied takeoff clearance. A yacht held by a port authority. A border closing just as you arrive. A crew withholding documentation because regulations have changed or because the vessel has a new beneficial owner. None of this is extraordinary in today's global environment. What *is* extraordinary is how unprepared most people are to face these situations calmly.

A mobility crisis is not a transportation problem; it is an interpretation problem. When an authority grounds an aircraft, withholds a passport, or requests additional verification, they are not questioning who you are—they are questioning how you fit into their regulatory framework. In fact, the initial reaction often determines the outcome. Individuals who become agitated, push for exceptions, or try to resolve the issue through status, urgency, or personal connections usually make things worse, because any behavior that looks impatient is easily interpreted as evasive. By contrast, those who present a clear narrative, coherent documentation, and a professional tone typically move through the process faster and with far less friction.

When a jet is grounded, the issue is rarely technical, it is almost always regulatory. A missing overflight permit, a change in the operator's classification, a newly updated security policy, or a request to confirm passenger identities. In these situations, the most important factor is that your documentation aligns perfectly with the story your movements tell. If your declared tax residence points to one country but your flight patterns suggest another; if the jet's operator structure conflicts with your business arrangements; or if the passenger manifest does not match your actual status, authorities will notice. The solution is not to explain more, but to contextualize precisely and without contradictions. Authorities need to see that your mobility fits within a legal framework–not improvisation.

Yachts follow the same logic. A yacht is a floating ecosystem combining immigration, maritime law, tax considerations, labor contracts, and ownership structures. Port authorities do not detain vessels arbitrarily; they do so when they see misalignment between flags, crew management, ownership details, routes, or technical documentation. Many crises originate from seemingly minor details: a change of beneficial owner not yet updated in the maritime registry, an improperly drafted crew agreement, or an insurance policy pending renewal. More than any other asset, the way you manage your yacht communicates who you are. Vessels with clean structures and professional crew management pass without friction. Those that mix personal life, leisure, business, and logistics without order create suspicion—even when everything is legal.

At borders, the situation is even more direct: an officer must interpret your presence. An entry decision can be affected by regulatory changes, regional alerts, new visa policies, or simple operational adjustments. Your purchasing power does not matter—what matters is the clarity of your profile. When an officer asks about your residence, your activity, the purpose of your visit, or your intended length of stay, they are not searching for mistakes; they are searching for coherence. If your answer aligns with your migration history, your documents, and your lifestyle pattern, the process continues. If it does not, the process stops. The best strategy is not to over-explain but to respond accurately and avoid improvisations that invite further questions.

In any blocked-transport scenario—jet, yacht, or border—the key is to reorganize mobility without undermining your documentary narrative. Moving to another country to "avoid problems" usually creates new ones, because it signals an intention to escape. Instead, adjusting routes within the legal framework, postponing travel, or requesting formal clarification has the opposite effect: it shows that you are willing to comply, that you understand the environment, and that your presence does not create risk.

What appears to be a mobility crisis is, in reality, a silent test: authorities are assessing whether your life fits within their system. If your structure is coherent, the interruption resolves. If it is not, the interruption becomes a signal. This is why every mobility incident should be treated not as an inconvenience, but as an audit—an opportunity to demonstrate that your system holds up not only when everything is smooth, but also when someone, legitimately, decides to examine it closely.

The four universal crisis principles

Every crisis, whether it begins with a headline, a legal notice, a frozen account, a leaked document, or an unexpected question from an authority, contains a single pivotal moment: the moment you feel the center of gravity shift away from you. Institutions ask for clarification. Journalists begin to circle. A regulator hesitates. A bank delays a transfer. A border official extends a review. Something that once felt routine suddenly becomes slower, heavier, and slightly more intense.

How you respond in that moment determines the entire trajectory of the crisis.

Despite the enormous variety of scenarios, every high-risk situation is governed by the same underlying mechanics: the system is testing the coherence of your architecture. And for that reason, the principles for surviving, and winning, are universal. They apply to any crisis, anywhere, regardless of the trigger.

These four principles decide who emerges stronger, and who becomes trapped in a cycle of reaction and escalation.

1. *Time* control: The first mistake in any crisis is to move too quickly. Urgency, when uncontrolled, is a form of exposure. Institutions, adversaries, and sophisticated observers all recognize the signs of someone who is afraid of time passing, because urgency always has a reason, and that reason becomes an interpretive signal.

Controlling time means reclaiming rhythm. Pausing long enough to observe. Requesting formal clarification instead of answering immediately. Asking for reasonable extensions. Creating strategic pauses rather than entering a reactive cycle.

When you control time, you send an unmistakable message: *my position is stable; I can afford to let this unfold.* Authorities respect that message. Opponents understand it. The system reads it as strength, not avoidance.

2. *Narrative* control through documentation: In every crisis, institutions do not interpret emotions. They interpret documents. They do not respond to your version of events. They respond to the structure supporting those events.

When there is no prepared narrative, people begin improvising. And improvisation creates noise. Noise becomes contradiction. Contradiction becomes interest. Interest prolongs the crisis.

Controlling the narrative means controlling the documents that speak for you. It does not mean providing more information; it means providing the *right* information, the information that allows the institution to reconcile what it sees with what it expects.

It also means ensuring that past documents, contracts, filings, travel patterns, income records, corporate structures, match the life you are presenting today. And it means reducing the number of voices communicating on your behalf so that the legal, fiscal, professional, and personal stories align perfectly. Correct documentation closes crises, while noisy documentation creates them.

3. *Exposure* control: Every crisis involves a boundary being crossed. Someone gains access to information they did not have before, or they interpret your behavior in a way that was never previously relevant.

Exposure increases when responses are unstructured, when explanations expand unnecessarily, or when secondary actors, staff, advisors, intermediaries, interact without coordination.

Controlling exposure means shrinking the surface area the crisis can touch. It means deciding which information belongs in the scope of the crisis and which does not. It means containing internal leakage, stopping staff from speculating, advisors from improvising, or providers from oversharing.

It also means avoiding abrupt movements: restructuring companies, moving funds, changing residency, modifying travel patterns, or altering your profile without a clear and documented reason. Abrupt shifts cause more damage than the original crisis.

Exposure is contained not by hiding, but by organizing. When your system is organized, there is nowhere for the crisis to grow.

4. *Continuity* control: A crisis stops being a crisis the moment you stop depending on its resolution to continue functioning. This is the dividing line between those who withstand pressure and those who collapse under it.

Controlling continuity means ensuring that your life and your structures keep moving even as the crisis unfolds. Your businesses stay operational. Your advisors keep working. Your mobility can be adjusted without looking evasive. Your accounts, assets, and obligations remain functional within legal boundaries.

When institutions see that your life continues without chaos, they interpret your architecture as strong. When adversaries see it, they lose leverage.

Continuity is the ultimate proof that your system is alive, coherent, and resilient.

Together, they form the foundation

These four principles are not tactics. They are disciplines, habits that reshape the way you manage uncertainty. A crisis does not destroy a well-designed system. It simply reveals it.

When your architecture is coherent, time becomes your ally, documents tell a consistent story, exposure remains contained, and continuity continues uninterrupted. And under those conditions, even an aggressive crisis becomes nothing more than a temporary audit, one that you pass by design.

Final note

A crisis is never just a disruption. It is an audit, one you did not request, but one that reveals the architecture of your life with absolute clarity. Every institution that asks for a document, every advisor who hesitates, every pattern that becomes visible, every inconsistency that suddenly matters, these are not attacks. They are tests of coherence.

This is why high-net-worth individuals often experience crises more intensely than others: their lives span jurisdictions, structures, assets, and relationships that must all align under pressure. When the question arises, whether from a bank, a regulator, a court, a journalist, or a border official, the system is not asking whether you are perfect. It is asking whether your architecture makes sense.

If it does, the crisis resolves, if it does not, the crisis expands.

The most important truth is that crises do not create weaknesses. They expose them. A structure that lacks substance, a residency that lacks documentation, a company without governance, a lifestyle inconsistent with declared geography, an advisor who improvises instead of coordinating, these weaknesses remain dormant until the moment the system begins paying attention. Then they surface all at once.

This is why the strongest individuals are not those who avoid crises, but those whose systems can withstand them. Coherence is a shield. Predictability is a defense. Legal clarity is a form of armor that no private conflict, institutional request, or unexpected event can break. A crisis cannot destabilize what is built on stable ground. It can only illuminate it.

And when your architecture is legitimately constructed, legally grounded, structurally sound, operationally clear, the crisis becomes an opportunity rather than a threat. Authorities recognize consistency. Banks reward transparency that is carefully designed, not excessive. Courts trust systems that are documented rather than improvised. Even adversaries recalibrate when they face someone whose life continues functioning without panic.

Legitimacy is not performative. It is procedural. It is built quietly through choices, discipline, and alignment long before any crisis appears. And when pressure arrives, legitimacy becomes visible in a way that no narrative, no explanation, and no defensive action can replicate. It is the difference between a person who survives a crisis and a person who emerges stronger from it.

Every crisis is an audit. Every audit is a mirror. And what the mirror reveals is not who you are, but how you built your world.

If your system is coherent, the world cannot break it. If it is legal, institutions cannot dismantle it. If it is aligned, no contradiction can be weaponized against you. A crisis, then, becomes not a threat but a moment of verification, a moment where the strength of your architecture becomes undeniable, to others and to yourself.

Chapter XIII. Sovereignty systems: designing a life that cannot break

Operational redundancy (a–b–c–d layers)

A sovereign life is not built on strength. It is built on layers. Strength depends on circumstances; layers survive them. Every high-net-worth individual who has endured pressure, litigation, political shifts, regulatory tightening, family conflict or institutional misunderstanding eventually discovers the same truth: you cannot control the world, but you can control the architecture that sustains you. Sovereignty begins the moment your life no longer depends on a single jurisdiction, a single advisor, a single bank, a single contract, a single asset, or a single narrative. The more pressure your environment can tolerate without breaking, the more sovereign you are.

Operational redundancy is the system that creates this resilience. It is not duplication for the sake of duplication. It is the deliberate design of parallel anchors that ensure continuity when one part of your system fails, freezes, collapses, or becomes compromised by circumstances beyond your control. Redundancy is not a luxury. It is the operating logic that separates those whose lives continue under pressure from those who collapse the moment the unexpected arrives.

Every sovereign system is built on four layers. The first is the a-layer: the world you live in every day. It includes your primary residence, your main bank, the structures that hold your operating companies, and the advisors who manage your core affairs. This layer must be fully lawful, coherent, and transparent. It is the layer most visible to institutions and the one that receives the majority of routine scrutiny. If the a-layer is weak, the rest of your system will spend its life compensating for its instability.

The second is the b-layer: the secondary environment that mirrors the essentials of your primary world without duplicating its vulnerabilities. If your a-layer provides residency, your b-layer provides an alternative path to lawful presence. If your a-layer holds operating accounts, your b-layer holds continuity accounts. If your a-layer relies on one advisor, your b-layer includes a second advisor capable of taking over if the first becomes unavailable or conflicted. The b-layer is not a backup; it is a parallel option that can activate instantly, without disruption.

The third is the c-layer: the strategic reserve. This is where you place what must remain protected from local pressure, jurisdictional politics, or administrative unpredictability. It is where you maintain relationships, accounts, or legal structures that you do not use in daily life but that come alive when the environment shifts. The c-layer is the insurance that prevents a crisis in one jurisdiction from becoming a crisis everywhere. It is not secretive; it is strategic. When designed correctly, it is fully compliant, fully lawful, and completely independent from the fluctuations of your primary operating base.

The fourth is the d-layer: the silent backup. This is not a structure you touch, nor a jurisdiction you rely on routinely. It is the final layer that prevents total collapse. The d-layer is where you place a small number of elements that guarantee continuity even in extreme circumstances: a safe jurisdiction where you can re-establish activity, a bank that remains untouched by regional instability, a legal mechanism that ensures authority transfers without contest, or a documented plan that activates if illness, disappearance, or litigation disrupts the normal flow of your life. The d-layer is rarely used, but its absence is catastrophic.

What makes redundancy powerful is not the existence of multiple layers, but the coherence between them. Each layer must be lawful on its own and mutually compatible with the others. A structure in the c-layer cannot contradict your a-layer narrative. A bank in the b-layer cannot operate in isolation from your tax reality. An alternative residency in the d-layer must reflect a plausible continuity plan, not improvisation. Sovereignty comes from alignment, not fragmentation.

Most HNWIs underestimate how fragile a global life becomes when everything depends on a single anchor. A change of government can freeze permits. A regulatory reform can question long-standing arrangements. A bank can tighten compliance and suspend access to funds without warning. A dispute with a partner can trigger asset freezes. An illness can leave you temporarily unable to execute decisions. A single system can fail overnight, simply because someone else has the authority to interpret your life.

Redundancy eliminates this fragility. When one layer freezes, another opens. When a system questions you, a parallel system confirms you. When one jurisdiction tightens, another absorbs the function. When one advisor becomes compromised, another steps in seamlessly. Redundancy removes the possibility of total failure.

This is the core of personal sovereignty. Sovereignty is not about control over others. It is about ensuring that no single actor, no institution, no country, no advisor, no event, can collapse the architecture of your life. It is the discipline of designing a system that bends when it must, adapts when required, and continues regardless of external pressures.

A life that cannot break is not built on optimism. It is built on the quiet certainty that, whatever happens next, the architecture has already prepared for it.

Reputation as infrastructure

Reputation is often misunderstood as perception, vanity, or public image. In reality, reputation is infrastructure. It is a structural element of your sovereignty, as essential as your legal architecture, your banking perimeter, or your jurisdictional layers. Institutions make decisions based on signals, not sentiment, and one of the strongest signals they rely on is the narrative surrounding your name. That narrative, accurate or not, affects access, treatment, scrutiny, and trust. A stable reputation reduces friction; a contradictory one multiplies it.

In the modern system, reputation is not built on publicity. It is built on consistency. Banks, regulators, courts, immigration authorities, and private-sector risk models all evaluate coherence before they evaluate merit. If your structures, movements, filings, and public footprint align, the system interprets you as low-risk. If they contradict each other, the system interprets you as unpredictable. Reputation emerges from whether your life can be understood at first glance by people who do not know you personally.

Reputation is not what the world says; it is what the system concludes. A wealthy individual who has no public visibility but maintains a flawless record of coherence often holds stronger institutional reputation than a well-known figure surrounded by ambiguity.

Conversely, someone who has never broken a law may still be classified as high-risk simply because their footprint is inconsistent. Inconsistency is treated as opacity, and opacity as potential exposure.

This is why reputation must be engineered with the same precision as any other component of your sovereignty system. Your corporate structures must reflect your profile rather than contradict it. Your public documents must match your private architecture. Your financial flows must align with your declared residency and economic presence. Your digital footprint must not undermine your legal position. Nothing damages reputation faster than being interpreted as someone who lives one story but files another.

Reputation is also cumulative. Small details that seem irrelevant to you, an outdated address in a filing, a dormant company that still appears in registries, a misplaced press mention from years ago, an advisor who represents conflicting clients, can shape institutional opinions. Algorithms process fragments, not context. They do not know which details matter and which do not. They treat everything as signal.

Your reputation becomes powerful when it becomes predictable. Not predictable in behavior, but predictable in logic. Institutions must be able to anticipate how you will operate, how you will document decisions, how you will react to compliance requests, and how your structures are designed to function. Predictability reduces the perceived cost of interacting with you. It accelerates approvals, simplifies reviews, and prevents escalation. A predictable profile is one that institutions trust.

Reputation also protects you in crisis. When an unexpected event occurs, litigation, media attention, regulatory tightening, or geopolitical changes, institutions fall back on the narrative they already hold about you. If your reputation is coherent, crises are interpreted as isolated events rather than reflections of your character or intentions. A strong reputation acts as a buffer, absorbing impact and reducing the likelihood of overreaction from systems that must always err on the side of caution.

Importantly, reputation must be managed without vanity. You are not trying to impress the world. You are trying to ensure that your life is legible to the systems that govern it. A sovereign individual does not seek followers, applause, or exposure. They seek stability. They seek the comfort of knowing that their name, when evaluated by any institution, automatically communicates reliability, legality, and structural clarity.

Reputation becomes detrimental only when it is performative. When you curate an image that does not reflect your reality, you build a narrative that cannot withstand scrutiny. This creates fragility instead of strength. The sovereign approach is the opposite: you construct a life so consistent, so lawful, and so coherent that the reputation emerges naturally. You do not need to defend it; it defends you.

A reputation designed as infrastructure does not ask the world to like you. It ensures the world can read you correctly. And once institutions read you correctly, you can operate across borders without unnecessary friction, suspicion, or noise. Reputation becomes a form of continuity, silent, durable, and always working in the background to protect the architecture you built.

Continuity without physical presence

One of the most powerful forms of sovereignty is the ability for your life, your structures, and your obligations to continue functioning even when you are not physically present. Wealth becomes fragile when it depends on your immediate intervention. It becomes resilient when it operates smoothly across distance, time zones, and moments of disruption. Continuity without physical presence is not a luxury, it is the operating system of a life that cannot break.

Most individuals, even wealthy ones, underestimate how much of their stability depends on proximity. They assume that presence equals control: being in the country to sign documents, being in the office to approve decisions, being available to advisors when questions arise. This model works until the first disruption, an unexpected border issue, a medical emergency, a geopolitical event, a family conflict, a sudden investigation, a travel restriction, or even something as simple as being on a long flight during a time-sensitive decision. Any life anchored to presence is a life that can be interrupted.

Continuity begins by decentralizing your operational capability. A company should not freeze because you cannot be reached. A bank should not delay a transfer because only you are authorized to execute it. Advisors should not halt work because they lack access to foundational documents. Staff should not improvise because the protocols depend on your input. The stronger your architecture, the less it needs immediate permission. Authority must exist, but it must be designed so that the system continues even in your absence.

This does not mean delegating power without control. It means designing governance that functions independently. A holding company with two authorized signatories is more resilient than one that relies exclusively on the founder. A trust with predefined distribution rules is more stable than one that depends on ad hoc instructions. A business with documented procedures, escalation paths, and role-based permissions can survive moments when the principal is unreachable. Every element of your structure should have a default mode that keeps things moving until you can intervene.

Continuity also requires geographic neutrality. If your life only works when you are in one jurisdiction, then your life is owned by that jurisdiction. Travel restrictions, political shifts, administrative delays, or institutional skepticism can interrupt your access at any moment. A sovereign architecture ensures that documents can be signed digitally or by authorized representatives, that entities have local governance, that financial operations can be executed from multiple locations, and that no single jurisdiction can immobilize your affairs simply by restricting your entry or presence.

The digital dimension is equally important. Your access must not depend on a single device, a single network, or a single point of authentication. Devices fail, networks collapse, borders impose controls. If you cannot authenticate into your financial systems while abroad, you do not have continuity, you have hope. Continuity requires redundancy: backup devices stored securely, mirrored access systems, alternative communication channels, and protected storage that remains available across borders. Not because you anticipate disaster, but because sovereignty demands independence from circumstance.

Your advisors must also be structured for continuity. A global life cannot rely on advisors who operate in isolation. They must communicate across jurisdictions, share the same core narrative, and understand the architecture well enough to make decisions that preserve coherence. When each advisor knows only a fragment, continuity collapses the moment you are not available to connect the pieces.

Conversely, when your advisors operate within an integrated framework, your absence is a logistical detail, not a liability.

Continuity without presence also means continuity without explanation. You should not have to defend your absence. If your documentation is consistent, if your structures have substance, if your residency is defensible, and if your governance is clear, institutions accept absence as part of a global life. Problems arise only when your footprint is inconsistent, when your travel patterns contradict your filings, when your assets do not match your declarations, or when your operations require your constant intervention. A well-designed life is one where absence does not generate suspicion because presence is not required to maintain legitimacy.

The ultimate test of continuity is whether your life would still function if you disappeared for thirty days without warning. Would your companies continue operating? Would your staff know what to do? Would your assets remain protected? Would institutions interpret the silence as instability, or as a normal variant of your mobility? If the answer is anything other than calm continuity, your architecture is not sovereign yet.

Continuity without physical presence is not about detachment or invisibility. It is about designing a system mature enough to survive distance, delays, unpredictability, and the natural limits of human availability. When you build this correctly, geography loses its power over you. You move through the world without fear of interruption. Your structures operate even when you cannot. And your life becomes something very few individuals, regardless of wealth, ever achieve: self-sustaining.

Becoming untouchable without becoming invisible

There is a common misconception among high-net-worth individuals: that protection requires invisibility. In reality, invisibility is neither attainable nor desirable. It raises suspicion, complicates compliance, and creates operational fragility. The goal of a sovereign life is not to disappear, it is to become structurally untouchable, meaning that no single actor, no single jurisdiction, and no single narrative can destabilize the architecture you have built.

Untouchability is not a matter of secrecy. It is the result of coherence. When your structures follow legal logic, when your governance is documented, when your financial flows match your declared life, and when your institutions see clarity instead of contradiction, you become extremely difficult to attack. Not because you are hidden, but because everything visible is lawful, consistent, and resistant to misinterpretation.

The first element of untouchability is legal defensibility. Every decision, residency, entity formation, asset transfer, governance model, must make sense in the jurisdiction where it exists. Many wealthy individuals try to optimize aggressively, choosing structures for tax reasons without matching them to real substance. These choices work only during calm periods. The moment a dispute, audit, or cross-border review occurs, the structure collapses under pressure because it cannot explain itself. Vulnerability begins where justification ends. If your architecture can speak for itself, through filings, operations, and substance, you no longer rely on persuasion. The structure defends you.

The second element is institutional confidence. Banks, regulators, courts, and border systems do not need to like you; they need to understand you. When institutions see a profile that is predictable, stable, and well documented, they treat you as low-risk. When they see anomalies, they treat you as a question mark. And the moment you become a question mark, you become touchable: transfers slow down, reviews intensify, permissions stall. Untouchability arises when institutions have no reason to hesitate. Clarity is not decoration. It is armor.

Redundancy is another pillar. You become touchable when one point of failure can immobilize you, one bank account, one jurisdiction, one advisor, one entity, one citizenship. A sovereign life is built on multiple layers: multiple access points, multiple operational bases, multiple pathways. You are not untouchable because you have many pieces. You are untouchable because no single piece can break the system. Even if one country tightens policy, one bank freezes an account, or one advisor becomes unavailable, continuity remains uninterrupted.

A further element is narrative discipline. Wealth attracts curiosity. Mobility attracts interpretation. Silence attracts speculation. You do not need to explain your life publicly, but you must avoid creating contradictions that others can weaponize. A divorce proceeding, a business dispute, a media article, a cross-border inquiry, all of these can expose parts of your architecture. The question is not whether they reveal something, but whether what they reveal is coherent. If your life tells the same story in every jurisdiction, you cannot be trapped by narratives others try to impose.

Emotional neutrality also contributes to untouchability. Many crises begin because individuals react impulsively: moving funds abruptly, restructuring in panic, sending poorly worded messages, or making decisions that contradict years of careful planning. Systems detect instability faster than people realize. An untouchable architecture includes not only legal structure but personal discipline: the ability to maintain rhythm, documentation, and consistency even under pressure. Crisis reveals architecture, but it also reveals character.

Finally, untouchability requires selective visibility. You do not avoid risk by hiding; you avoid risk by being visible in the right places and invisible in the ones that create unnecessary exposure. Your residency must be visible to the jurisdiction that governs it. Your substance must be visible where your companies operate. Your compliance must be visible to the institutions that rely on it. But your private life, your internal governance, your travel patterns, your relationships, and your personal assets do not need to exist as public knowledge. Untouchability is not darkness. It is calibration.

The paradox of sovereign life is this: the individuals who appear the most stable are not the ones who have minimized contact with the world, but the ones whose architecture remains unshakeable regardless of contact. Attacks become irrelevant because they have nowhere meaningful to land. Pressure becomes noise because the system is built to absorb it. And visibility becomes safe because the visible parts are clean, lawful, and structurally reinforced.

Becoming untouchable without becoming invisible is the highest expression of personal sovereignty. It is the moment when your presence does not create vulnerability, your absence does not create interruption, and your profile cannot be destabilized by curiosity, conflict, or institutional review. You are not hiding from the world. You are operating above its pressure points.

Ending power correctly, exit architecture

Power is never lost in a single moment. It fades through poorly executed endings, neglected structures, unresolved obligations, and transitions handled without strategy. Wealthy individuals tend to plan for expansion, new companies, new projects, new jurisdictions, but they rarely plan for endings. And yet, endings are where most legal, financial, and reputational damage occurs. Beginning well is important. Ending cleanly is essential.

An exit is not an interruption. It is a structural event. It reshapes how institutions interpret you, how your architecture is classified, and how future decisions will be examined. When you close a structure, a residency, a company, or a relationship with a jurisdiction, you are not simply "stopping activity." You are creating a new chapter of your profile, one that institutions will evaluate long after your attention has moved elsewhere. For this reason, exit architecture is one of the most powerful forms of sovereignty.

A correct exit begins with legal completeness. Many high-net-worth individuals assume that an entity becomes irrelevant once it stops being useful. In reality, dormant structures are among the most common sources of future exposure. A company that is inactive is still an entity; it still carries reporting duties, potential liabilities, and a formal existence in the eyes of the jurisdiction. When it is not properly closed, through resolutions, deregistration, audits, corporate filings, and documented cessation, it becomes a risk that survives your intentions. An unfinished exit is not an oversight. It is a vulnerability disguised as convenience.

The second element of a correct exit is narrative consistency. Every jurisdiction, tax, immigration, regulatory, banking, forms an internal narrative about you. When you close a structure or leave a country, your actions must align with that narrative. If the timing contradicts your declared center of life, if asset transfers occur immediately after a residency change, if companies dissolve the moment you move to a different tax system, institutions may interpret the exit as avoidance. They do not need proof of wrongdoing; structural contradiction is enough to trigger scrutiny. A strategic exit therefore respects the rhythm of your documented life. It happens when the facts already support it.

The third element is continuity. Ending one structure does not exempt you from the function it previously served. If you dissolve a holding company, the governance responsibilities must migrate somewhere. If a trust reaches the end of its term, succession planning must already exist with precision. If you relocate your residency, your economic footprint must follow in a way that is defensible. A structure should never disappear without the next one being ready. Hard edges create gaps. Gaps create exposure. Continuity is the discipline that prevents both.

Tax finality is the fourth element, and one of the most overlooked. Exiting a jurisdiction or dissolving a structure has tax consequences even when your intentions are clean. Some countries impose exit taxes; others interpret the end of presence as a taxable event; others reassess the last years of activity before closing the file. The danger arises when individuals move too quickly, assuming that physical relocation equals tax disengagement. Jurisdictions judge your exit by the coherence of your documentation, not by your intention. When the exit is clean and timed with legal knowledge, the jurisdiction releases you. When it is rushed, the jurisdiction holds on.

Reputational closure forms the fifth pillar. Endings leave trails, in public records, corporate registries, media environments, osint ecosystems, and the internal systems of banks and regulators. When a structure closes abruptly or without apparent reason, observers fill the gap with speculation. When a partnership ends without formalization, the absence of documentation becomes a story on its own. Reputation does not suffer from endings; it suffers from endings without logic. A well-designed exit makes the narrative self-explanatory, even without disclosure.

The sixth element, and the one most often ignored, is human detachment. People maintain old access because no one revoked it. Advisors continue using outdated documents because no one provided new ones. Staff make decisions based on previous authority. Former partners speak as if the connection still exists. Old accounts remain open "just in case." These residues of past structures accumulate silently until they create contradiction. Ending power correctly requires closing the human perimeter as carefully as the legal one.

Finally, a correct exit demands psychological discipline. Wealth creates attachment. People keep entities longer than needed. They maintain accounts they no longer use. They leave assets in jurisdictions they no longer understand. They postpone dissolution because it feels like admitting change. This is how complexity accumulates, not through ambition, but through hesitation. Sovereignty requires the ability to end without emotional residue. Letting go of structures that no longer serve you is not a loss. It is a refinement of control.

A well-executed exit becomes part of your protection. It demonstrates to institutions that your architecture is intentional, not improvised. It shows that your governance is mature, not reactive. It signals that your life is structured through law, not sentiment. And most importantly, it ensures that nothing from the past remains open long enough to become a future vulnerability.

Sovereignty is not only the capacity to build. It is the wisdom to end.

Final note

Sovereignty as a lifelong discipline

Sovereignty is not a destination. It is a discipline, a way of structuring your life so that nothing essential depends on improvisation, and no critical part of your identity can be destabilized by pressure, misunderstanding, or the decisions of others. You reach this form of stability not by isolating yourself, but by designing your architecture with precision and honesty.

When you look back at the system you have built, you will notice that the strongest parts were never the most complex ones. They were the ones shaped by clarity: clear jurisdictional anchors, clear ownership structures, clear residency logic, clear governance, and clear documentation. Complexity protects only when it is coherent. Coherence protects even when life becomes complex.

Throughout these chapters, you have seen that exposure does not emerge from wealth, visibility, mobility, or ambition. It emerges from contradiction. When the story you live and the story your documents tell diverge, institutions respond with force, because they must. When they align, the world reads you without confusion, and your life moves forward without resistance.

Sovereignty is not about being unreachable. It is about being understood correctly.

A system built with intention survives pressure because every part of it can be defended without performance, without panic, and without improvisation. Your legal footprint, your financial architecture, your reputation, your mobility, and your personal world all become predictable in the best sense of the word: not repetitive, but stable enough that no single event can break the structure.

What you have designed is not invisibility. It is resilience. Not defensiveness. Stability. Not secrecy. Legitimacy.

A strong architecture does not eliminate risk. It absorbs it. A coherent identity does not prevent crises. It neutralizes them. A well-designed exit does not erase the past. It prevents the past from governing you.

In the end, sovereignty is the art of ensuring that life continues on your terms, even when circumstances shift unexpectedly. It is the discipline of building now what you will need later, of preparing for endings before they arrive, and of maintaining a system that works even on the days when you do not.

Nothing in this book protects you unless you apply it. But once applied, every layer of your life becomes part of a structure that endures, quietly, lawfully, and without dependence on chance.

Sovereignty is not the absence of vulnerability. It is the presence of design.

Chapter XIV. The strategist: the missing architect in a global life

Why a strategist exists

In a global life, complexity does not come from wealth itself. It comes from movement, from the number of systems that respond to your presence, and from the way institutions interpret your choices. A high-net-worth individual rarely lives inside a single legal, financial, or social environment. Residence sits in one country, citizenship in another, assets in several, professional activity in a third, and personal relationships across borders. Each of these elements is managed by different professionals, each working within their own discipline. What is missing is the person who sees the entire picture.

This is where a strategist exists. The strategist is not another advisor. The strategist is the person who understands that your life behaves like a system, one where law, finance, mobility, reputation, governance, personal decisions, and timing interact constantly. Most advisors work in straight lines. A strategist works in networks. While others focus on the rules of their field, the strategist interprets how those rules collide or align when applied to your actual life.

A strategist becomes necessary because modern institutions do not evaluate you in isolation. They read patterns: your residency, your movements, your companies, your filings, your relationships, your public footprint, your digital traces. When these elements contradict each other, institutions react. Banks ask for clarification. Tax authorities investigate. Immigration systems tighten. Civil disputes escalate. Reputation becomes fragile. None of this happens because of malice or illegality; it happens because the life of a global individual produces more data than most people can manage.

Traditional advisors are not trained to integrate these realities. A tax lawyer cannot predict how a bank's risk algorithm interprets your file. An immigration expert does not consider how your corporate governance will affect a residency renewal. A wealth manager may not recognize how civil exposure or a potential criminal misunderstanding could influence access to accounts. Each specialist sees a piece, and each piece may be correct. But a piece does not guarantee coherence.

The strategist exists to preserve that coherence. Their work begins where other advisors end. They identify the invisible gaps between jurisdictions, detect contradictions before institutions discover them, and bring order to the narrative that your file presents to the world. They operate in the space where legal rules, financial structures, personal intentions, and institutional perception intersect. Their role is not to replace specialists, but to make specialists work together—so that the decisions you make in one area do not create risk in another.

A strategist also exists because global lives are vulnerable to timing. A structure created too late, a contract signed without context, a move between countries that does not match your footprint, an asset placed in the wrong entity, a relationship not disclosed at the right moment—all these decisions may be perfectly legal, yet be interpreted through a different lens if the context is unclear. A strategist anticipates these patterns. They ensure that your decisions make sense not only today but also when viewed in hindsight by an institution, a regulator, or a court.

Above all, a strategist exists because no HNWI can carry the weight of coherence alone. The more complex the life, the more moving parts must align. The strategist is the person who translates complexity into order, risk into structure, and visibility into something manageable. Their purpose is simple: to keep your life functioning as a single, coherent system rather than a collection of disconnected decisions.

When your world spans borders, industries, relationships, and obligations, a strategist becomes the stabilizing force that connects everything. They are not there to add layers. They are there to ensure that the life you have built can withstand pressure, change, and scrutiny without collapsing under its own weight.

What a strategist actually does

A strategist works in the space where most advisors do not look: the space between the rules. Their work is not theoretical. It is practical, continuous, and deeply connected to the way institutions interpret a global life. While lawyers, tax advisors, bankers, and consultants each manage their own technical universe, the strategist manages the alignment of all those universes so that your life reads as coherent, lawful, and stable no matter how complex it becomes.

The strategist begins by mapping the full architecture of your life. They study your residency, your citizenships, your companies, your structures, your sources of income, your digital footprint, and your mobility patterns. They review how each element appears to institutions, not only how it appears to you. They identify contradictions that you may not see—an asset held in a jurisdiction incompatible with your tax position, a holding without substance, an operating company whose governance contradicts your residency, a relationship that creates exposure, or a pattern of travel that does not match your declared center of life. Their first task is always clarity: before anything can be designed, they must understand what already exists.

Once clarity is established, the strategist transitions to alignment. They work quietly in the background with your tax lawyer, your corporate counsel, your immigration advisor, your bankers, and your fiduciaries. They review drafts, anticipate consequences, and verify that every move in one jurisdiction remains compatible with the obligations in another. Their job is not to repeat technical advice but to ensure that the advice of one expert does not undermine the work of another. In a global life, most risks are born from misalignment. The strategist prevents these collisions before they occur.

A strategist also monitors timing. Institutions interpret decisions differently depending on when they occur. A structure created just before a change of residency reads differently from one created years earlier. A large transfer made during litigation has a different meaning from one made during calm. The strategist manages this context. They design timelines that avoid institutional misunderstanding. They coordinate actions across advisors so that nothing appears rushed, reactive, or defensive. Their work ensures that your decisions follow a rhythm that institutions interpret as stable, credible, and legitimate.

They also manage narrative coherence. Every global individual projects a story through filings, transactions, travel, contracts, and public information. Institutions read that story long before speaking with you. The strategist curates that narrative. They ensure that what appears in bank records, immigration files, company registries, and tax returns all tells the same story. When inconsistencies appear, they address them immediately, before they become institutional questions. They understand that narrative is not publicity; it is the quiet trail of information that defines how the system perceives you.

Beyond governance, the strategist anticipates pressure. They test your structures as a regulator would test them. They review substance as a judge would review it in litigation. They examine your mobility as an immigration officer would interpret it. They look at your companies as a risk algorithm would score them. They identify the weaknesses that would emerge during crisis, long before crisis arrives. Their function is preventive. They ensure that your life can withstand pressure without frantic reactions or sudden restructuring.

The strategist also deals with environments you may not consider. They monitor geopolitical shifts that affect your nationality. They anticipate tax reforms in jurisdictions connected to your structures. They analyze banking trends that may affect access to accounts. They identify new disclosure obligations before they become mandatory. Their work evolves with the world. A strategist who stops adapting is no longer a strategist.

Finally, the strategist builds the operational framework that keeps your architecture alive. They maintain communication between advisors. They ensure that board meetings occur on time, that filings match reality, that documentation is updated, that entities have substance, and that decision-making follows the legal path that each jurisdiction expects. They create the procedures that give your life continuity, even when you are unavailable or when circumstances change suddenly.

In essence, a strategist does not manage wealth. They manage coherence. They make sure that every part of your global life functions as a single, logical system that institutions can understand without difficulty. Their work protects not only your assets but your mobility, your reputation, and your long-term stability. They are the person who stands between you and the friction created by a world that is increasingly interconnected, increasingly regulated, and increasingly demanding of clarity.

The Difference Between Advisors and Strategists

Advisors solve problems. Strategists prevent them. That is the simplest way to describe the distinction, but the reality is more nuanced. Most individuals with global lives work with excellent advisors: tax lawyers, corporate counsel, private bankers, fiduciaries, risk consultants, immigration experts, and accountants. Each one operates at a high technical level. Each one sees a specific angle of your life. But none of them see the whole. A strategist operates in the full space between those angles. They do not replace your advisors; they connect them. They make sure that the work of one does not contradict the work of another, and that no decision—no matter how small—creates unintended consequences across borders.

Before moving forward, it is important to correct a misconception that affects many global clients: working with advisors does not automatically mean that everything you share with them is protected by professional secrecy. Confidentiality depends on the jurisdiction, the profession, and the specific task being performed. In Switzerland, for example, attorney–client privilege applies only when a lawyer is acting in a strictly legal capacity; it does not extend to fiduciary, corporate-administrative, or family-office functions. In France and Italy, lawyers also benefit from strong secrecy rules, yet these protections weaken when the professional is involved in operational or financial tasks rather than legal defense. In the United Kingdom and the United States, accountants, financial advisors, and corporate service providers have no general privilege at all, and can be compelled to disclose information in tax investigations, regulatory reviews, or court proceedings. Across the European Union, intermediaries—including tax advisors, consultants, and even certain lawyers—must report specific cross-border arrangements under the DAC6 directive, regardless of client preference.

The same pattern exists with financial institutions. Bankers around the world, from Switzerland and Luxembourg to Singapore, the UAE, and the United States, are bound by AML and KYC obligations that require them to report suspicious transactions, unusual activity, large cash movements, or anything involving politically exposed persons. These duties override any expectation of confidentiality. Notaries in civil-law jurisdictions such as Spain, France, Italy, Germany, and the Netherlands must report irregular or high-risk transactions under anti-money-laundering rules. Trustees and fiduciaries in common-law jurisdictions (Jersey, Guernsey, Cayman, BVI, Singapore) must disclose information to regulators when required under tax-transparency frameworks such as CRS, FATCA, BO registers, and economic-substance laws. Corporate formation agents, registered agents, real-estate brokers, luxury-asset intermediaries, and even some wealth-management consultants are subject to mandatory reporting obligations in multiple jurisdictions.

In practice, many professionals act with integrity and protect your information as much as the law allows, but the law does not always allow as much as clients imagine. In several countries, their first duty is to the regulator or the state, not to the client. A strategist understands these boundaries intimately and ensures that your architecture does not rely on an assumption of secrecy that may not exist in reality.

The core difference between advisors and strategists lies in perspective. Advisors look at your life through the lens of their discipline. A tax lawyer sees tax exposure. A banker sees risk scoring. A corporate lawyer sees governance. An immigration advisor sees residency compliance. None of them is wrong, but each sees only one frame of a much larger picture. A strategist looks at the whole picture first, then at the details, and then back at the whole again. They understand that one signature in one country can trigger scrutiny in another; that your mobility pattern affects tax interpretation; that your residency interacts with your corporate structure; and that your public footprint influences how institutions evaluate your transactions.

Advisors provide expertise; strategists provide context. Expertise answers technical questions. Context answers operational questions: What will this look like to a bank? How will a regulator interpret it? Does this decision align with the rest of your architecture? Will this create inconsistencies that may trigger reviews or audits? These are questions only a strategist is trained to ask.

An advisor gives you rules; a strategist gives you direction. Advisors interpret legislation, case law, regulations, and procedures. They map what is possible. But they do not tell you which path creates the least friction, which choice aligns with your long-term plan, or which option preserves coherence across all jurisdictions. A strategist helps you decide not just *what* you can do, but *what you should do* if you want your architecture to remain stable over time.

The difference becomes especially visible during moments of pressure. When an institution questions your residency, freezes an account, delays a transfer, requests additional information, or initiates a review, your advisors respond according to their field. The strategist coordinates the entire response, ensuring that what you tell the bank aligns with your immigration record, your tax filings, your corporate documentation, your mobility pattern, and your existing narrative across systems. They build the version of your story that institutions will believe because it is coherent, consistent, and supported by real structure. Without this coordination, even innocent lives can appear contradictory.

Another distinction is chronology. Advisors enter your life when you ask them to. Strategists stay before, during, and after each decision. They monitor the evolution of laws, regulatory standards, the risk appetite of banks, geopolitical shifts, and changes in reporting rules. They help you adjust before anyone asks for clarification, before a structure becomes obsolete, and before a jurisdiction becomes unstable. Advisors react; strategists anticipate.

Advisors are specialists; strategists are integrators. The specialist perfects a single mechanism. The integrator ensures the mechanism does not break the system. You may have the best advisors in the world, but without someone connecting their work, your architecture becomes a collection of isolated decisions—sound individually, but vulnerable when placed together.

What makes the strategist indispensable is their ability to translate complexity into coherence. They work quietly, aligning facts, documents, jurisdictions, relationships, and timing. Their goal is simple: to keep your life interpretable. Not dramatic, not defensive, not opaque—just clear. In a world where institutions judge you by the coherence of your information rather than the sophistication of your intentions, that clarity becomes the highest form of protection.

Multi-Domain Competence: The Core Requirement

A strategist cannot operate from a single discipline. Their work requires moving across legal systems, financial structures, mobility rules, digital environments, and human dynamics with enough clarity to understand how each piece affects the others. They do not need to be the best lawyer, the best banker, or the best tax specialist in the room, but they must understand each field well enough to connect dots that specialists, working alone, do not see.

This multi-domain view is what turns a fragmented life into a coherent system. A strategist reads civil, criminal, tax, corporate, and private-international law not as isolated categories, but as interacting forces that shape how a high-net-worth individual is interpreted across jurisdictions. They understand banking logic, compliance thresholds, due-diligence patterns, and the way institutions detect inconsistencies long before they are visible to the client. They also understand how residency rules, visas, citizenships, and cross-border movement influence tax exposure, mobility, and institutional perception.

Their competence extends into corporate structuring, trusts, fiduciary frameworks, and the operational requirements that make these vehicles credible. They follow how digital footprints accumulate, how metadata reveals patterns, and how online behavior can contradict a narrative built elsewhere. They are attentive to reputation—both public and private—and how a single inconsistency can shift the way an entire system reads a person.

A strategist also needs a practical understanding of personal and asset security, because risks often emerge from proximity: people, logistics, properties, staff, service providers, or travel routines. They study the psychology of high-net-worth individuals, recognizing patterns of decision fatigue, emotional exposure, or over-reliance on advisors. They understand how private relationships and public relationships interact, how conflict or loyalty can influence risk, and how power dynamics shape behavior around wealth.

Finally, they must read geopolitics in operational terms. Not theoretical geopolitics, but the type that influences how certain nationalities are treated at borders, how banks classify clients from different regions, how sanctions and political tensions shape visibility, and how global narratives can suddenly shift the ground under a person's life.

A strategist is not a universal expert. They are the only professional tasked with understanding how these domains meet, overlap, and sometimes clash. Their competence lies in their ability to see patterns, anticipate contradictions, and design a life architecture where every piece—legal, fiscal, corporate, digital, and personal—moves in the same direction. Their role is also operational: they identify the right specialists in every jurisdiction, select the professionals whose expertise is genuinely necessary, and coordinate their work so that each action strengthens the overall design rather than pulling it apart. Specialists protect their field. A strategist protects the whole system.

The Strategic Map: How Your Life Is Actually Analyzed

A strategist does not begin with documents, structures, or tax positions. They begin with the person. The first step is always a diagnostic phase in which your life is examined as a system rather than a list of isolated facts. This diagnostic process is quiet, methodical, and highly revealing. A strategist looks for patterns that repeat, contradictions that signal risk, and silent exposures you may not have noticed because they never created a problem—yet. They study how your decisions fit together, how your assets move, how your residencies and relationships have evolved, and how your daily behavior aligns with the image institutions have already formed of you. The goal is not judgment. It is clarity. Before solving anything, a strategist needs to understand the architecture you are already living inside.

A core part of this analysis is the comparison between your real life and your institutional narrative. Every individual leaves two versions of themselves behind: the person they believe they are, and the person institutions think they are. Your passports, visas, residencies, tax filings, employment contracts, corporate roles, travel patterns, financial flows, and digital footprint all feed into that narrative. When these pieces align, your life is stable. When they do not, you enter a zone where even innocent behavior can be misinterpreted. A strategist reads those discrepancies early, identifying where you appear resident, active, or economically connected—sometimes without realizing it. The goal is to detect exposure before an authority, bank, or foreign jurisdiction detects it for you.

The strategist then performs an internal audit of all structures surrounding you. Companies, trusts, foundations, partnerships, SPVs, real estate vehicles, bank accounts, insurance structures, and even informal arrangements all form part of your operational skeleton. Many structures that appear functional are silent liabilities: outdated shareholders' agreements, dormant companies with no substance, trusts that were never administered correctly, foundations with inconsistent documentation, or corporate positions that no longer match your life. An internal audit reveals these fractures. It shows where substance is missing, where governance has deteriorated, or where a small inconsistency could trigger institutional curiosity later. This audit is not about cleaning the past; it is about understanding the present.

Digital exposure is another layer of analysis. A strategist studies your electronic footprint with the same seriousness as your legal and financial one. Emails, public information, social media, company registries, flight data, leaked databases, advisory records, and metadata all create patterns that institutions can interpret even when you are unaware of their existence. A strategist maps these elements to determine what parts of your life are already visible, what parts could be inferred, and what parts contradict the narrative you intend to maintain. In the modern environment, digital exposure is no longer optional. It is a silent dossier that grows with every interaction.

Mobility is equally revealing. Travel patterns, visa histories, entry and exit stamps, flight logs, private jet manifests, yacht movements, and habitual destinations all tell a story. A strategist examines whether your mobility aligns with your declared residency, your corporate interests, your lifestyle, and your stated commitments. Mobility can strengthen your narrative if it matches your legal frameworks. It destroys your narrative if it contradicts them. The strategist evaluates each of your nationalities, the risk level associated with each passport, the jurisdictions that may interpret your presence as taxable or reportable, and the countries where your arrival could trigger scrutiny. Mobility is not just movement; it is data.

The strategist also assesses the people around you. Personal relationships, family members, romantic partners, key employees, advisors, drivers, assistants, captains, pilots, and business partners all create second-degree exposure. Their actions, mistakes, loyalties, and circumstances can either support your architecture or undermine it. A strategist evaluates who introduces risk, who strengthens coherence, and who may unintentionally create vulnerabilities. They consider interpersonal dynamics, conflicts, pressures, and the hidden influence that people close to you may hold. Many problems in the lives of high-net-worth individuals originate not from their own actions, but from the actions of people operating in their shadow.

Finally, the strategist determines the vulnerabilities that matter most. Some risks are immediate: an incoherent residency position, a dormant structure that could draw attention, a bank account with inconsistent activity, an unexamined tax footprint, or a mobility pattern that contradicts your legal framework. Other risks are structural: an outdated family arrangement, a corporate architecture that no longer fits your life, a foundation created under old laws, an exposure created by political ties, or a narrative that institutions could misinterpret if pressure arises. The strategist does not eliminate every risk; they prioritize the risks that can destabilize your system.

By the end of this process, the strategist does not simply know your life. They understand its mechanics. They see how each part interacts with the others, where the system supports you, and where it could collapse under scrutiny. This map becomes the basis for everything that follows: your structures, your governance, your mobility, your trajectory, and the strategy that protects you across borders and over time.

Designing a Coherent Life Architecture

Once the strategist understands the full map of your life, the next step is to build an architecture that holds together under real-world conditions. This is not a theoretical exercise. It is the practical construction of a system that matches who you are, where you live, how you move, how you earn, how you invest, and how institutions will interpret you. Coherence is the foundation of everything: your structures, your financial footprint, your digital presence, your mobility, and your long-term intentions must tell the same story. When these elements align, they form a stable, predictable, and defensible life pattern. When they do not, even perfectly legal arrangements can be misunderstood.

The creation of this architecture begins with your asset structure. A strategist designs a framework that reflects your real economic activity rather than an outdated snapshot of your past. Assets must be located in jurisdictions that make sense for your residency, your family, your business operations, and your exposure level. Companies must have substance. Trusts and foundations must have governance that matches their purpose. Holdings must be proportional to the scale of your assets. Every vehicle you use should have a function that can be explained without effort, and every decision should leave a documented trail that institutions can understand if they ever need to review it.

Residency, domicile, citizenship, and your geographic footprint must then be aligned. Many individuals try to treat these elements separately, but institutions never do. They interpret all four together, and any contradiction between them can trigger unnecessary questions. A strategist ensures that your declared residency matches your lifestyle, that your domicile is consistent with your long-term intentions, that your citizenships do not create avoidable risk, and that your travel patterns reinforce rather than undermine your legal profile. When these anchors work together, they form the backbone of your narrative.

Corporate structure is another pillar. A strategist evaluates whether your companies are proportionate to your needs, whether they have real activity, whether their governance is credible, and whether their economic purpose is clear. A company created for convenience but left dormant becomes a liability when examined. A company that reflects your real business logic becomes a stabilizer. The strategist ensures that your corporate presence matches the jurisdictions where you operate, the scale of your income, and the expectations of the financial institutions you rely on.

Banking relationships must also fit the architecture. Banks do not judge you solely by your wealth; they judge you by the clarity of your position. A strategist ensures that your accounts, structures, investment profiles, and financial flows are coherent, transparent, and compatible with the risk frameworks of the institutions that serve you. This means choosing banks whose compliance culture matches your global life, maintaining documentation that supports every pattern, and ensuring that no account contradicts your declared residency or corporate activity. A coherent banking profile is often the difference between stability and disruption.

Visibility is another dimension. A strategist helps you maintain a controlled public profile that does not create unnecessary exposure. This does not mean hiding. It means shaping the small pieces of information that institutions can see so that they align with your legal and financial reality. A clear public narrative reduces misinterpretation. It also protects you from the distortions that arise when the digital ecosystem fills in the blanks with incomplete or misleading information.

Mobility is equally strategic. A strategist evaluates how your travel patterns interact with your residencies, visas, structures, and risk profile. They help design mobility routes that do not conflict with tax residency rules, banking expectations, or immigration systems. The objective is not to limit movement, but to ensure that every movement strengthens the architecture rather than weakening it. Mobility that matches your legal and financial life is read as stability. Mobility that contradicts it is read as risk.

Finally, every decision must be built to survive future scrutiny. A strategist designs your life architecture with the understanding that at some point—a bank, a regulator, a tax authority, or a foreign jurisdiction may review your file. When that day comes, the goal is for the system to explain itself. A structure that reflects your real life, your real patterns, and your real obligations can withstand examination without friction. A structure that contradicts these elements becomes fragile.

A coherent life architecture is not a privilege reserved for a few. It is the natural consequence of matching your legal, financial, and personal realities with the world that interprets you. When designed correctly, it gives you stability across borders, predictability in uncertain environments, and the freedom to operate without the constant fear of being misunderstood. It is the invisible framework that allows a global life to remain both powerful and peaceful.

The Strategist as Interpreter Between Experts

In a global life, no single professional sees the whole picture. Lawyers see legal frameworks. Tax specialists see reporting obligations. Bankers see risk and patterns of financial behavior. Immigration advisors see residence and mobility requirements. Security consultants see vulnerabilities in your environment. Reputation advisors see how the public narrative can affect institutional perception. Each expert is indispensable within their domain, but each one operates with a narrow lens. If no one unifies their work, the result is fragmentation: separate recommendations that contradict one another, duplicated structures, mismatched filings, and decisions that expose you unintentionally. A strategist prevents that fragmentation by acting as the interpreter who translates every expert's work into a coordinated system.

A strategist is not trying to replace specialists. Their primary task is to ensure that each expert's contribution fits into the architecture of your life. They do this by understanding the logic of every field—legal, fiscal, corporate, banking, immigration, security, and digital—and by seeing how these fields interact in practice. A corporate lawyer may draft a structure that is legally correct but incompatible with your tax residency. A wealth manager may recommend an investment that conflicts with your mobility pattern. An immigration advisor may suggest a residency strategy that creates banking inconsistencies. None of these professionals are wrong in isolation; the problem appears only when their recommendations collide. The strategist prevents those collisions.

To do this effectively, the strategist works as a coordinator, bringing in the right specialists for each jurisdiction, sector, and problem. Their job is not simply to advise but to find, select, and manage the professionals who will execute the technical work. They ensure that every lawyer, accountant, trustee, banker, or consultant is chosen because they fit the architecture—not because they happen to be available or familiar. The strategist becomes the person who holds the global puzzle and makes sure each piece is placed where it belongs.

This role requires continuous translation. Experts speak different languages—not linguistically, but conceptually. A tax advisor has a different logic than a criminal lawyer. A corporate director operates with a different mindset than a banker. A strategist translates one domain into terms another domain can understand, ensuring that the system remains coherent. They explain to lawyers how a banking decision affects legal standing, explain to bankers how a residency plan affects risk classification, and explain to trustees how governance decisions affect future audits or reporting obligations. Without this bridge, each professional works in a vacuum, and a vacuum is dangerous for someone with a global footprint.

The strategist also protects you from being overwhelmed. High-net-worth individuals often receive conflicting advice because experts only see their portion of the map. A strategist filters, integrates, and sequences the recommendations so that you do not have to guess which one is correct. They evaluate whether a proposed structure is functional, whether it aligns with your jurisdictional anchors, and whether it creates exposure in other parts of your life. They prevent overengineering and eliminate unnecessary complexity, knowing that complexity without purpose is a source of suspicion rather than protection.

When pressure arrives—an audit, a dispute, a regulatory inquiry, a block on an account—the strategist is the one who coordinates the response. They ensure that every expert acts in harmony, that information is consistent across jurisdictions, and that no professional contradicts another inadvertently. They keep the perimeter tight, the narrative stable, and the sequence of actions clean. This is where their role becomes indispensable: institutions interpret contradictions as risk, and a strategist's job is to make sure none appear.

A strategist's value is not measured by what they do alone, but by how well they orchestrate the talents of others. They make sure your lawyers, tax advisors, bankers, corporate directors, immigration specialists, trustees, security consultants, and communication teams all move within a unified framework. They keep your system stable, coherent, and functional over time.

In the world of global individuals, specialists protect the details, but the strategist protects the whole.

Crisis management: why strategy is tested under pressure

Strategy is never tested in calm environments. It is tested when something breaks, when a system reacts unpredictably, or when an institution suddenly focuses its attention on you. A crisis can take many forms: an unexpected audit, a criminal investigation, a cross-border divorce, a lawsuit in a jurisdiction you barely know, a frozen bank account, a reputational attack, the loss of mobility due to visa restrictions, or the political instability of a country where you hold assets or family ties. These events do not merely disrupt your routine—they reveal whether the architecture of your life was built with real coherence or whether it depended on improvised decisions that collapse under pressure.

A strategist becomes essential at precisely this moment because they do not experience a crisis the way a specialist does. A lawyer sees legal exposure. A banker sees compliance risk. A tax advisor sees reporting inconsistencies. A security consultant sees threats. The strategist sees *the system reacting as a whole*. They understand how a single event—an inquiry letter, a journalist's question, a PEP classification, a regulator's request, a residency audit—can ripple across borders, affect structures, disrupt banking relationships, or trigger further scrutiny in jurisdictions that were previously asleep.

When a crisis emerges, the strategist does not improvise; they reorganize. They assess which parts of your architecture can hold under scrutiny, which ones need immediate reinforcement, and which ones require reconfiguration. They know how to adapt structures without creating noise, how to shift governance without triggering institutional suspicion, and how to sequence actions so that every response is defensible and proportionate. Adaptation is not creativity; it is precision. It requires knowing what each jurisdiction expects, how banks interpret timing, how regulators perceive narrative, and how to maintain stability even when the environment becomes unpredictable.

The first step in crisis management is containment. The strategist centralizes communication, limits exposure, and prevents conflicting messages from emerging through advisors who are not coordinated. They ensure that no one answers questions informally, no document is shared prematurely, no structural change is executed without understanding its consequences in other jurisdictions. Containment preserves options. A scattered response destroys them.

The strategist then builds the legal perimeter. They bring in litigators, regulatory defense lawyers, cross-border enforcement experts, or specialized forensic accountants when necessary. But they do so with quiet discipline, protecting confidentiality, avoiding unnecessary visibility, and ensuring that each professional understands not just the case, but the role it plays within the larger system. A crisis handled by isolated professionals becomes fragmented. A crisis handled by a strategist becomes coherent.

Adaptation is the next phase. Structures created years ago may no longer be defensible under new standards. Mobility patterns may need to be recalibrated. Governance might require reinforcement. A trust may need clearer decision protocols; a holding company may need renewed substance; a corporate structure may need a revised board; a bank relationship may need a strategic switch to a jurisdiction with better procedural guarantees. The strategist reconfigures these elements while ensuring that each modification appears natural, timely, and aligned with your long-term narrative—not as a reaction to pressure.

Crises also reveal the importance of timing. A strategist knows that dissolving a company or moving assets at the wrong moment can generate institutional alarms stronger than the original issue. They understand that staying in or leaving a jurisdiction must be evaluated not only legally but symbolically. They know that certain actions, even legal ones, can be interpreted as avoidance if executed too close to a triggering event. Their role is to protect your position by choosing the sequence that minimizes interpretation and maximizes stability.

Throughout the crisis, the strategist preserves emotional clarity. Wealth often magnifies fear, and fear leads to decisions that make problems worse: unnecessary statements, contradictory explanations, impulsive restructurings, aggressive reactions. A strategist neutralizes these impulses. They maintain a stable narrative, filter noise, and ensure that every move–legal, corporate, financial, or personal–serves the architecture and not the emotion of the moment.

What makes a strategist indispensable in times of crisis is not their access to experts, but their ability to reorganize the entire system while keeping it coherent. They hold the map, even when parts of the landscape change suddenly. They protect your options. They preserve your mobility. They safeguard your structures. They maintain the line between visibility and exposure. And once the crisis subsides, they ensure that the lessons learned become part of a stronger architecture, one that is harder to destabilize in the future.

A specialist defends a position, and the strategist defends your life as a system.

The strategist as guardian of coherence

Once a system is built, the real work begins. A life spread across jurisdictions, advisors, companies, residences, and personal relationships cannot stay coherent on its own. The architecture will slowly drift unless someone maintains it with intention. Laws change. Banks revise their policies. Visas shift. Personal circumstances evolve. Economic cycles pressure certain assets. Family dynamics introduce new variables. Digital footprints expand. Every part of the system ages at its own pace. A strategist exists to ensure that the architecture of your life does not age into inconsistency.

The strategist becomes the guardian of coherence, the professional who ensures that every component—legal, fiscal, operational, corporate, personal—continues to align with the logic that holds your system together. They do not replace specialists; they monitor the interaction between specialists to make sure that each one contributes without contradicting another. They revisit the assumptions underlying your structures, validate whether governance still reflects reality, and verify that your residency, domicile, citizenship, mobility, and financial footprint all tell the same story through institutional eyes.

A large part of this work involves periodic structural review. Entities constructed years earlier may have drifted away from their intended function. Trusts may require updated letters of wishes or clarified decision protocols. Holding companies may need renewed substance, documented governance, or rebalanced asset composition. Foundations may require adjustment in board composition or philanthropic activity. Even your personal contracts—employment, consultancy, investment agreements—may need revision as your life evolves. A strategist ensures that every structure remains proportionate, compliant, and narratively consistent with who you are today.

Coherence also depends on anticipating external changes. Regulatory environments shift quickly, especially in areas such as tax transparency, reporting obligations, beneficial ownership rules, capital controls, and cross-border movements. A strategist keeps a permanent eye on these movements. They track geopolitical developments that may affect your citizenships or residencies. They monitor jurisdictions where you hold assets, checking for changes in enforcement practices or compliance expectations. They analyze emerging banking trends—de-risking, offboarding, PEP classifications—to protect your access to financial systems. Their role is to adjust your architecture before change becomes pressure.

Another essential task is maintaining clean institutional narrative. Your life leaves a trail across borders: filings, bank records, immigration entries, contracts, digital traces. These fragments create the story that institutions use to evaluate you. If this story becomes inconsistent, you become exposed. A strategist ensures that residency declarations match real presence, that mobility patterns support your tax positions, that companies operate in the jurisdictions where they claim to be based, and that your banking footprint reflects your structural logic. Narrative misalignment is one of the main causes of institutional suspicion. A strategist prevents it by keeping your storyline straight.

The strategist also updates your personal and corporate protocols. Over time, your digital practices may need reinforcement, your privacy settings may require revision, your travel routines may need adaptation, or your communication patterns may need restructuring. On the corporate side, internal reporting, document management, board procedures, and contractual workflows may need adjustments to ensure they can withstand scrutiny. A strategist keeps these moving parts synchronized so that nothing drifts into contradiction.

This role extends to day-to-day decisions. Most exposure is created not by large events but by small, repeated choices that slowly break alignment: an informal instruction to a trustee, an impulsive investment, a casual email, a sudden change of travel pattern, an unplanned relationship, a donation that triggers reporting obligations. A strategist reviews these decisions in light of the entire architecture, ensuring that each step reinforces the system instead of weakening it. Their work is not to control your life, but to keep your life coherent as it evolves.

Being a strategist is not about designing a plan and walking away. It is about accompanying a living architecture as it grows, shifts, and reacts to the world. The strategist keeps all the parts of your system breathing in rhythm, ensuring that your structures, your behaviors, your footprint, and your narrative remain aligned. In a global environment where institutions read patterns rather than explanations, this coherence is not a luxury. It is the foundation of resilience.

A specialist protects a domain, while the strategist protects continuity.

Why most HNWIs need a strategist but don't know it

Most high-net-worth individuals go through life assuming that their advisors already cover everything. They believe that a good lawyer protects them legally, a good accountant protects them fiscally, a good banker protects their assets, and a good family office protects their structure. On paper, this looks reasonable. In reality, it creates some of the most dangerous blind spots in the world of private wealth.

The truth is simple: specialists do not speak to each other, and even when they do, they do not fully understand the implications of each other's work. A tax advisor may optimize a structure that creates problems for immigration. A banker may request documentation that contradicts a legal position. A corporate lawyer may draft governance that clashes with the client's residency status. An investment advisor may recommend transactions that trigger reporting obligations in several jurisdictions. None of this happens because the advisors are incompetent. It happens because each one protects their field without seeing the whole system.

Most HNWIs believe they are protected because each advisor is competent in isolation. What they fail to see is that their life is not isolated. It is fragmented across borders, entities, relationships, and obligations. Complexity itself becomes the risk. The more successful the individual, the more scattered the system becomes—and the more likely it is that contradictions will appear where nobody expected them.

Another reason most HNWIs underestimate their need for a strategist is that their success has often shielded them from institutional friction. Wealth creates efficiency. Doors open. Delays disappear. Many never experience real scrutiny until a specific event places them under a different light: a divorce, a liquidity event, a conflict with a partner, a compliance review, a blocked account, a political shift, or a tax authority that suddenly becomes curious. It is only in these moments that they realize their system was never designed to withstand pressure.

There is also a psychological factor. Many HNWIs assume that their intelligence or business acumen transfers naturally to legal, regulatory, geopolitical, or institutional fields. They believe they "understand enough," and therefore underestimate the complexity of cross-border life. That confidence becomes a liability when decisions are made without understanding their long-term institutional consequences. A strategist exists precisely to protect clients from the invisible gaps in areas they do not see.

Another common misconception is the belief that problems will be visible when they appear. In reality, institutional risk builds quietly. A residency inconsistency flagged in one country may sit unnoticed for years before triggering an audit. A dormant company may become problematic the moment a bank updates its compliance criteria. A trust that has functioned perfectly for a decade may be questioned after a change in reporting rules. Most exposure does not announce itself. It accumulates silently until it becomes unavoidable. A strategist detects these shifts long before they materialize.

Most importantly, HNWIs often assume that with enough wealth, protection becomes automatic. But visibility, not wealth, is what draws attention – regulators, banks, journalists, political actors, competitors. You do not need to be famous to be noticed; you only need to be inconsistent. When your world touches multiple jurisdictions, inconsistency becomes the one thing you cannot afford. A strategist exists to prevent exactly that.

High-net-worth individuals do not lack intelligence or resources. What they lack is someone who sees the whole picture, someone who understands how institutions interpret their behavior, someone who can read the system from above and ensure that every decision, structure, and movement aligns. Most need a strategist long before they realize it because the system only reveals its weaknesses under pressure. And by the time pressure arrives, it is often too late to fix the inconsistencies that took years to accumulate.

The strategist does not replace your advisors. They make sure your advisors do not accidentally create risk for each other. They identify the gaps you do not see, the contradictions you cannot detect, and the patterns institutions will interpret long before you realize they exist. In a world where every decision leaves a trace, the strategist is the one who ensures that all those traces form a coherent line rather than a series of red flags.

Most HNWIs think they don't need a strategist – until the moment they realize they always did.

Choosing the right strategist

Choosing a strategist is not like choosing a lawyer, a banker, or a consultant. Those roles operate within defined boundaries. A strategist operates above them. They are the one person who must understand how every piece of your life interacts—your structures, your movements, your risks, your narrative, your digital footprint, your relationships, your jurisdictions. This is why choosing the wrong person can create more damage than having no strategist at all.

A true strategist has one essential quality: they see your life as a system, not as a collection of tasks. They can read patterns in your decisions, detect contradictions in your structures, foresee pressure points that your advisors do not even notice, and anticipate institutional responses before they happen. This perspective is not learned from books. It is earned through years of working inside the environments that interpret people like you—banks, courts, tax authorities, corporate boards, immigration systems, regulatory regimes, and international negotiations.

Competence begins with experience. A strategist must have real exposure to global lives, not theoretical knowledge or second-hand stories. They must have seen how institutions behave when something goes wrong, how files are read behind closed doors, how banks classify risk, how authorities interpret contradictions, and how a small oversight can expand into a full-blown crisis. Without this background, they cannot protect you; they can only guess.

Systemic thinking is equally essential. A strategist must understand law, finance, compliance, geopolitics, digital intelligence, and human behavior—not as isolated disciplines, but as interconnected forces. They do not need to be the best tax lawyer or the best migration expert. They need to understand how tax interacts with residence, how residence interacts with visibility, how visibility interacts with digital exposure, and how all of that interacts with your long-term intentions. A strategist is the only professional whose job is to integrate everything.

Operational and psychological judgment is another core requirement. Wealth does not eliminate pressure; it amplifies it. Decisions must be taken quickly, without panic, and always within the boundaries of what institutions can accept. A strategist must maintain clarity under stress, neutrality during conflict, and stability when the client is overwhelmed. Not every advisor can manage this. Many collapse under the emotional load. A strategist cannot afford to.

Communication is also critical. A strategist must be able to translate complex risks into simple decisions, to explain consequences without alarming you, to prepare you without overwhelming you. They must communicate with your advisors in their own technical language, while communicating with you in a way that keeps you grounded. If they cannot communicate with precision, they cannot coordinate your system.

Independence is non-negotiable. A strategist must sit outside the interests of your advisors, your businesses, your family, and your entourage. They cannot be influenced by the fees of a law firm, the preferences of a banker, or the internal politics of a family office. Their loyalty must be to the architecture—not to any stakeholder within it. A strategist who depends financially on one advisor or one institution cannot protect you from that advisor or institution.

The ability to anticipate is perhaps the rarest skill of all. The strategist must see risks before they materialize, understand which small details can evolve into structural problems, and measure decisions not only by their immediate effect but by their future interpretation. Most advisors think in terms of tasks. A strategist thinks in timelines.

Emotional maturity matters more than most HNWIs realize. A strategist must not be impressed by wealth, intimidated by complexity, or distracted by noise. They must maintain calm when others lose it, neutrality when others react, and discipline when others improvise. Stability is part of their function. You cannot entrust your sovereignty to someone who is unstable in their own life.

Zero sensationalism is essential. A strategist who sells fear, conspiracy theories, or "secret techniques" is not a strategist; they are a liability. The real work is sober, methodical, legal, and predictable. There are no tricks. There is only coherence. The strategist who promises magic will destroy your system faster than any advisor who makes a mistake.

Finally, choosing a strategist requires honesty—from you. You must be prepared to share information, to follow advice, and to commit to coherence. A strategist can only protect what you allow them to see. Many clients want miracles while hiding key details. No strategist can operate under those conditions. The relationship only works when both sides act with discipline.

The right strategist will not impress you with dramatic language. They will impress you with clarity, stability, judgment, and the quiet sense that your world makes more sense when they are in the room. They will see risks you did not see, align advisors who never spoke to each other, stabilize decisions that felt chaotic, and build a system where every piece finally works together.

The wrong strategist creates chaos, while the right strategist removes it entirely.

What a strategist cannot do

A strategist holds a rare position in a global life, but that position has clear limits. Defining those limits is not a matter of humility; it is a matter of accuracy. A strategist protects coherence, anticipates risks, connects disciplines, and designs systems that can withstand pressure. But they do not replace the professionals who live inside each domain. Confusing these roles leads to mistakes that no architecture can absorb.

A strategist cannot help you if you step outside the structure designed to protect you. Many of the problems HNWIs face do not come from external threats, but from small decisions made at the wrong moment, sharing information with the wrong person, improvising because "nothing will happen," or assuming that wealth alone will absorb the impact. No architecture can withstand that. The strategist's job is not to repair damage that has already been created, nor to perform miracles. Their job is to make your goals possible—legally, calmly, and with continuity. But that only works if you remain within the system built for you and communicate before making decisions that carry consequences.

A strategist cannot replace lawyers. They understand legal logic—civil, corporate, criminal, tax, or cross-border—but they do not draft litigation strategies, argue cases, or act as legal representatives. Their value lies in knowing which lawyer to activate, in which jurisdiction, at which moment, and with which instructions. They ensure the legal work is coherent with the entire system, but they never perform it themselves.

A strategist cannot replace tax specialists. They understand how tax interacts with residency, domicile, citizenship, and corporate structure, but they do not calculate liabilities or prepare filings. They do not create tax schemes, optimize rates through loopholes, or promise outcomes they cannot control. Their work is to ensure tax advisors operate with accurate information, consistent assumptions, and realistic constraints.

A strategist cannot create opacity. They do not hide assets, disguise ownership, or bypass reporting obligations. They do not design structures for secrecy; they design structures that survive visibility. Any professional who offers "tricks," "confidential methods," or "invisible systems" does not understand the modern world. A strategist works within the law because only lawful structures remain stable when exposed to light.

A strategist cannot perform magic. They cannot undo years of poor decisions overnight. They cannot transform a chaotic financial footprint into a coherent architecture unless the client commits to discipline. They cannot make institutions ignore contradictions or rewrite the past. Their work begins the moment clarity becomes possible, not the moment consequences disappear.

A strategist cannot clean a life without cooperation. They cannot impose order on someone who does not want to change patterns, align advisors, review structures, or confront uncomfortable truths. The architecture only works when the client accepts that sovereignty requires responsibility. A strategist can design the system, but the client must live inside it.

A strategist cannot guarantee outcomes. They cannot promise visa approvals, tax rulings, bank acceptance, or judicial interpretations. They operate by increasing probability, reducing friction, and shaping a narrative that institutions can understand. But the final decision always belongs to the authority, the bank, or the court. The strategist prepares the ground; they do not control it.

A strategist cannot override reality. If a structure lacks substance, if a residence is fictitious, if a company has no governance, if reporting is inconsistent, no amount of coordination will make it defensible. Their work is to identify these flaws, correct what can be corrected, dismantle what cannot, and rebuild in a way that reflects the truth of the client's life.

A strategist cannot protect you from yourself if you refuse structure, take decisions without consulting or analyzing its effects, or act in any irrational way or worse, act foolishly. Many HNWIs fall into problems not because the world targets them, but because they act without coherence—multiple advisors who do not speak to each other, structures created without purpose, movements that contradict their filings, relationships unmanaged, risks ignored. A strategist can guide, warn, and prepare, but they cannot impose discipline.

A strategist does not serve to "hide" anything. They serve to align everything. They ensure that lawyers, bankers, tax experts, immigration specialists, corporate directors, trustees, security advisors and any other professional part of the structure operate inside a unified logic rather than in isolated silos. They protect against contradictions, not against rules.

Understanding these limits is essential. The strategist is not the architect of illusions. They are the architect of coherence. Their power comes not from the ability to bend systems, but from the ability to align your life with how systems actually work. When those limits are respected, the strategist becomes the one figure capable of sustaining your sovereignty in a world where every mistake creates consequences.

The strategist as long-term protector of sovereignty

A strategist's work does not end once the system is built. The value of their role becomes most visible over time, when life shifts, jurisdictions evolve, laws tighten, and institutions reinterpret patterns that once went unnoticed. A global life does not remain still, and an architecture that is not maintained eventually loses the very stability it was designed to create. The strategist prevents that drift.

Their primary function is continuity. They revisit structures to ensure that governance remains consistent with the client's current circumstances. They verify that trusts, companies, foundations, and residency positions still make sense under new legal standards. They examine whether documentation aligns with recent activity, whether decision-making remains coherent, and whether the system still reflects the client's narrative in the eyes of institutions. A structure that was defensible ten years ago may no longer be enough today; the strategist keeps it alive, updated, and legally defensible.

Risk does not remain static. Personal relationships change, business ventures expand or dissolve, jurisdictions tighten their reporting rules, banks become more conservative, and geopolitical shifts alter how certain passports, transactions, or industries are interpreted. The strategist continuously reassesses these variables and adjusts the client's architecture accordingly. They do not wait for pressure to reveal the weakness; they identify it early, present options, and integrate corrections before institutions force a reaction.

Narrative is another element that evolves. A global life produces digital footprints, travel patterns, contractual relationships, professional ties, family developments, and public exposure. A strategist ensures that these elements do not contradict the structure that supports them. They update the institutional narrative so that banks, authorities, and compliance systems see a life that makes sense on paper and in practice. They preserve alignment between the client's reality and the interpretation that systems inevitably make of it.

The strategist also anticipates legislative and geopolitical shifts. When a country reforms its tax code, restructures immigration routes, introduces new reporting rules, or becomes politically unstable, the strategist prepares the ground in advance. They adjust residency positions, corporate arrangements, or banking relationships before the change becomes a problem. Their value lies not in reacting quickly but in forecasting correctly—creating options when the environment is still calm, not when the window has already closed.

On the personal side, the strategist helps maintain stability across relationships, teams, and advisors. People change, services deteriorate, and professionals rotate in and out of a client's circle. The strategist monitors this ecosystem, replacing advisors when necessary, managing transitions, and ensuring that no sudden gap undermines a structure.

They protect the architecture from becoming dependent on one individual whose departure could destabilize the system.

The strategist's work is not decorative. It is operational. They preserve the line between power and exposure, ensuring that influence does not turn into vulnerability and that success does not create blind spots. They correct small inconsistencies before they become institutional contradictions. They maintain the discipline that allows a global life to remain coherent under pressure.

Ultimately, sovereignty is not a moment–it is a condition that must be preserved. Wealthy individuals lose sovereignty not because of a single decision, but because of the gradual accumulation of unmanaged risks, outdated structures, and conflicting narratives. A strategist acts as the guardian of that sovereignty. They hold the system together, maintain its logic, adapt it to change, and ensure that every piece continues to function without noise or contradiction.

Their role is long-term because exposure is long-term. Their work is continuous because risk is continuous. And their purpose is simple: to keep the client's life stable, coherent, and protected in a world where rules shift faster than most people can follow. When done correctly, the strategist becomes the quiet force that preserves legacy, continuity, and the freedom to act without fear.

A Global life made possible

A global life becomes stable not because it is simple, but because someone is watching all the moving parts and keeping them aligned. Wealth, mobility, visibility, and responsibility inevitably create pressure points. Some are predictable; others appear without warning. What determines whether these moments become crises or mere inconveniences is the quality of the system you have built around you — and the person who ensures that the system keeps working.

A strategist does not eliminate risk; they make risk manageable. They do not remove complexity; they give it structure. They do not promise invulnerability; they create a life where vulnerabilities are identified early, corrected calmly, and absorbed without destabilizing the whole. Their role lives in the background, often unnoticed, yet it is this quiet presence that allows everything else to move without friction.

The essence of strategy in a high-net-worth life is not theatrics or secrecy. It is discipline. It is continuity. It is the ability to anticipate change, adapt without fear, and maintain coherence even when the world shifts direction. In an environment shaped by regulation, information exchange, compliance filters, political volatility, and institutional scrutiny, coherence is not a luxury — it is survival.

No architect builds a structure and walks away. The same is true for the architecture of a global life. It must be reviewed, maintained, and adjusted as you evolve, as your assets grow, as your visibility increases, and as jurisdictions reinterpret the rules. A strategist becomes the guardian of that evolution, ensuring that every decision fits the bigger picture and that the bigger picture remains stable over time.

If there is one idea to carry with you from this chapter, it is this: *wealth gives you possibilities, but only strategy gives you continuity.*

A strategist preserves that continuity — not by force, but by clarity; not by hiding, but by aligning; not by reacting, but by preparing. And in a world where everything can change overnight, that quiet form of protection becomes one of the strongest expressions of sovereignty you can have.

Final Note

A strategist is not a symbol of power. They are a safeguard of coherence. Their work is quiet, often invisible, and intentionally unglamorous. It lives in the background, in the decisions no one sees, in the conflicts that never escalate, in the structures that remain stable because someone is watching the whole system instead of a single piece. Most people only understand the value of a strategist when something has already gone wrong. The irony is that the strategist's greatest achievements are the problems that never appear.

The role demands discipline, distance, and an unusual combination of technical and human understanding. It requires seeing life as a structure, not as a series of events; reading jurisdictions the way others read maps; and understanding how institutions interpret a person's actions long before those actions become files, flags, or headlines. Above all, it requires the ability to adapt without panic and to reorganize without creating noise, building continuity even when circumstances shift abruptly.

A strategist cannot replace lawyers, bankers, or advisors, and they cannot compensate for a client who refuses structure or acts without thinking. What they can do—and what very few people can—is hold all the pieces at once, ensuring that nothing collapses simply because one specialist failed to see what another one created.

In a world where visibility is constant, where systems talk to one another, and where consequences travel faster than intentions, the strategist exists for one purpose: to preserve your sovereignty. Not the abstract idea of freedom, but the practical ability to act without fear, to move without contradiction, and to build a future without being slowed by the past.

Their work begins long before the pressure arrives and continues long after the immediate threats fade. Continuity is their measure of success. Stability is their signature. And coherence—the alignment between your life, your structures, and your obligations—is the legacy they leave behind.

If there is one idea to carry from this chapter, it is this: you do not hire a strategist for the crisis you see. You hire a strategist for the crisis that never reaches you.

Closing Note

Reaching the end of this book does not mean you have reached the end of your learning. It means you now see the landscape with the clarity that most people never acquire. You understand how institutions interpret a life that crosses borders, how exposure forms long before it becomes visible, and how stability depends on structure rather than secrecy or instinct. What appeared abstract at the beginning now reads like a system—one where every choice, every pattern, and every piece of documentation shapes the way the world assesses you.

A global life is not automatically risky. It becomes risky when the elements that compose it move in different directions. You have learned how residency, citizenship, corporate substance, digital footprints, and patterns of mobility create your institutional identity. You have seen how banks, regulators, and jurisdictions read those signals, and how they react when something does not align. You have also seen why coherence is not a luxury but the condition that allows you to operate freely without generating unnecessary attention.

Throughout these chapters, you have studied the internal mechanics of exposure, the silent vulnerabilities inside families, companies, and political environments, and the pace at which a small inconsistency can become a jurisdictional event. You have learned how structures fail when they are neglected, how they survive when substance is real, and how legality—not opacity—has become the only foundation that endures pressure.

You now understand that a system built correctly does not need drama or secrecy to function. It simply needs alignment. When your structures match your life, when your documentation reflects your reality, and when your strategy evolves as circumstances shift, you stop being reactive. You move with stability, even when the environment is unstable. You stop depending on improvisation. You stop relying on luck. Your system no longer collapses because someone else misinterprets you.

What you have gained here is not a set of tactics. It is a framework for building a life that can withstand light. A way of thinking that turns complexity into something manageable. A method for navigating institutions without fear, and for adapting your architecture without signaling panic. It is a form of self-protection that does not depend on hiding but on being structurally sound. The goal was never to make you invisible. It was to make you unshakeable.

If there is one idea to carry forward, it is this: stability is not born from secrecy—it is born from coherence. And coherence is something you can design, maintain, and protect every day, no matter how many jurisdictions you touch or how visible your life becomes.

Your architecture is now yours. What you build from this point forward rests on a foundation that can hold.

Thank You

Thank you for reading this edition and for giving your time to a subject that most people never pause to examine. A book like this only becomes useful when it meets a reader who wants to understand not just the world, but their place inside it. If you have reached this page, you belong to that small group of people who value clarity, structure, and the quiet strength that comes from knowing how things actually work.

Writing this book required revisiting years of experience, conversations, crises, and patterns that repeat themselves across countries, families, industries, and generations. None of it would mean anything without someone on the other side willing to reflect, question, and build a better architecture for their own life.

I am grateful for your trust. You allowed me to accompany you, even briefly, into areas of life that few discuss openly: exposure, coherence, jurisdiction, substance, identity, strategy. These are not easy subjects, and they have no definitive end. But every reader who understands them—even partially—reduces their vulnerability and increases their freedom.

If anything in these pages helped you see your world differently, or helped you protect what matters with more confidence and less noise, then the work has served its purpose.

Thank you for choosing this book, for your patience, and for allowing these ideas to become part of your thinking. Wherever you go next, I hope you carry with you a sense of order, calm, and agency in a world that often feels engineered for the opposite.

– Mia Galgau

Legal notice and copyright protection

Title: ***HNWI Survival Manual Enhanced Edition – When your wealth becomes a target.***

ISBN: Assigned.

Second edition: Enhanced edition. Geneva, Switzerland.

© Mia Galgau | Taxhells. All rights reserved.

This publication, including all its contents, structure, and distinctive concepts, is an original work protected under Swiss copyright law (*Loi fédérale sur le droit d'auteur et les droits voisins*, lda, rs 231.1).

The entire text is digitally watermarked and traceable.

No part of this document may be reproduced, distributed, transmitted, translated, stored in a retrieval system, or adapted in any form or by any means, electronic, mechanical, photocopying, recording, or otherwise, without the prior written permission of the copyright holder.

Unauthorized use, resale, or public circulation of this work, in whole or in part, constitutes a breach of intellectual property and may result in legal action under Swiss civil and criminal law.

This document has been registered and timestamped as intellectual property in accordance with Swiss and international standards. Verification and enforcement measures are in place.

This is a strategic publication. You are not allowed to copy it. You are allowed to *build from it.*

Thank you.

www.ingramcontent.com/pod-product-compliance
Lightning Source LLC
Chambersburg PA
CBHW051400240926
51852CB00002B/72
9782940835386